Nature and Grace

Nature and Grace

A New Approach to Thomistic Ressourcement

Andrew Dean Swafford

Foreword by Edward T. Oakes, SJ

PICKWICK *Publications* · Eugene, Oregon

NATURE AND GRACE
A New Approach to Thomistic Ressourcement

Pickwick Publications
An Imprint of Wipf and Stock Publishers
199 W. 8th Av.e, Suite 3
Eugene, OR 97401

www.wipfandstock.com

ISBN 13: 978-1-62564-424-4

Cataloging-in-Publication data:

Swafford, Andrew Dean.

    Nature and grace : a new approach to Thomistic ressourcement / Andrew Dean
Swafford ; foreword by Edward T. Oakes, SJ.

    xiv + 206 p. ; 23 cm. Includes bibliographical references and index.

    ISBN 13: 978-1-62564-424-4

    1. Nature—History of doctrines. 2. Grace (Theology)—History of doctrines.
3. Catholic Church—Doctrines. 4. Scheeben, Matthias Joseph, 1835–1888. 5.
Philosophical theology. I. Oakes, Edward T. II. Title.

BT761.3 .S92 2014

To my wife Sarah and our children,

Thomas, Fulton, and Cate

But in a special way, I also dedicate this work with fondest memory to Father Edward T. Oakes, SJ (b. May 18, 1948, d. Dec. 6, 2013), without whom this work this work would never have seen the light of day.

Mysticism keeps men sane. As long as you have mystery you have health; when you destroy mystery you create morbidity. The ordinary man has always been sane because the ordinary man has always been a mystic . . . If he saw two truths that seemed to contradict each other, he would take the two truths and the contradiction along with them. His spiritual sight is stereoscopic, like his physical sight: he sees two different pictures at once and yet sees all the better for that.

—G. K. Chesterton, *Orthodoxy*

Contents

Foreword—Edward T. Oakes, SJ   *ix*

Preface   *xiii*

1   Introduction   1

PART ONE: Henri de Lubac

2   De Lubac on Nature and Grace: The Historical and
      Theological Context   25

3   Foundations for Nature and Grace   67

**PART TWO: The Contemporary Resurgence
of the Pure-Nature Tradition**

4   Lawrence Feingold and the Defense of the Pure-Nature
      Tradition   87

5   Steven A. Long on Natural and Eternal Law   117

**PART THREE: The Reconciliation of Extrinsicism
and Intrinsicism in Matthias Joseph Scheeben**

6   Matthias J. Scheeben on the Relationship of Nature and
      Grace   143

7   Conclusion   195

Bibliography   199

Foreword

IF EVER IT WERE true that missteps on first principles reap enormous consequences further on down the line, this most certainly applies to the nature-grace question. Very often this debate has seemed needlessly pedantic and far from the core of the Christian story. However, Dr. Swafford brings out well in this fine text how the question of the relationship between nature and grace is intimately tied to the following questions: the engagement with secularism and the question of evangelization; the relationship between faith and reason; the uniqueness of Jesus Christ and the question of religious pluralism—in other words, what did the Person and Work of Christ actually accomplish for humanity? Or, is the grace of salvation simply something that bubbles up from within our very humanity, in which case Jesus is perhaps inspiring, but by no means necessary. Dr. Swafford returns again and again to these and like questions as the proper motivation and context for the central importance of this issue of nature's relation to grace.

The history of the question tends to have been something of a see-saw where one or another aspect has received emphasis. For example, the medieval scholastics and their commentators tended to emphasize the integral autonomy of nature and the natural order; they did so, on their account, in order to preserve the supernatural dignity of the grace of Christ; in other words, it was felt that nature had to stand in no strict and inherent *need* of grace in order for grace to truly be *gratuitous*. Conversely, if nature stood in need of grace, it would seem that God's gift of grace would become in some way obligatory (and thus no longer gratuitous).

Henri de Lubac saw this trajectory of a self-enclosed natural order (however benign its origin) as coming into full blossom in the Enlightenment period and in the birth of modern secularism. In other words, de Lubac saw that such an emphasis upon an autonomous natural order found a natural home in secularism—because it appeared that the supernatural was in the end simply *unnecessary*. In this way, Neo-Scholastic apologetics (which placed a heavy emphasis on the autonomy of the natural order) found an odd fraternity with the very secularism it so despised.

For this reason, de Lubac made his case in the twentieth century that secular humanism was something of a contradiction in terms; that deeply rooted in human nature was a desire for God, and that true and authentic human fulfillment was tied up with man's relationship with the divine. Thus, the notion of a closed and autonomous natural order was for him a fiction: all things were created *in* and *for* Jesus Christ (cf. Col 1:16), leaving no domain beyond the reach of the God-Man—that is, leaving no *purely* secular domain.

At least in Catholic circles, de Lubac's analysis carried the day after the Second Vatican Council (1962–1965), whereas the more robust (Neo-Scholastic) emphasis on the integral natural order was predominant from Cajetan in sixteenth century to eve of Vatican II. Perhaps surprisingly, however, in the last fifteen years or so there has been a revival in this question, and most of it has come as a pushback against de Lubac. Modern Thomistic scholars such as Lawrence Feingold and Steven A. Long have argued that de Lubac's analysis pushed the balance too far; that in de Lubac's account grace has swallowed up nature, and strange as it may sound, secularism has once again become the unintentional result: if human nature is so tuned to the divine, grace need not come to us from the *outside*, as it were, in which case this divinization proceeds from *within*; and therefore one need not emphasize the singularity of Jesus Christ, making all religions more or the less the same with respect to their access to the divine—the root of which again stems from human nature itself, not from God coming to us from the outside.

But this Thomistic revival has once again brought the debate to a stalemate. And here is where Dr. Swafford is especially poised to make his contribution: in this work, he shows convincingly that the resources to resolve this debate existed all along in the relatively little known German theologian of the nineteenth century, Matthias Joseph Scheeben. What Dr. Swafford captures is that Scheeben's analysis is able to pull together the chief contributions of each side, while at the same time avoiding the chief pitfalls characteristic of each respective side. Scheeben, in short, is able to distinguish the orders of nature and grace, so as to bring to light the true sublime grandeur of supernatural grace and the singularity of the Cross of Jesus Christ; but he does so in order to show forth the splendor of their *union* in the heart of each believer. And so Scheeben exemplifies the phrase: "distinguish in order to unite." As with the Incarnation, Christ's human and divine nature are properly distinguished, but no less important is their union in the Divine Person of the Son; the same goes for the mystery of nature and grace: they are intelligibly distinguished, but they are divinely-ordained to come together in a nuptial union.

It is for this reason that Scheeben is praised by the likes of thinkers as diverse as Hans Urs von Balthasar and Réginald Garrigou Lagrange—no mean feat, to be sure; but such is the strength of Scheeben's ability to synthesize and reconcile diverse viewpoints. And such is likewise the merit of Dr. Swafford's analysis here; whatever the cause, Scheeben is seldom if ever brought into this debate. For this reason, I believe Dr. Swafford's work will bear fruit for years to come, if only for the reason that he has been able to move this debate forward, so to speak, beyond the impasse of rival groups and their competing accounts of nature and grace.

For the first time, it seems, Scheeben has entered the discussion; and if we follow Dr. Swafford's account, Scheeben just may hold the key to resolving this issue. If such is the case, Dr. Swafford's work will have brought us to a new threshold, at least as it concerns the Catholic discussion of nature and grace over the last seventy years or so and beyond.

Edward T. Oakes, SJ
University of St. Mary of the Lake
Mundelein, Illinois
Aug. 8, 2013

Preface

THE TOPIC OF NATURE and grace touches virtually any and every theological and even human question; it was this far-reaching aspect of the issue which first drew me to consider the question in more detail. Difficult as this topic undoubtedly is, deviations in either direction are so devastating that it is worth spending whatever time and energy we have on the matter. For the very issues of secularism, pluralism, and even relativism all trace back to the issue of nature and grace at some point, and for this reason the issue of nature and grace has certainly not lost any of its relevance at the contemporary time.

Before we begin, let me acknowledge my enormous debt to the University of St. Mary of the Lake; I wish especially to thank the director of my dissertation, Fr. Edward T. Oakes, S.J., for his extraordinary diligence, patience, and leadership in seeing this project to completion; without question, I would not be where I am without his support, and I have learned immensely from him both as a scholar and as a Christian disciple. And in recent times, I have learned from him not just how to live, but also how to die as a Christian disciple in the arms of our Lord Jesus.

I would also like to thank Fr. Emery de Gaál for patiently working through each chapter of the manuscript along the way. Thanks also to the rest of my dissertation committee for agreeing to take on this project: Fr. Patrick Boyle, Sr. Sara Butler, M.S.B.T., and Fr. John G. Lodge; I certainly benefited a great deal from their expertise and generous feedback.

I would also like to thank my good friend Father Cajetan Cuddy, O.P., for his more remote contribution to this project. When I began graduate studies in Old Testament and Semitic Languages, I can vividly recall—for better or worse—discussing with him the issues of nature and grace for hours on end, no doubt when my time should have been spent studying Hebrew. It was Brother Cajetan who first showed me the fundamental importance of this issue, and in fact I first learned of the work of Lawrence Feingold and Steven A. Long from him at this time—both of whom have figured largely in the present work, particularly in chapters four and five.

Let me also acknowledge my debt to two of my current colleagues at Benedictine College, Edward Macierowski, who helped me enormously with the French text of Henri de Lubac; and Jamie Spiering, who was kind enough to assist me with the German texts of Matthias Scheeben. They were of enormous help in this undertaking.

I would also like to thank Jane Schuele and Angie Gomez of the library staff at Benedictine College for their wonderful support in helping me acquire articles and interlibrary loan materials.

Of course, I could not fail to mention here my parents, Larry and Anna, without whose support I would not be where I am; I am forever grateful for their love and encouragement. I would also like to thank my wife's parents, Jerry and Linda Henry; their support has also been invaluable throughout this whole process.

Finally, my wife and children have to be considered as virtually co-authors of this manuscript—first of all, because my wife has patiently read every draft along the way; but secondly, on account of the patience and encouragement shown to me by her and my children: my debt to them, and especially my wife, is incalculable.

Last but not least, this work in Sacred Theology is dedicated to Almighty God—the Author of both the orders of nature and of grace—Who has revealed Himself in and through His Son, our Lord and Savior, Jesus Christ.

1

Introduction

It is rightly said that the topic of nature and grace touches almost any and every theological and even human question, for one's appraisal of this issue transforms the way in which one understands the very encounter between man and God. For this reason, twentieth-century French theologian Henri de Lubac (1896–1991)—regarded as one of the primary inspirations of Vatican II—contends that this issue: "is at the heart of all great Christian thought . . . at the bottom of discussions with modern unbelief, and form[s] the crux of . . . Christian humanism."[1] Hence, the formulation of the nature-grace relation has far-reaching consequences, affecting no less than the meta-narrative—not just of Christianity—but of humanity itself.

In what follows, we will see that there are two basic aspects of the Christian mystery of nature and grace: (1) Christocentrism, which is to say that Christ is the center and end of *all* things; and (2) the necessity of distinguishing between nature and grace for the purpose of preserving the supernatural transcendence and gratuity of grace.

The Christocentric aspect of nature and grace appears in the opening of the very first encyclical of the late Bl. Pope John Paul II when he writes: "Jesus Christ is the *center* of the universe and of history."[2] This theme in fact goes all the way back to Sacred Scripture, as can be seen here in the Letter to the Colossians: "For in him all things were created

1. De Lubac, *At the Service of the Church*, 35; "au cœur de toute grande pensée chrétienne . . . au fond des discussions avec l'incroyance moderne, qu'il formait le nœd du problème de l'humanisme chrétien" (De Lubac, *Mémoire sur l'occasion de mes écrits*, 33).

2. John Paul II, *Redeemer of Man*, no. 1.

1

. . . all things were created *through him* and *for him* . . . [and] *in him*
all things hold together" (Col 1:16–17). And similarly, the Letter to the
Ephesians states:

> For he has made known to us in all wisdom and insight the mys-
> tery of his will, according to his purpose which he set forth in
> Christ as a plan [οἰκονομίαν] for the fullness of time [πληρώματος
> τῶν καιρῶν] to *unite* [ἀνακεφαλαιώσασθαι] *all things in him*,
> things in heaven and things on earth" (Eph 1:9–10).[3]

In the second century, St. Irenaeus likewise echoes this Christocentric Pauline theme:

> So the Lord now manifestly came to his own, and, born by his
> own created order which he himself bears, he by his obedience
> on the tree *renewed* [ἀνακεφαλαιόω] [and reversed] what was
> done by disobedience in [connection with] a tree; and [the power
> of] that seduction by which the virgin Eve, already betrothed to
> a man, had been wickedly seduced was broken when the angel
> in truth brought good tidings to the Virgin Mary, who already
> [by her betrothal] belonged to a man. . . . Therefore he *renews*
> [ἀνακεφαλαιόω] these things in himself, uniting man to the
> Spirit. . . . He therefore completely *renewed* [ἀνακεφαλαιόω] *all
> things*.[4]

Contemporary patristic scholar Robert Louis Wilken comments on
St. Irenaeus' use of Ephesians 1:10 here, observing that Christ brings
to "completion" what was originally begun in creation, suggesting that
Christ is not just the beginning, but also the *end* of all creation—the one
in whom creation reaches its final goal:

> [St. Irenaeus] favors terms like *renew* and *restore*. . . . Drawing
> on the language of Saint Paul in Ephesians, he says that Christ
> "summed up" or "united" all things in himself (Eph 1:10). . . .

---

3. See also the prologue in the Gospel of John: "all things were made *through him*,
and without him was not anything made that was made" (1:2–3), and also the Letter to
the Hebrews: "in these last days he has spoken to us by a Son, whom he appointed the
heir of all things, *through whom* also he created the ages" (Heb 1:2).

4. Irenaeus, *Against Heresies*, bk. V, ch. 19–20, emphasis added, cited from
Richardson, *Early Christian Fathers*, 389–90; brackets with Greek text are added, other
brackets with English are original in translation. Note: the "recapitulation" motif is here
translated as "renew" (see ibid., 389 n. 93).

Christ does not simply reverse what had been lost in the fall: he brings to *completion* what had been partial and imperfect.[5]

Similarly, in the medieval period, St. Thomas Aquinas (1225–1274)—though perhaps better known for his emphasis upon the *distinction* between nature and grace—also shares this same Christocentric perspective which is apparent in his correlation of the eternal Law with the Person of the Word (i.e., the Son). This association is significant since for Aquinas the very notion of nature and the natural order finds its ontological root in the eternal law—here correlated with the Person of the Word—in which case the "natural" order is *itself* Christocentric in its very foundation. In this light, St. Thomas writes: "Among other things expressed by this Word, the eternal law itself is expressed thereby."[6]

St. Thomas is here stating implicitly—not only that the natural order does not exist apart from Christ—but that the very notion of the natural order is itself *Christological.* Such a view is incompatible with the very notion of secularism, if by this term one means a certain domain of reality somehow independent of Christ. This point is emphasized by twentieth-century Eastern theologian Vladimir Lossky (1903–1958) in the following:

> The Eastern tradition knows nothing of "pure nature" to which grace is added as a supernatural gift. For [Eastern theology], there is no natural or "normal" state, since grace is implied in

5. Wilken, *The Spirit of Early Christian Thought*, 66–67, first italics original, emphasis added on the word "completion." See also Jaroslav Pelikan who comments on these themes in the pre-Nicene period: "The reason the incarnation was necessary was that man had not merely done wrong—for this, repentance would have sufficed—but had fallen into a corruption, a transiency that threatened him with annihilation. As the agent of creation who called man out of nothing, the Logos was also the one to rescue him from annihilation. This the Logos did by taking flesh. For this theology, it was the universality of death, not the inevitability of sin, which was fundamental. . . . It was death and corruption that stood in the way of man's participation in the divine nature, and these had to be overcome in the incarnation by the Logos" (Pelikan, *The Christian Tradition*, 1:285).

6. *ST* I-IIae, .q. 93, a. 1, ad 2. We will return to this issue later on, but for now let us note that the "eternal law" is simply God's overarching providence governing all things. The importance here, then, is that the eternal law includes both what might be called the "order of nature" *and* the "order of grace." Accordingly, correlating Christ with the former softens the force of the radical distinction between nature and grace. In this light, St. Thomas becomes something of a model for holding both aspects of the mystery of nature and grace together in proper balance, the Christocentric aspect of unity and the need to distinguish nature and grace from one another.

the act of creation itself. . . . "Pure nature" . . . would thus be a philosophical fiction. . . . The world [has been] created in order that it might be deified . . . [and] its center [is] in the Word, the hypostatic Wisdom of the Father. . . . For there is no "natural beatitude" for creation [and it] has no other end than deification. All the distinctions which we may try to make between the state which was proper to the first creatures, according to their natures, and that which was conferred upon them by their ever-increasing participation in the divine energies [i.e., grace] can never be more than fictions.[7]

While Lossky clearly accentuates the Christocentric aspect of nature and grace, let us now turn to establish the importance of the second aspect of nature and grace, namely, the necessity of *distinguishing* between nature and grace, for the purpose of preserving the supernatural character of divine grace. This distinction can likewise be traced back to Sacred Scripture, as for example when St. Paul portrays the grace of salvation as vastly surpassing the created natural order: "No eye has seen, nor ear heard, nor the heart of man conceived, what God has prepared for those who love him" (1 Cor 2:9; cf. Isa 64:4). Let us note that in order for grace to "surpass" the natural order, or be considered "supernatural," we must presuppose some notion of the "natural."[8]

Though man is gratuitously created in the image and likeness of God (Gen 1:26), this original creation is surpassed by man's new creation in Christ (cf. 2 Cor 5:17). Hence, the sublime grandeur of man's supernatural participation through divine grace surpasses man's original creation in *imago Dei*, since by the grace of Christ man now shares in the very filiation of the Eternal Son. For this reason, St. John the Evangelist can write the following: "See what love the Father has given us that we should be called children of God, *and so we are*" (1 John 3:1).[9] While

7. Lossky, *The Mystical Theology of the Eastern Church*, 101.

8. Let us also observe that the very word "supernatural" presupposes an understanding of the word "natural," since the former is strictly speaking intelligible only in relation to the latter.

9. This theme of "sonship" is scattered throughout the New Testament: "For you did not receive the spirit of slavery to fall back into fear, but you have received the spirit of sonship. When we cry 'Abba! Father!' it is the Spirit himself bearing witness with our spirit that we are children of God, and if children, then heirs, heirs of God and fellow heirs with Christ, provided we suffer with him in order that we may also be glorified with him" (Rom 8:14–17). Similarly, the Letter to the Galatians states: "But when the time had fully come, God sent forth his Son, born of a woman, born under the law, to

the original *imago Dei* is restored in Christ, the New Testament goes beyond this primordial restoration: in Christ man is now "conformed to the image of his Son" (Rom 8:29)—man has become "a son in the Son," as the traditional language of the Church has it.[10] This salvation in Christ is quintessentially a supernatural work of divine grace, since it is a gift above and beyond the parameters of human nature, as classically stated here in the Letter to the Ephesians: "by *grace* [we] have been saved" (Eph 2:8).[11]

The point we wish to emphasize at this juncture is that this distinction between the first creation and the new creation (or between nature and grace) is necessary for the purpose of preserving the supernatural transcendence of grace; this distinction between nature and grace further presupposes the independent coherence of the natural order—or else it could not be distinguished from grace.

Twentieth-century literary scholar and apologist C. S. Lewis presupposes this line of reasoning when he describes Christianity as a religion in which God encounters man from the "outside," that is, in terms of God's pursuit of man and not the other way around. In other words, supernatural grace comes to man from without, as something over and above his nature, and so Lewis writes:

> To be frank, we do not at all like the idea of a "chosen people." Democrats by birth and education, we should prefer to think that all nations and individuals start level in the search for God, or even that all religions are equally true. It must be admitted at once that Christianity makes no concessions to this point of view. It does not tell of a human search for God at all, but of something done by God for, to, and about, Man [i.e., God's search for man].[12]

_____

redeem those who were under the law, so that we might receive adoption as sons. And because you are sons, God has sent the Spirit of his Son into our hearts, crying 'Abba! Father!' So through God you are no longer a slave but a son, and if a son then an heir" (Gal 4:4–7). Likewise, we read in the Book of Revelation: "I am the Alpha and the Omega, the beginning and the end. To the thirsty I will give water without price from the fountain of the water of life. He who conquers shall have this *heritage*, and I will be his God and he shall be my *son*" (Rev 21:6b–7).

10. John Paul II, *Veritatis Splendor*, no. 17.

11. Similarly, emphasizing the gratuity of the grace of salvation, St. Paul writes: "While we were yet helpless . . . Christ died for the ungodly. . . . God shows his love for us in that while we were yet sinners Christ died for us" (Rom 5:6–8).

12. Lewis, *Miracles*, 187.

Here Lewis' point is that Christianity presents itself as a supernatural religion precisely because it is founded upon a divine entrance into the created order, from the top down, as it were, as a matter of divine *descent*, rather than man's progressive *ascent*. But in order to understand grace as something "over and above" human nature, we must first have some prior conception of human nature—in relation to which grace then stands as "over and above." For without a sense of the coherence of nature, *as* nature, grace necessarily loses its specificity: that is, without a coherent view of nature and the "natural," the unique signification of the term "*super*-natural" becomes unclear.

Now *how* this independent coherence and integrity of the natural order can be reconciled with the Christocentrism mentioned above is itself an interesting question, and one which we will take up in due course. For now, let us simply note that both aspects of the nature-grace relation are essential for preserving the integrity of the Christian mystery of nature and grace.

And so with this preliminary assessment in mind, let us now turn to introduce the nature-grace debate more specifically, noting especially the implications which follow from various positions.

Parameters of the Nature-Grace Debate

Corresponding to the two dimensions of the nature-grace mystery— Christocentrism and the necessary distinction between nature and grace—are two poles comprising the nature-grace debate more generally: *extrinsicism* and *intrinsicism*. They are so named on account of the closeness (or lack of closeness) with which they correlate the orders of nature and grace—or more specifically, the closeness or lack of closeness with which they correlate human nature with the gift of grace.

Extrinsicism emphasizes the distinction of nature and grace for the purpose of preserving the supernatural and transcendent gratuity of grace, over against human nature. Intrinsicism, on the other hand, holds that human nature is inherently open-ended and oriented to the supernatural order of grace, in which case man's fulfillment lies only in and through Christ—with the result that a purely "natural beatitude" is simply out of the question—much as Lossky stressed above. For this reason, intrinsicism is more incompatible with secularism than is the case with extrinsicism; and in fact, the latter has been alleged to have subtly reinforced secularism in the modern era, on account of its emphasis upon the self-contained and independent coherence of the natural order.[13]

Accordingly, as we mentioned at the outset, this debate has clear implications for secularism, and even for religious pluralism. As for the latter, in its extreme form, intrinsicism can serve as a catalyst for relativizing the uniqueness of Christ, as well as that of the sacraments—relativizing their status as privileged channels of grace. The reason is due to the fact that in its extreme form, intrinsicism correlates nature and grace *so* closely that it *identifies* nature and grace as one and the same—with the result that the order of grace ultimately becomes something that "bubbles" up from *within* human nature, quite contrary to C. S. Lewis' comments above. If we were to follow this intrinsicist train of thought, it would ultimately imply that the grace of Christ is not substantially different from that of non-Christian religions, in which case the newness or uniqueness of Christ is thereby diminished.[14]

While we should note that this more extreme form of intrinsicism is certainly not that of the Christian tradition rooted in St. Paul, it is still the case that the problems resulting here illustrate the importance of extrinsicist aspects of the nature-grace relation. For as we have said, if the term "grace" is applied so broadly that it covers all that might otherwise have been considered "natural," the exceptional character of grace inevitably fades away. For this reason, a more specific awareness as to what constitutes the natural and supernatural orders—by way of their

---

13. Cf. De Lubac, *Surnaturel*, 153–54.

14. Edward T. Oakes summarizes well the anomaly that the extreme forms of extrinsicism and intrinsicism ultimately yield similar results regarding the issue of secularism: "Intrinsicism so *fuses* nature and grace that anything natural becomes, by the very fact that it *is* natural, a form of grace . . . Again we are faced with the irony of history . . . Admittedly, intrinsicism comes to the opposite conclusion from that drawn by extrinsicism—that grace more or less automatically wells up from within nature rather than confronting it extrinsically from the outside—but, in one of those ironies that have marked the life of the Church after Vatican II, this 'naturalized grace' ends up justifying secular independence from religion, too" (Oakes, "The Paradox of Nature and Grace," 667–96, here 693, emphasis original). On the other hand, we should also note that extrinsicism in its extreme form so separates nature and grace that the natural order appears as an autonomous and independent order of existence so completely set apart from the order of grace that the natural order seems to be self-sufficient in its own right; in this view, while the order of grace may "add" to the perfection of the order of nature, grace seems to be, strictly speaking, unnecessary. In this light, too, the order of grace diminishes in its importance, making secularism once again the ironic but logical result.

intelligible distinction—actually serves to preserve the singular unique-ness of supernatural grace.

For now, with this general outline of the two main schools of thought before us, let us turn to set the stage for what will follow in greater detail. Here we will define key principles and terms to be used throughout, most of which refer to the extrinsicist tradition, but which also serve as the backdrop for the intrinsicist critique against the extrin-sicist tradition in the twentieth century—led first and foremost by Henri de Lubac.

Preliminary Definitions

Nature

In what follows, "nature" will be understood in its Aristotelian sense as follows: "nature is a principle [ἀρχῆς] or cause [αἰτίας] of being moved and of being at rest in that to which it belongs primarily, in virtue of itself and not accidentally."[15] The collection of things which have such a principle (i.e., a "nature") constitutes the order of nature.[16]

Importantly, let us observe here that "nature" is a principle *in* things—it is not a thing itself. As we will see, this point is of the utmost importance because it illustrates the fact that the notion of the natural order—as intelligibly distinct from the supernatural—need not be taken to imply that this natural order actually *exists* independent of the order of grace. On the contrary, the notion of the natural order's coherence entails nothing more than the conceptual distinction between its intel-ligibility, *as* natural—as distinct from the supernatural order of grace, which is something over and above human nature.

Aristotle's definition of nature only implies that there are different kinds of things, with different principles of activity (that is, different "na-tures")—in virtue of which each is intelligible in its own right.[17] Again,

---

15. Aristotle, *Physics*, bk. II, ch. 1 (192b 21–23), cited in Barnes, *The Complete Works of Aristotle*, 329: "ὡς οὔσης τῆς φύσεως ἀρχῆς τινὸς καὶ αἰτίας τοῦ κινεῖσθαι καὶ ἠρεμεῖν ἐν ᾧ ὑπάρχει πρώτως καθ᾽ αὑτὸ καὶ μὴ κατὰ συμβεβηκός."

16. The medieval maxim *agere sequitur esse* ("act follows being") draws from this definition. In other words, a thing's characteristic behavior or activity reveals its essence or nature—its nature being simply the ultimate source or principle underlying a thing's characteristic powers.

17. A good analogy to illustrate this point is to take the notion of substance and

the independent *intelligibility* of the natural order in no way entails the independent *existence* of the natural order; recognizing this fact is the first step toward reconciling the above-mentioned Christocentrism with the extrinsicist emphasis upon the nature-grace distinction.

The Divine Economy and the End(s) of Man

The divine "economy" refers to God's providential ordering and governance over all things. When we refer to the "actual" or "concrete" divine economy, we are referring to the present order of God's providence, over against a "hypothetical" ordering of things which might have been possible, but which does not actually exist. This discussion plays directly into the question regarding man's ultimate end, since in the actual divine economy (the actual ordering of God's providence), man's last end is the beatific vision. Since this vision of God is a *supernatural* end, it raises the question as to whether or not the beatific vision is man's *only* possible end—or whether man could have been ordained to a purely *natural* end in a hypothetical divine economy. If a purely natural end would have been possible in a hypothetical economy, then there is a further question as to whether man's purely natural end is still possible in the present economy, despite the fact that man is actually and concretely ordered to God in the beatific vision.

If one holds that the beatific vision is man's *only* possible end, there are further questions regarding both God's justice, as well as the gratuity of grace and the beatific vision. In other words, one is left with the following question: could God have *refused* the offer of the beatific vision—if this were man's *only* possible end? If we say that God could

---

accident: this distinction is intelligible and is rooted in reality, yet a particular substance and its accidents are never physically separable from one another, in the sense that I could never hold the bare substance of a thing with no accidents whatever; in other words, a substance cannot physically exist without *some* accidents, though many of these can be gained or lost throughout the course of a thing's existence. In other words, I could not ask someone to hand me the "weight" of a rock (an accident) without also handing me the rock itself (the substance), nor could they hand me the bare "substance" of the rock, without also handing me its accompanying accidents along with it. In this light, there is nothing incompatible in adhering to the notion of an independently *intelligible* order of nature, on the one hand, juxtaposed alongside the above-mentioned Christocentrism, on the other. We can acknowledge two separate intelligible orders of reality, while simultaneously acknowledging the inseparable *existential* interplay between the two orders; though intelligibly distinct, they exist inseparably from one another in the concrete order of things.

not have refused man the beatific vision—since it is man's only possible end—then it would appear that the beatific vision is no longer a *free* gift, since it would seem to be necessary on account of man's nature.

On the other hand, if we hold that God could have refused the beatific vision, we retain the essential gratuity of man's supernatural end, but we likely would have to accept the possibility of a purely natural end; otherwise, we are committed to the possibility that God could have created man with only the possibility of the beatific vision as a final end— an end which He could refuse man—in which case man could have been created with only the final prospect of suffering and frustration as his final end. The question, then, of course, is whether this view squares with God's justice, or if it tends toward some form of Voluntarism which is perhaps incompatible with the Christian tradition.

For these reasons, thinkers in the extrinsicist tradition insist that man has *two* final ends: one natural, accessible by way of his natural powers; and the other supernatural, accessible only by way of supernatural grace. Strictly speaking, only the latter is gratuitous (and is therefore not necessary)—which is to say that God could have refused the beatific vision (since this supernatural end requires the gift of grace) without any injustice on His part; all that is necessary on God's part as a matter of justice is that He supply for man's *natural* end, which is the end flowing from his nature.

This leads us directly to our next topic, namely, the *debitum naturae*, or the "debt of nature," which in the extrinsicist tradition signifies what God *owes* to the creature as a matter of justice, in virtue of what flows from the natural order.

The Debitum Naturae

As implied above, the *debitum naturae* stipulates that some things are in fact *due* to the creature on account of the creature's nature or essence. God's justice to the creature entails that He provides whatever is necessary for a given creature to reach its *natural* end—which is the end given to it on account of its nature, and which is accessible by way of its own natural principles. In this light, God is *not* free in His offer of man's natural end; that is, He could not have withheld this end from man without injustice on His part.

A frequent objection to this notion of the *debitum naturae* is that creation itself is gratuitous, a point which underlies Lossky's statement above—in which case, God cannot be said to *owe* anything to any creature whatsoever. Extrinsicist thinkers respond by conceding that creation is of course gratuitous in that it is a free act on God's part; but once God chooses to create, there is a natural order which He has brought into existence—and which is intelligible in its own right—and which therefore should be taken as an expression of divine wisdom and providence. For this reason, according to extrinsicist proponents, God is not so much "indebted" to the creature, as He is to Himself, and to the manifestation of His own divine wisdom in the natural order—an order which He freely willed into existence. In other words, it is God—not the creature—who is the source of the *debitum naturae*. Thus, the *debitum naturae* is nothing more than the recognition of the natural order as (1) independently intelligible and as (2) a manifestation of divine wisdom and divine providence.

Further, since man's elevation in Christ *surpasses* the order of nature, we can speak of at least *two* levels of gratuity, one of creation, and another surpassing the natural order of creation. It is in fact the *debitum naturae* which preserves this twofold gratuity: for "gratuity" can refer to (1) that which is not owed, simply speaking, in which case creation itself is gratuitous; (2) "gratuity" can also refer to a divine gift which is *over and above* the natural order. In this second sense, supernatural grace is "doubly" gratuitous, as it were, because it elevates man over and above the endowment implied by his specific nature.

But if "gratuity" is reduced simply to *what is not owed*, this twofold distinction of gratuity collapses. For this reason, while extrinsicist thinkers readily concede that the natural order is gratuitous in the first sense above, it is not gratuitous in the second sense; hence, only the gifts of grace and glory are gratuitous in *both* senses.

Hence, the notions of *dependence* and *gratuity* are not exactly the same thing, and it is generally the blurring of these two issues which lies behind objections against the *debitum naturae*. While it is the case that all of creation is *dependent* upon God and His providence, as we just pointed out, the *gratuity* of creation and the *gratuity* of supernatural grace are not on the same level. Accordingly, this "dependence" of creation upon God can be registered in two ways, which correlates with the two aforementioned levels of gratuity: namely, (1) creaturely dependence upon God, in accordance with His *natural* providence in the natural order; and (2) creaturely dependence upon God, in accordance with His supernatural providence and supernatural elevation by way of divine grace.

In the following, St. Thomas witnesses to the importance of the *debitum naturae* when he answers the following objection in the *Summa Theologiae*: "The act of justice is to pay what is due. But God is no man's debtor."[18] To which Aquinas responds this way:

> In the divine operations debt may be regarded in two ways, as due either to God, or to creatures, and in either way God pays what is due. It is due to God that there should be fulfilled in creatures what His will and wisdom require, and what manifests His goodness. In this respect God's justice regards what befits Him, inasmuch as He renders to Himself what is due to Himself. It is also due to a created thing that it should possess what is ordered to it. . . . Thus also God exercises justice when He gives to each thing what is *due* to it by its *nature* and *condition*.[19]

The point implied here is that what is due to a creature in accordance with its "nature and condition" refers to the natural order, and stands in contrast to the transcendent gift of supernatural grace. Similarly, this line of thinking lies behind the following from St. Thomas when he addresses the need for predestination, which arises precisely because God's providence has *supernaturally* ordered man to an end beyond the powers and parameters of his nature:

> The end towards which created things are directed by God is *twofold*, one which *exceeds all proportion* and faculty of created nature; and this end is life eternal, that consists in seeing God which is above every creature. . . . The other end, however, is *proportionate* to created nature, to which end created being can attain according to the power of its nature. . . . Hence the type of the aforesaid direction of a rational creature towards the end of life eternal is called predestination.[20]

Natural Desire

In the extrinsicist tradition, man's natural desire is contained within the natural order, the possible fulfillment of which is included in the

---

18. *ST* I, q. 21, a. 1, obj. 3.

19. *ST* I, q. 21, a. 1, ad 3, emphasis added.

20. *ST* I, q. 23, a. 1, emphasis added.

debitum naturae. For this reason, the fulfillment of man's natural desire (or at least the possibility thereof) is necessarily *due* to the creature— as a matter of justice—as something included in the *debitum naturae.* Accordingly, for the extrinsicist tradition, man cannot be said to have a *natural* desire for the beatific vision, since that would thereby nullify the *gratuity* of this supernatural end.

The reasoning behind the extrinsicist tradition at this point draws largely from a principle found in Aristotle (384–322 BC), namely, that *nature does nothing in vain,* illustrated here in the following examples: "A shoe is pointless [μάτην] when it is not worn. But God and nature create nothing that is pointless [μάτην]."[21] Similarly: "Whenever the sexes are separate the female cannot generate perfectly by herself alone, for then the male would exist in vain [μάτην], and *nature makes nothing in vain* [μάτην]."[22] And finally: "Animals must be endowed with sensation, since *Nature does nothing in vain* [μάτην]."[23]

The appropriation of this principle by the extrinsicist tradition and its application to man's natural desire solidified what would become the principal opposition against de Lubac in the twentieth century. As we will see in the next two chapters, de Lubac argued that man has a *natural* desire for the beatific vision; but still, he insisted that this supernatural end retained its gratuity. For the extrinsicist tradition, however, these two positions are incompatible: since a *natural* desire cannot be in vain, the fulfillment of a natural desire—on account of the *debitum naturae*— is therefore *not* gratuitous.[24]

21. Aristotle, *On the Heavens* bk. I, ch. 4 (271a 32–33), cited in *The Complete Works of Aristotle,* 452: "μάτην γὰρ ὑπόδημα τοῦτο λέγομεν, οὗ μή ἐστιν ὑπόδεσις. ὁ δὲ Θεὸς καὶ ἡ φύσις οὐδὲν μάτην ποιοῦσιν."

22. Aristotle, *On the Generation of Animals,* bk. II, ch. 5 (741b 2–3), cited in *The Complete Works of Aristotle,* 1150, emphasis added: "ἐν ὅσοις δὲ κεχώρισται τὸ θῆλυ καὶ τὸ ἄρρεν, ἀδύνατον αὐτὸ καθ᾽ αὑτὸ τὸ θῆλυ γεννᾶν εἰς τέλος· τὸ γὰρ ἄρρεν μάτην ἂν ἦν, δὲ φύσις οὐδὲν ποιεῖ μάτην."

23. Aristotle, *De anima,* bk. III, ch.12 (434a 30–31), cited in *The Complete Works of Aristotle,* 690, emphasis added: "τὸ δὲ ζῷον ἀναγκαῖον αἴσθησιν ἔχειν ... εἰ μηθὲν μάτην ποιεῖ ἡ φύσις."

24. See Louis Dupré's "Introduction" to de Lubac, *Augustinianism and Modern Theology,* xiv where he writes: "To a theology that had accepted the existence of two relatively independent orders of reality the idea of a natural desire for a supernatural end was *a priori* excluded. The principal objection against it the new theologians strangely derived from Aristotle's static cosmology. In *De Caeol II* the philosopher had written that heavenly bodies stay their course, because no being desires what its nature has no means to attain. If the stars had the power to move beyond their course, nature

For de Lubac on the other hand, the beatific vision is man's *only* final end; any other final end results only in man's permanent frustration and suffering, as he writes here: "In me . . . in my concrete nature—that nature I have in common with all real men . . . the 'desire to see God' cannot be permanently frustrated without an essential suffering. To deny this is to undermine my entire Credo."[25]

To complicate matters further, Pope Pius XII's 1950 encyclical *Humani generis* seems to teach along the very lines of the extrinsicist tradition above—or so at least it would appear at first glance—since he seemed to condemn de Lubac's teaching on the matter. Pope Pius XII writes: "Others destroy the gratuity of the supernatural order, since God, they say, cannot create intellectual beings without ordering and calling them to the Beatific Vision."[26] Here the pope seems to condemn the position which would deny the possibility of a purely natural end, as de Lubac seems to do so in the above when he states that there can be only *one* end for man. For this reason, it is alleged that *Humani generis* targeted de Lubac specifically, an issue which we will take up in the following chapter.

For now, let us simply observe the apparent tension between de Lubac and *Humani generis* on this point. Consider, for example, the pope's remarks in comparison to the following from de Lubac, which represents his cardinal thesis in his 1946 *Surnaturel*: "L'esprit est donc désir de Dieu."[27] Clearly, de Lubac is here precluding the very possibility of a purely natural end—since the created spirit, of which man is no doubt a prime example—inherently and inexorably desires the beatific vision, on account of its very nature.

---

would have given them the means to do so. In the same way, Cajetan and Suárez [key thinkers in the extrinsicist tradition], and their followers argued a human being can feel no desire for what its nature [cannot] attain."

25. De Lubac, *The Mystery of the Supernatural*, 54. "En moi . . . en ma nature concrète, dans cette nature que j'ai en commun avec tous les hommes réels . . . le 'désir de voir Dieu' ne saurait être éternellement frustré sans une souffrance essentielle. Je ne saurais nier cela sans faire une brèche à mon *Credo*" (De Lubac, *Le Mystère du Surnaturel*, 80, italics original).

26. DH 3875–99. Pius XII, *Humani generis* (1950), no. 26.

27. De Lubac, *Surnaturel*, 483: "The spirit is desire for God." I would like to thank my colleague, Dr. Edward Macierowski, for help in translating passages from de Lubac's *Surnaturel*. He is currently translating volume four of de Lubac's *Medieval Exegesis*, and has already completed volumes 2 and 3 for publication.

For further complexity and even irony here, however, let us note that the Second Vatican Council appears to have weighed in on this issue as well, and this time undoubtedly in favor of de Lubac. The Council states: "Christ died for everyone, and . . . all are in fact called to *one* and the same destiny, which is divine . . ."[28] Thus, while at mid-twentieth century de Lubac looked to be a man condemned, by the close of the Second Vatican Council he was recognized as one of its leading influences—and this especially pertains to the Council's general framework on nature and grace.

Obediential Potency

For the extrinsicist tradition, man's capacity for the beatific vision cannot be described as a natural potency or natural inclination (both of which are closely related to natural desire), since a natural potency inclines a thing to its *natural* end—the fulfillment of which is contained within the *debitum naturae*, which would therefore be due to the creature according to divine justice. In this light, the extrinsicist tradition employs the concept of obediential potency for the purpose of accounting for the precise relationship between human nature and the beatific vision.

At a basic level, the meaning of "obediential potency" refers to the capacity of a creature to "obey" the Creator, since the finite creature is always susceptible to being elevated or transformed by divine omnipotence. Accordingly, at one level obediential potency is used to explain God's working of miracles, the transforming of finite creatures in such a manner that would have been impossible on the part of the creatures taken by themselves, in virtue of their natural powers alone.

However, in contrast to the case of a miracle, obediential potency as applied to man's capacity for the beatific vision is slightly different because man remains *man* throughout this divine elevation. In other words, while the case of a miracle appears to have no specific relation to the nature of the creature as such—since God could transform anything into any other thing whatever—the capacity for the beatific vision *does* have some relation to human nature, since not every creature can be elevated in such a manner (that is, not *as* that particular creature). In this light, though it is impossible for man to actualize the beatific vision by

28. *Gaudium et Spes*, no. 22, in *Vatican Council II: Constitutions, Decrees, Declarations,* emphasis added.

virtue of his natural powers alone, this capacity is nonetheless rooted in the very dynamism of human nature itself.

For this reason, "obediential potency" has two distinct meanings: (1) "generic" obediential potency which corresponds to the case of a miracle, and which indicates no real relation between the specific nature of the creature and its miraculous transformation; and (2) "specific" obediential potency which corresponds to man's specific capacity for the beatific vision, and which stipulates that the capacity for a certain elevation *is* in fact rooted in the very nature of the creature in question; this elevation is therefore perfective of that particular nature, albeit in a way that transcends the powers of its nature, strictly speaking.

As for an illustration of generic obediential potency, let us consider the following from the Gospel of Matthew: "God is able from these stones to raise up children of Abraham" (Matt 3:9); this is an example of a generic obediential potency because the stones are no longer *stones* by the end of the change; and supposing that these hypothetical stones, now-turned-human, were to receive the beatific vision, they certainly would not do so *as* stones. Hence, these stones have no *specific* obediential potency for the beatific vision (though they could be said to have a generic one).

On the other hand, as we have said, the capacity of human nature to be elevated to the beatific vision is a specific obediential potency precisely because this capacity is rooted in man's *specific* nature: not every nature can be elevated to any end whatsoever, for only spiritual and intellectual nature possesses the capacity for the beatific vision; any other creature would have to be first transformed into an intellectual and spiritual creature, and only then elevated to the beatific vision.

Accordingly, the reason that the extrinsicist tradition insists upon the designation of man's potency for the beatific vision as *obediential* (as opposed to natural) stems only from the fact that human nature cannot actualize this potency by itself. Moreover, since obediential potency refers to a capacity to be elevated beyond what is possible in virtue of the natural order, its actualization is not contained within the *debitum naturae*—in which case its fulfillment is always gratuitous (in contrast to *natural* potency, or natural desire which is contained within the *debitum naturae* and therefore would not be gratuitous). In this light, the extrinsicist tradition contends that the notion of specific obediential potency masterfully captures the balance of on the one hand, rooting the capacity for the beatific vision in human nature, while simultaneously preserving on the other hand the sublime gratuity of this elevation, as supernaturally transcending the powers of human nature.

The Supernatural Order of Grace

In what follows supernatural "grace" will be understood with reference to man's participation in the divine nature (cf. 2 Pet 1:4) in such a way that transcends what is signified in the notion of creation.[29] Accordingly, we will seek to point out the distinctively Trinitarian aspect of supernatural grace which elevates man to share in God's Triune life, over against that participation in which all creatures partake by way of creation. This point will come to light most fully in chapter 6.

At this point, let us now turn to outline the procedure to be undertaken as follows, introducing in summary fashion the task of each successive chapter.

Chapter Précis

In what follows, we will proceed in three parts: (1) Part One (chapters 2 and 3) will introduce Henri de Lubac and the overarching historical and theological context for the nature-grace debate, particularly as it took place in the twentieth century. The remote but relevant historical context goes back at least to the French Revolution of 1789 and the Church's ongoing struggle with the rising tide of secularism. As we will see, ecclesial thinkers throughout France in the nineteenth century tended to align with conservative political theorists—those most opposed to the heirs of the Revolution—harboring hopes of forestalling the triumph of secularism. In the end, this alignment turned out to discredit the Church's engagement with modernity and actually bolstered the growth of secularism. For as the European monarchies of old lost credibility—to which the Church seemed so intimately intertwined—it seemed almost inevitable that the Church's fate would share in the ebb and flow of Europe's political fortunes, for better or worse.

In the twentieth-century, the Church in France found itself in a similar position when Nazi Germany defeated France in 1940, which

---

29. Through the grace of Christ, we become "partakers of the divine nature" (2 Pet 1:4).

resulted in four subsequent years of German occupation. Hitler installed
Marshal Henri Philippe Pétain (1856–1951) who governed France from
Vichy, and he would do so under the auspices of National Socialism.

Despite the ominous fact that he governed under Hitler's watch-
ful eye, Pétain's rule appeared to give some semblance of a return to a
more traditional form of government, one which ostensibly looked to
reverse some of the French Revolution's heritage of strident secularism
and anti-clericalism. For this reason—failing to recognize the full situation at hand—many Catholics were actually friendly to the conservative
political arrangement with Pétain, hoping that his rule would undo the
secularist trajectory of French society. However, de Lubac took strong
exception here, as he perspicaciously saw the true colors of Pétain's regime. In fact, his friend and fellow Jesuit, Yves de Montcheuil (1899–
1944), professor of theology at the Institute Catholique in Paris, paid the
ultimate price for his intellectual resistance against the Nazi regime: de
Montcheuil was shot and killed in 1944.[30] And de Lubac, too, had to flee
from the Gestapo on occasion, and it was precisely in this context that
his epochal work, *Surnaturel*, took final form, as he recounts here:

> In June 1940, leaving in haste with a group of companions for La
> Louvesc, after having evaded the Germans who were approach-
> ing Lyons, I carried along a bag with a parcel of notes in it, among
> which was the notebook for *Surnaturel*. I spent several days up
> there putting a little order into it. Soon there was the return from
> our exodus (when Lyons was south of the famous "line of demar-
> cation"), and I gave no more thought to it. But when, in 1943,
> being hunted by the Gestapo, I had to flee once more, I again
> carried along my notebook.[31]

His thinking on nature and grace is certainly not unrelated to this
dark period of European history, for de Lubac's aim is no other than to
articulate the foundations of a genuinely Christian humanism. In his
mind, the horror of the Nazi regime represented nothing short of the disastrous implications which follow when the nature and mystery of man

30. See de Lubac, *At the Service of the Church*, 47–49.
31. Ibid., 35. Many Jesuits heroically held their ground against the Nazi agenda
in France at this time. See Lapomarda, *Jesuits and the Third Reich*, 315–16. In the
epilogue, he summarizes the results of his research: "The Jesuits as an organization and
as individuals in service to others, Christians as well as Jews, did not remain silent but
resisted the evil policies of the Third Reich and, as a consequence, suffered very much
for such opposition to the Nazis in Europe" (ibid., 359).

is misapprehended—when we fail to see the innate dignity of every human person, as created in the image and likeness of God, and ultimately ordered to a supernatural union with God in Christ Jesus.

The Catholic intellectual backdrop for de Lubac at this time is the theology of pure nature (also known as the extrinsicist tradition) which stretched back to the time of the sixteenth-century Reformation. It developed rapidly against the backdrop of the condemnation of Michael Baius (1513–1589) in 1567 in Pope Pius V's papal bull *Ex omnibus afflictionibus*.[32] As we will see, Baius had a very low view of post-lapsarian human nature, not unlike that of Martin Luther (1483–1546).[33] Accordingly, Baius emphasized man's depravity to the point that man's nature seemed to take on an utter exigency for grace—an utter *need* for grace—in which case grace would seem to be no longer *gratuitous*.

The pure-nature tradition emerged forthrightly in this context, appearing to have on hand the ideal solution: namely, the need to ground theology upon the prior conception of "pure nature," that is, a conception of "human nature" considered abstractly, apart from the order of grace. This notion of pure nature allowed Catholic theologians to explain the coherent integrity of human nature—apart from the gift of grace—giving them the conceptual tools necessary to preserve the gratuity of grace, over against Baius' teaching on man's post-lapsarian condition. Consequently, when St. Pius V condemned several of Baius' propositions regarding nature and grace, the pure-nature tradition appeared to receive something of a papal endorsement. Largely for this reason, it quickly rose to hegemonic status, going virtually unchallenged for centuries—that is, until de Lubac called it into question at mid-twentieth century.

After setting up this historical context of de Lubac's work, chapter 3 will take up the foundational and methodological principles which govern de Lubac's teaching on nature and grace; here we will seek to

---

32. Denzinger, *Enchiridion symbolorum*, DH 1901–1980.

33. In *Bondage of the Will*, Luther writes: "Our will principally because of its corruption can do no good of itself." And similarly: "Free-will without God's grace is not free at all, but is the permanent prisoner and bondslave of evil, since it cannot turn itself to good" (Luther, *Selections from His Writings*, 182, 187, respectively). Similar to Luther's position on free will here, the following is a proposition attributed to Baius which was condemned by Pope Pius V in his Bull *Ex omnibus afflictionibus*: "It is a Pelagian error to say that free will is capable of avoiding sin" (Denzinger, *Enchiridion symbolorum*, DH 1901–1980).

show the contrast between him and the pure-nature tradition, as it manifests itself at a basic hermeneutical level. For example, de Lubac places a great deal of emphasis upon the theological category of paradox and he sees his efforts here as diverging sharply from his counterparts in the pure-nature tradition. With this methodological hermeneutic in hand, de Lubac simply refuses to restrict himself to mutually exclusive categories—such as *either* "natural desire" (for the beatific vision), *or* its "gratuitous" fulfillment. The category of paradox, in other words, enables de Lubac to transcend such conventional dichotomies, in which case one can affirm both man's *natural* desire for the beatific vision and its *gratuitous* fulfillment—no doubt, much to the chagrin of his pure-nature interlocutors. As we will see, this *modus operandi* of de Lubac is central to the logic of de Lubac's overall position on nature and grace.

This is but one example of the basic difference in theological posture and *prolegomena* of de Lubac over against the pure-nature tradition; their differences here initiate the fundamental trajectory of their disagreements more generally, which largely accounts for their apparent stalemate at mid-twentieth century. Thus, the treatment of de Lubac here will help to inform our treatment of both his overall position, as well as more precisely delineate where and how he differs from the pure-nature tradition.

Next, we will begin Part Two (chapters 4 and 5), where we will take up the recent resurgence of the pure-nature tradition, which has taken place largely over the last decade. Chapters 4 and 5 will treat two of its leading representatives, Lawrence Feingold and Steven A. Long, respectively.[34]

As we will see, it appears that the Church's shift from extrinsicism before the Council to intrinsicism after the Council may have gone too far—at least so it may seem by way of perception; and it is just this perception that explains this resurgence of the pure-nature tradition. Accordingly, these chapters will take up the pure-nature tradition's contemporary articulation, as well as their assessment of de Lubac.

At this point, let us state our thesis clearly: it is our contention that the resolution of these issues, as they have emerged in the contemporary form of the debate over nature and grace, can best be found in the theology of Matthias J. Scheeben (1835–1888). Accordingly, Part Three (chapter 6) will treat Scheeben's masterful combination of extrinsicism and

---

34. Feingold, *Natural Desire to See God*; and Long, *Natura Pura*.

intrinsicism, a synthesis which captures both dimensions of the mystery of nature and grace. Scheeben's thought, we contend, can reconcile the most important contributions of both the pure-nature tradition, as well as those of de Lubac; and for this reason, the recovery of his thought can move the present debate beyond its current stalemate, which has not yet moved substantially from its mid-century form, despite the increase in activity on this issue.

As an indication of Scheeben's potential to accomplish this mediating task, let us take note of the fact that quite diverse thinkers—on both sides of the nature-grace issue—praise his work and find in him something of an ally. This diversity points to a common convergence in Scheeben, one which we will explore throughout and which Aidan Nichols captures here:

> The sympathetic citation of his [Scheeben's] work by twentieth-century theologians as different as Hans Urs von Balthasar [1905–1988], a child of the so-called "new theology" [of which de Lubac is perhaps *the* representative] of the 1940s and 50s, and Réginald Garrigou-Lagrange [1877–1964], champion, in the years immediately preceding the Second Vatican Council, of "strict observance" Thomism [perhaps *the* intellectual opponent of de Lubac in the 1940s on nature and grace], attests to his mediating role.[35]

It will be the task of chapter 6 to bear out Scheeben's achievement here, which we will undertake in four phases: (1) we will introduce Scheeben and his credentials for successfully bringing about this reconciliation; (2) we will demonstrate his basic congruity with the pure-nature tradition; (3) we will survey his teaching on the grace of divine sonship (which will eminently distill the sublime and supernatural character of divine grace); finally, (4) we will demonstrate Scheeben's

---

35. Nichols, *Romance and System*, 19. Balthasar describes Scheeben's thought as: "truly and in the highest sense and degree a theology of the 'glories of divine grace'" (Balthasar, *Seeing the Form*, 116). Scheeben's Jesuit translator, Cyril Vollert, praises him in a similar vein: "His most notable contribution to Neo-Scholasticism is his service in bringing the supernatural, in its full purity and beauty, back to the center of theological thought. By his doctrine as well as by his method he sought to destroy the lingering influence that rationalism and the Enlightenment had exerted on Catholic theology. He was neither philosopher nor apologist but a theologian . . . He tried to attract men to the faith, not by proofs built on historical or apologetic foundations, but by opening and displaying its inner treasures" (Vollert, "Introduction," in Scheeben, *Nature and Grace*, xiii).

ability to accommodate the intrinsicist contribution of de Lubac by way of his teaching on the Incarnation, where Scheeben captures the very Christocentrism mentioned at the outset of this chapter.

Let us conclude here by observing that Scheeben's thought on nature and grace is yet to be considered a critical part of this debate. For this reason, it is our modest hope and conviction that the present argument will rectify this lacuna; for Scheeben, it seems, has a tremendous contribution to make to this discussion—and perhaps unlike any other, he can reconcile both sides together and move the debate beyond its current impasse. With this overarching and timely task before us, let us begin our journey with Henri de Lubac.

PART ONE

Henri de Lubac

2

De Lubac on Nature and Grace

The Historical and Theological Context

A s we saw briefly in chapter 1, the context motivating Henri de
Lubac's thinking on nature and grace is undoubtedly the secularization of the European heart and mind.[1] His aim was to re-articulate
a Christian humanism for post-war Europe, one which aimed to link
man's beatitude inherently to the supernatural order of grace. This push
toward a more intrinsic alignment of nature and grace first appears in
his 1946 work *Surnaturel* which called into question the centuries-long
hegemony of the pure-nature tradition; as we have seen, the central thesis of this work is as powerful as it is straightforward: "L'esprit est donc
désir de Dieu."[2]

This *obiter dictum* serves as the foundation of his vision for an un-
relenting Christian humanism, a point which especially comes out later
in life when he describes the evangelical purpose underlying *Surnaturel*:
"The work thus constituted a sort of attempt to reestablish contact between Catholic theology and contemporary thought, or at least to elimi-
nate one basic obstacle to that contact . . . with a view to engaging in
dialogue with it."[3]

1. See Chadwick, *Secularization of the European Mind*, 107–60.
2. De Lubac, *Surnaturel*, 483; English translation: "The spirit is desire for God."
3. De Lubac, *At the Service of the Church*, 36. "L'ouvrage constituait donc une sorte
d'essai pour rétablir le contact entre la théologie catholique et la pensée contemporaine,
ou du moins pour éliminer un obstacle de base à ce contact, non pas en vue d'une
'adaptation' quelconque à cette pensée, mais plutôt en vue de permettre d'engager
avec elle un dialogue,—lequel, commme toujours lorsqu'il s'agit d'idées sérieuses, no

The need for Catholic theology to engage the culture in this manner had been apparent for some time, for by the dawn of the twentieth century it was clear that de Lubac's own native France was no longer desirous of the titular honor, "eldest daughter of the Church." To a large extent, this sentiment was shared by Western Europe as well, as many European countries attempted to sort out the relationship between their newly-won secular identity and their long Catholic past.

Not just the French Revolution, but the upheavals of the widespread revolutions of 1848 are significant moments in this European narrative,[4] not to mention the profoundly symbolic meaning behind the Spanish Civil War of 1936: as the monarchies of the *ancien régime* were overthrown, so too was Europe's former religious identity. For in both perception and reality, ecclesial structures were so tied to the political arrangements of the past that their fate seemed inextricably bound up with one another. For this reason, "Europe," as something evocative of a common Catholic and Christian patrimony was coming to an end, a transition which Pope Benedict Emeritus describes here from his contemporary vantage point:

> Europe has developed a culture that, in a manner hitherto unknown to mankind, excludes God from public awareness. His existence may be denied altogether or considered unprovable and uncertain and, hence, as something belonging to the sphere of subjective choices. In either case, God is irrelevant to public life.[5]

For de Lubac, the Church's inability to engage the culture constructively was directly affected by its predominant nature-grace framework. His more intrinsicist vision for Christian humanism, however, was met

---

pourrait être qu'un affrontement, un combat" (De Lubac, *Mémorie sur l'occasion de mes écrits*, 34–35). See Komonchak, "Theology and Culture at Mid-Century," 580.

4. Chadwick, *Secularization of the European Mind*, 45: "During the middle years of the nineteenth century, churches, old-established and conservative, stood against liberalism. Liberals wished to dismantle or adapt the ancien régime, of which these churches were part. The mortal enmity between the Church of Rome and Italian liberals was only a tense example of a clash which was found in Prussia, Austria, France, Spain, and sometimes England." See also Derfler, *Socialism since Marx*, 3–12.

5. See Ratzinger, *Christianity and the Crisis of Cultures*, 30. The emeritus pope is here dealing with the "debate about the definition of Europe and its new political shape" (ibid., 31)—particularly, as this debate concerned the preamble of the European Constitution (ibid., 32) and the "Christian roots of Europe" (ibid.).

with resistance—and not just from his secular interlocutors—but from his fellow Catholic theologians in the pure-nature tradition.

As we noted in the previous chapter, this resistance seems to have found its way even into papal teaching in *Humani generis* in 1950, the immediate aftermath of which resulted in the stripping of de Lubac's faculties for teaching Catholic theology, as well as the removal of several of his works from the shelves of Jesuit libraries—not the least of which was the monumental *Surnaturel*. This would constitute no less than an intellectual exile for de Lubac, and one which would last throughout most of the 1950s.[6]

This isolation would eventually come to an end with the dawn of a new decade, and remarkably de Lubac would find himself fast becoming one of the foremost inspirations behind the Second Vatican Council (1962–1965). Given the controversy that surrounded *Surnaturel*, the affinity between him and the Council is certainly noteworthy, especially where the Council's teaches regarding man's *single* final end: "All are in fact called to *one* and the same destiny, which is divine."[7]

This development is indicative of a larger shift in the Church's thinking on nature and grace—a shift *from* extrinsicism, *to* the more intrinsicist alignment of de Lubac. This development is important not only for our treatment of de Lubac here, but also for the larger task at hand, since it was this ecclesial swing in the intrinsicist direction—and the perception that it went *too* far—that constitutes the *raison d'être* for the resurgence of the pure-nature tradition, as we have noted earlier.

---

6. Between the years of 1950–58 de Lubac was effectively terminated from his teaching of Catholic theology, and his texts *Surnaturel*; *Discovery of God*; and *Corpus Mysticum* were removed from Jesuit libraries. It is in this period that de Lubac published his three books on Buddhism. By 1953, however, restrictions seemed to have been relaxed somewhat, allowing for the publication of *Méditation sur l'Église*; in English: *Splendor of the Church*. In 1950, apparently before restrictions were fully in place, he was able to publish his work on Origen: De Lubac, *Histoire et Esprit: L'Intelligence de l'Écriture d'après Origène*; in English: De Lubac, *History and Spirit: The Understanding of Scripture according to Origen*. See Voderholzer, *Meet Henri de Lubac*, 69; originally published in German, 1999, as *Henri de Lubac begegnen*. In 1956, de Lubac began work on his monumental, *Exégèse médiéval*, which came out in four volumes between the years of 1959–1964 (see Voderholzer, *Meet Henri de Lubac*, 79). De Lubac, *Exégèse médiévale, Les quatre sens de l'Ecriture*. De Lubac, *Exégèse médiéval: Les quatre sens de l'Ecriture*. De Lubac, *Exégèse médiévale, Les quatre sens de l'Ecriture*.

7. *Gaudium et Spes*, no. 22, in *Vatican Council II: Constitutions, Decrees, Declarations*, emphasis added.

At this point, let us now turn to the historical background of de Lubac's teaching on nature and grace. This background, both remote and proximate, is critical for understanding the ultimate import and motivation of de Lubac's teaching—which from beginning to end is none other than the establishment of a genuine Christian humanism as a response to the strident secularism of his day.

Henri de Lubac in Historical Context

Nineteenth Century

Perhaps irrevocably, the very identity of France was reshaped in the French Revolution. For from the first convocation of the Estates General in May of 1789, to the Tennis Court Oath taken by the Constitutional Clergy in late 1790 (obliging their allegiance to the state)—and on to the Reign of Terror in 1792–93 (where populism turned violent, shedding the blood of many priests and religious)—a battle ensued over the very heart and soul of France; Sunday rest was set aside as symbolic of the superstition of the past, only to be replaced by the more metric and rationally evocative *decadi* (ten-day week);[8] the worship of "Reason" was quite literally enshrined in the Cathedral of Notre Dame with its own newly-devised enlightened cult.[9] While these events seem quite distant from our experience, they constituted nothing short of France's disavowal of its Catholic past, a disavowal which set in motion a train of events that are still running their course in the present time.[10].

In the aftermath of the French Revolution, Napoléon Bonaparte (1769–1821) sought to reign in this revolutionary spirit, bringing about a rapprochement of sorts between Church and State. He sought the anointing of approbation from Pope Pius VII, much as Pope Leo III had done for Charlemagne in the year 800. Hence, Napoléon established a Concordat with the Church in 1801, instituting an order of reconcili-

8. Dansette, *Religious History of Modern France*, 1:90; originally published in French as *Histoire Religieuse de la France Contemporaine: de la Révolution à la Troisième République*.

9. Ibid., 94–95.

10. Ibid., 52–57, 70–72, 90, 94, 96, 113.

ation which would govern Church-State relations for approximately a century.[11]

However, this reconciliation was no unmitigated good for the Church: though it halted the onslaught of overt persecution, the French clergy would now become state employees, and Napoléon would enjoy the prerogative of appointing bishops.[12] In this context, religious orders would receive the brunt of persecution, since their allegiance inevitably lay directly with their religious superiors or the Holy Father himself—making them generally more resistant to state influence. This state of affairs continued even in de Lubac's day, which is in fact the reason why he had to undertake his novitiate in England in 1921, outside of his native France.[13]

The critical culmination of this secularist trajectory of France occurred under the administration of the French Prime Minister Émile Combes (1835–1921). A former seminarian—now-turned-Freemason—unilaterally severed diplomatic ties with the Vatican in 1904.[14] This action took on the form of a legal decree on 9 December 1905 when this outright secularization became law.[15] Its promulgation represented France's self-proclaimed emancipation from its Catholic past, as twentieth-century French historian Adrian Dansette explains here:

> The separation bill . . . became the law of 9th December, 1905. Today, it still governs relations between Church and State. The concordat [of Napoleon, 1801] had described Catholicism as "the religion of the majority of French people." The new law proclaimed that the Republic did not recognize any form of religion, nor did it pay the salaries of its ministers. . . . The State ceased to give it an official position in the order of precedence and to concern itself with the appointment of the Church's ministers or with their salaries.[16]

11. Larkin, *Church and State*, 2. See also Dansette, *Religious History of Modern France*, 1:149–56.

12. Dansette, *Religious History of Modern France*, 1:157–68. See also Larkin, *Church and State*, 48.

13. Voderholzer, *Meet Henri de Lubac*, 28–30.

14. Pope Leo XIII had died on July 20, 1903. See Dansette, *Religious History of Modern France*, 2:214–19. See also Larkin, *Church and State*, 183. Voderholzer, *Meet Henri de Lubac*, 29–30. Aubert, *Church in a Secularised Society*, 75–76.

15. Dansette, *Religious History of Modern France*, 2:205–6.

16. Ibid., 2:231.

More was at stake than simply a Church-State separation, however. For Combes, this constituted a *rejection* of France's public and Christian identity, and especially its previous ties to the Church:

> He [Combes] declared war on the old religion and tried to sub-stitute for it another. . . . Thus, the [more positive] idea of secular-ism as a guarantee of liberty and equality in a country divided in its beliefs was being substituted [for a much more pernicious and militant] secularist ideology, denying Catholicism and promot-ing a rationalist religion, which put man in the place of God.[17]

The Church did not adapt well in this changing context, and its failure to do so reinforced the burgeoning secular thrust of French society. Perhaps no event captures this better than what is known as the "Dreyfus Affair," so named after Alfred Dreyfus (1859–1935), a Jewish officer who was falsely accused of treason toward the end of the nineteenth century. The significance of this event goes well beyond the specific details of the trial, for it became truly emblematic of this French (and European) cultural struggle between its Catholic past and its burgeoning secular future.[18]

In 1894, Alfred Dreyfus was convicted of treason for supposedly revealing intelligence secrets to the German army; the case was re-opened after questions were raised regarding the justice of the convic-tion.[19] Anti-Semitic sentiment was rife, and unfortunately prominent Churchmen constituted no serious exception;[20] it soon became apparent that a significant piece of evidence brought against Dreyfus was in fact a forgery—no doubt, the result of the anti-Semitic machinations of the day.[21] And in fact, it was advocates of the liberal Republic (heirs of the Revolution) that led the charge in vindicating Dreyfus, while the tradi-tional nobility of French society—those symbolic of the *ancien régime* (exemplified here in the army)—came out *against* Dreyfus. Hence, at least by perception, the Church was on the wrong side of the issue, as many of her intellectual representatives rushed to the army's defense against the purportedly treasonous Jewish officer. Dansette writes:

17. Ibid., 2:205–6.

18. See Derfler, *Third French Republic*, 48–59.

19. McManners, *Church and State in France*, 124–25.

20. Ibid., 122–23. Dansette, *Religious History of Modern France*, 2:167. See also Derfler, *The Dreyfus Affair*, 26.

21. McManners, *Church and State in France*, 125. Dansette, *Religious History of Modern France*, 2:169, 172.

"Almost all the Church's friends were opposed to Dreyfus, and almost all her enemies, the Jews, the Protestants, and the free-thinkers, were on the other side."[22]

This attachment to the *ancien régime* on the part of the Church continued long into the twentieth century and can be readily observed in the sympathies many Churchmen had for the French political movement known as *Action Française*; this was a conservative political movement which emerged at the end of the nineteenth century, largely in response to the fallout of the Dreyfus affair. As proponents of the liberal republic gained momentum, *Action Française* became a rallying point of resistance and a vocal proponent of France's Catholic and conservative past. However, *Action Française* actually had very little to do with the Gospel; in fact, its founder Charles Maurras was no less than a committed *atheist*.[23] Still, many churchmen of high clerical repute had strong sympathies for the movement on account of its opposition to the liberal sentiments of the day, as Dansette recounts here:

> There can be no doubt that Pius X . . . felt some sympathy for the Action Française whose opponents, modernism and the *Sillon* [a pro-democratic newspaper founded by Marc Sangnier and rival of *Action Française*], were also his own. He remarked . . . that Maurras [founder of *Action Française* and atheist] was "a doughty defender of the Church and the Holy See". . . .The Pope looked on Maurras as a defender of the Church from outside.[24]

World War II

The volatility of this more remote context for de Lubac's writings is compounded by his more proximate setting—writing as he did, right in the very heart of World War II.[25] Contemporary German de Lubac

22. Dansette, *Religious History of Modern France*, 2:181.

23. Ibid., 2:380, 383.

24. Ibid., 2:385. See also Aubert, *Church in a Secularised Society*, 52, 79.

25. Thus, the Nazi occupation (1940–1944) of France and the trials of World War II provide the overarching context in which many of de Lubac's seminal works matured into final form, the exception being *Catholicisme*, which he published in 1938; in English: *Catholicism*. Published initially in 1944 is de Lubac, *Corpus Mysticum: L'Eucharistie et l'Église au Moyen Âge*; English translation: Henri de Lubac, *Corpus Mysticum: The Eucharist and the Church in the Middle Ages*; and published initially in the same year (1944) also: de Lubac, *Le drame l'humanisme athée*; English translation: de Lubac, *The*

scholar, Rudolf Voderholzer, describes this more immediate context for de Lubac's work this way:

> De Lubac expressly denied that he was repeatedly arrested by the Germans, as has sometimes been reported. It is true, however, that after the German troops had marched into the hitherto free zone, including Lyons, in the fall of 1942, he had to flee the city again in 1943 because the Gestapo were looking for him. This time he found refuge in a religious house in Vals (a spa south of Lyons). He used this time of complete seclusion to rework and expand his book *Surnaturel*. "Taking advantage of the resources offered by the Vals library, the manuscript swelled. When I came back to Lyons soon after the departure of the German army, it was ready to be delivered to the printer."[26]

Once again, in this proximate setting we find a lingering penchant on the Church's part for traditional forms of government. Thus, as with the Church's involvement in the Dreyfus affair—and with *Action Française*—and so also here: in this context, the Church's lingering attachment to the *anciene régime* led many French Catholics to sympathize with the government of Pétain in Vichy, France, a government which ruled under the auspices of no less an ominous figure than Adolf Hitler during the Nazi occupation of France from 1940 to 1944.

In order to consider some of the roots of this lingering attachment and their relation to the issue of nature and grace, let us observe their expression in the political thought of the great Neoscholastic Thomist, Réginald Garrigou-Lagrange (1877–1964). His biographer, Richard Peddicord, captures his political sentiments this way:

> His fidelity to St. Thomas, witnessed in his preface to the Angelic Doctor's *De regimine principum*, kept him from being friendly toward democracy. The call to restore the monarchy . . . and to restore the Catholic Church's traditional position in French society made it easy for him to overlook Maurras's own atheism and his purely pragmatic use of the symbols and ethos of Catholicism.[27]

Drama of Atheist Humanism. The other two works that originate in this period are: de Lubac, *Proudhon et le Christianisme*; in English, *The Un-Marxian Socialist*; and de Lubac, *De la connaissance de Dieu*. A revised edition came out in 1956, entitled *Sur les chemins de Dieu*; English translation: Henri de Lubac, *The Discovery of God*.

26. Voderholzer, *Meet Henri de Lubac*, 57; the quotation is from de Lubac, *At the Service of the Church*, 35.

27. Peddicord, *The Sacred Monster of Thomism*, 93.

At this point, let us pause to notice a certain anomaly here: namely, that one unabashedly formed in the tradition of extrinsicism (as Garrigou-Lagrange certainly was) would seem to be more logically in favor of a political arrangement built upon the *autonomy* of the natural order—in which case one would have expected him to have been a *friend* of secular democracy, seeing in it something of a *purely* natural political arrangement, built upon natural justice and the like. In fact, this logical connection between secular politics and an extrinsicist emphasis upon a strong nature-grace distinction can be observed (of all places!) in Vatican II:

> Many of our contemporaries seem to fear that a close association between human activity and religion will endanger the autonomy of humanity, of organizations and of science. If by the autonomy of earthly affairs is meant the gradual discovery, utilization and ordering of the laws and values of matter and society, then the demand for autonomy is perfectly in order: it is at once the claim of humankind today and the desire of the creator. *By the very nature of creation, material being is endowed with its own stability, truth and excellence, its own order and laws.* These, as the methods proper to every science and technique must be respected. . . . We cannot but deplore certain attitudes not unknown among Christians deriving from a shortsighted view of the rightful autonomy of science; they have occasioned conflict and controversy and have misled many into opposing faith and science.[28]

In other words, Garrigou-Lagrange's political views are really more consonant with the supernaturalizing tendency of *intrinsicism*, which tends to align nature and grace so closely that the "natural" loses its abiding and independent integrity. Accordingly, some versions of this thoroughgoing intrinsicism would be favorable to something like a religious state, certainly not a secular one.

The following statement from contemporary philosopher Stanley Hauerwas illustrates this type of intrinsicism—when he advocates for (or at least suggests the legitimacy of advocating for) a "*Christian*" physics, of all things. Such a position is indicative of a radical intrinsicism because it negates the independent coherence and intelligibility of the natural order—here even at the level of mathematical physics. Hauerwas writes:

28. *Gaudium et Spes*, no. 36, in *Vatican Council II: Constitutions, Decrees, Declarations*, emphasis added.

It is at least possible that the very content of physics, history, or economics shaped by faith may be different. I need to be very clear about what I am saying about how the Christian faith may shape the material conditions that make what Christians mean by physics quite different from what physics might mean if it is produced by those who do not share our faith. Am I really suggesting that there might be something like a "Christian physics" or a "Christian economics"? I can only say, "It depends on the character of what is meant by physics or economics in the societies in which the church finds herself."[29]

Thus, there is a certain logical inconsistency exhibited here between extrinsicism and the above-mentioned attachment to the *anciene régime*; nonetheless, many Churchmen at mid-century embraced this very juxtaposition, despite its logical tension.

This intellectual context helped turn Catholic hopes naively to Marshal Henri Philippe Pétain (1856–1951)—the next in the line of conservative political hopefuls appearing sympathetic to Church-state collaboration. Once again, as was the case in the Dreyfus affair, not to mention *Action Française,* and so also here: the fear of strident French secularism led many Catholics to support Pétain, overlooking the very tragedy unfolding before their eyes. Robert O. Paxton explains:

As the godless Third Republic lost its legitimacy, few groups found revenge sweeter than the French clergy and the faithful, nursing long grudges against the results of the French Revolution and against sixty years of official republican anticlericalism. . . . Most Catholics longed for official support for religious values and for undoing old wrongs that still smarted: the "expulsion of God" from public schools in the 1880s, the quarrel over church property at the time of the separation of church and state in 1905, laws that discriminated against religious orders. . . . And so Monseigneur Delay was speaking for most Catholics when he told Pétain at the end of 1940 during one of the marshal's triumphal tours, "God is at work through you . . . to save France."[30]

Though of course tragically misguided in hindsight, the already-aged Pétain did provide fodder for these misguided Catholic sympathies—just as Charles Mauras had done earlier with *Action Française.*

29. Hauerwas, "How Risky is *The Risk of Education?*," 79–94, here 88.

30. Paxton, *Vichy France,* 149. Paxton notes that French and German records reveal no serious dissent against the regime prior to 1941 (ibid., 38). See also Larkin, *France since the Popular Front,* 93–94.

For example, Pétain reinstated religious education in state schools, over-
turning the anti-clerical educational reforms of Jules Ferry in the early
1880s, which had especially targeted schools run by religious orders.[31]
Pétain even granted state funding for parochial schools.[32] Nonetheless,
the benign nature of this political arrangement quickly showed its true
colors: anti-Semitic laws were already in place by the end of 1940, and
the deportation of the Jews took place on French soil by the year 1942.
While Marshal Pétain may have governed France from Vichy, he certainly did so at the behest of Adolf Hitler.[33]

De Lubac stood aghast at the ignorance of many of his fellow
Catholics in this period; in the words of Joseph Komonchak: "Many
Thomists . . . [simply continued their] unfortunate alliance [with] . . .
right-wing politics."[34] But the passion with which de Lubac took opposition to this Catholic acquiescence to Pétain is readily seen in the following excerpt from a letter he wrote to his superiors on 25 April 1941:

> In the face of so tragic a situation, how can we fail to be surprised
> to perceive only so few signs of uneasiness in Catholic and even
> ecclesiastical circles? Without stopping their intrigues in other
> respects, the Nazis seek to put our vigilance to sleep, and nearly
> everything is taking place as if they were succeeding. It seems
> that we have become, in large measure, dupes of the necessity
> in which we find ourselves of participating in the official lie. . . .
> Many priests are extremely ignorant of the situation or prove to
> be skeptical about facts that are nevertheless, unfortunately, well
> established. . . . For a long time a very skillful propaganda has

31. Aubert, *Church in a Secularized Society*, 73. Also Dansette, *Religious History of Modern France*, 2:41.

32. Paxton, *Vichy France*, 151.

33. Ibid., 173–74. Leslie Derfler draws out the connection between the Dreyfus affair, *Action Française*, and the situation here in Vichy, France at mid-twentieth century in the following: "The anti-Semitism and nationalist policies of the collaborationist Vichy regime [is] the 'tragic sequel' to the Dreyfus Affair. . . . The general who allied himself with the people sympathetic to Hitler's Germany, Marshal Philippe Pétain, did so . . . out of hatred for the Republic, like the generals at the time of the [Dreyfus] Affair. . . . [Pétain's] ideology was nourished by his friend, the implacable anti-Dreyfusard [one *against* the side of Dreyfus] Charles Maurras [founder of *Action Française*]. . . . During the Vichy period (1940–1943), all anti-Dreyfusards defended—at least initially—the [Vichy] regime and all Dreyfusards opposed it, [and so] the old cleavages that distinguished the two camps endured well into the twentieth century" (Derfler, *Dreyfus Affair*, 61–62).

34. Komonchak, "Theology and Culture at Mid-Century," 579–602, here 602.

been exercised over them, and as most do not suspect how far
the art of Hitler's lie goes, it has often had only too much success.
. . . *Today, moreover, the old, ever-recurring illusion of the support
of authority makes us forget all the rest.*[35]

In de Lubac's mind, the atrocities of this period have everything to
do with the issue of nature and grace, for these unconscionable events
showcase the disastrous fruits of the then-regnant secular and atheistic
humanism, as well as the inability of the pure-nature tradition to respond adequately in this secularist milieu. As we have said, de Lubac's
teaching on nature and grace must be understood within the context of
his engagement with secular modernity, with the express aim of grounding a veritable *Christian* humanism—which in his mind constitutes the
only true *humanism*. For him, anything less inevitably loses sight of
man's intrinsic dignity and the true nobility of his calling. Accordingly,
during the Christmas of 1943 in the midst of World War II, he writes:
"It is not true, as is sometimes said, that man cannot organize the world
without God. What is true is that, without God, he can ultimately only
organize it *against* man. Exclusive humanism is *inhuman* humanism."[36]

Let us now turn to introduce the pure-nature tradition more fully.
In so doing, we will better understand why de Lubac was met with such
opposition, despite his otherwise laudable intentions. An entire theological culture was perceived to hang in the balance upon the publication of *Surnaturel* in 1946; and for thinkers in the pure-nature tradition,
a verdict favorable to de Lubac could only spell disaster for the very
integrity of the faith.

Introduction to the Pure-Nature Tradition

According to its proponents, the pure-nature tradition is rooted in the
teaching of St. Thomas Aquinas, although this point is especially disputed by de Lubac in *Surnaturel*—the full title of which suggests innocu-
ously enough that it is merely a "historical study" (*Surnaturel: Études
historiques*). This mere "historical study," however, made startling claims
to say the least, as it leveled an indictment against the whole theological

35. De Lubac "Letter to My Superiors," (Lyons, April 25, 1941) cited in *Theology
in History*, 432–34, emphasis added; originally published in French as *Théologie dans
l'histoire*.

36. De Lubac, *The Drama of Atheist Humanism*, 14, emphasis added.

tradition of pure nature for their misunderstanding of Aquinas' teaching on nature and grace. According to de Lubac—contrary to the pure-nature tradition—Aquinas actually held to *one* final end for man.

Moreover, not only did de Lubac challenge the pure-nature tradition's standard interpretation of Aquinas—and not only did he suggest that the pure-nature tradition was ill-equipped to respond to modern secularism—but even further: he argues that the pure-nature tradition actually *abetted* the rise of modern secularism, on account of its excessive emphasis upon the independent integrity of the natural order.

In the following sections, we will take up the pure-nature tradition's relationship to each of the following: (1) St. Thomas Aquinas; (2) Michael Baius (1513–1589); and (3) modern secularism. We should note that the teaching of St. Thomas will reappear in the second and third sections as well, since the interpretation and application of his thought always remains in the background of these issues.

The Relation of St. Thomas to the Pure-Nature Tradition

Let us begin by noting that St. Thomas was certainly no exponent of the pure-nature tradition, pure and simple; contemporary pure-nature advocates concede as much when they argue—not so much that their teaching can be read off the pages of St. Thomas—but that their interpretive tradition develops organically from principles readily found within St. Thomas. For this reason, let us state upfront that the exegetical question is largely insoluble, since it all depends on which texts are interpretively privileged over others. One set of texts lends support to the legitimacy of the pure-nature tradition, while others clearly favor de Lubac.[37]

As an example of the latter, St. Thomas writes: "Final and perfect happiness can consist in nothing else than the vision of the Divine

37. See contemporary pure-nature advocate, Steven A. Long who writes: "It helps to put to rest the exegetic difficulty. It is without doubt true that there is a problem in the very texts of Aquinas, and a problem which seemingly does not allow much room for maneuver with respect to its solution because the doctrinal points that constitute the elements of the problem—one is almost tempted to say 'constitute the contradiction'—are starkly and clearly stated in St. Thomas's text. Yet the realization that there are indeed *two* sets of texts, one of which was not merely an interposed corruption, itself marks a decisive advance toward correct interpretation of Thomas's teaching" (Long, *Natura Pura*, 13, emphasis original). Edward T. Oakes makes the same point in "The *Surnaturel* Controversy," 625–56, here 644–45.

Essence."[38] To the same effect, he states again: "There resides in every man a natural desire to know the cause of any effect which he sees. . . . But if the intellect of the rational creature could not reach so far as to the first cause of things, the natural desire would remain void."[39] And likewise in another work, he states:

> Now, a person has not attained his ultimate end until natural desire comes to rest. Therefore, for human happiness which is the ultimate end it is not enough to have merely any kind of intelligible knowledge; there must be *divine* knowledge, as an ultimate end, to terminate the natural desire. So, the ultimate end of man is the knowledge of God.[40]

For St. Thomas, man's final end must consist in the vision of God: "Natural desire does not come to rest as a result of this knowledge which separate substances have of God; rather, it further arouses the desire to see the divine substance."[41] Moreover, man has a natural desire for this supernatural end—and yet such a natural desire cannot be in vain—and so here we can see something of the crux of de Lubac's teaching right in the thought of the Angelic Doctor: namely, that man has a natural desire for his supernatural end, the only end in which man's beatitude consists—but yet this supernatural end is nonetheless gratuitous. Accordingly, St. Thomas writes:

> Since it is impossible for a natural desire to be incapable of fulfillment, and since it would be so, if it were not possible to reach an understanding of divine substance *such as all minds naturally desire*, we must say that it is possible for the substance of God to be seen intellectually, both by separate intellectual substances and by our souls.[42]

After asserting that man has a natural desire for the beatific vision—and after asserting that natural desires cannot be in vain—Aquinas then turns to defend the necessity of grace in order for man to attain his supernatural end. Hence, for Aquinas and for de Lubac, man's *natural* desire for the beatific vision is juxtaposed alongside an

---

38. *ST* I-IIae, q. 3, a. 8.
39. *ST* I, q. 12, a. 1.
40. *ScG* III, q. 25, ch. 12, emphasis added.
41. *ScG* III, q. 50, ch. 2.
42. *ScG* III, q. 51, ch. 1, emphasis added.

unequivocal affirmation of the *gratuity* of this very supernatural end. St. Thomas states:

> Moreover, whatever exceeds the limitations of a nature cannot accrue to it except through the action of another being. For instance, water does not tend upward unless it is moved by something else. Now, seeing God's substance transcends the limitations of every created nature; indeed, it is proper for each created intellectual nature to understand according to the manner of its own substance. But divine substance cannot be understood in this way, as we showed above. Therefore, the attainment by a created intellect to the vision of divine substance is not possible except through the action of God, Who transcends all creatures.
>
> Thus, it is said: "The grace of God is life everlasting" (Rom 6:23). In fact, we have shown that man's happiness, which is called life everlasting, consists in this divine vision, and we are said to attain it by God's grace alone, because such a vision exceeds all the capacity of a creature and it is not possible to reach it without divine assistance. Now, when such things happen to a creature, they are attributed to God's grace. And the Lord says: "I will manifest Myself to him" (John 14:21).[43]

On the other side of things, the only real basis for asserting that St. Thomas affirms the possibility of a purely natural end—as still possible in the present divine economy—usually stems from passages dealing with limbo as a final state. The pure-nature tradition's interpretation infers from the lack of suffering in limbo that it is tantamount to a purely natural beatitude. Aquinas touches on this issue in the following from *de Malo*, which is often cited in support of the pure-nature tradition:

> Man endowed with only natural powers would be without the divine vision if he were to die in this state, but nevertheless the debt of not having it would not be applicable to him. For it is one thing not to be bound to have, which does not have the nature of punishment but of defect only, and it is another thing to be bound not to have, which does have the nature of punishment.[44]

However, let us state clearly that the speculative question regarding man's purely natural end—in contradistinction to the historical and exegetical one—is probably not best adjudicated by recourse to the final

43. *ScG* III, q. 52, ch. 6–7.
44. *De Malo*, q. 5, a. 15, ad 1 cited in *On Evil*, 214.

state of limbo, since such a premise is less universally viable in the present context than it used to be in a previous era of the Church. Likely, it is the case that St. Thomas considered limbo to be established Church teaching, and so one might suppose that—had it not been for the customary acceptance of the doctrine of limbo—he would not have come so close to affirming the possibility of man's purely natural end in the present economy. On this issue, we will see that Steven A. Long (whom we will treat in chapter 5) is much closer to the spirit of St. Thomas than is his fellow pure-nature advocate Lawrence Feingold (whom we will treat in chapter 4). For the latter employs limbo as a *premise* in his argument in order to defend the possibility of man's purely natural end, while the former is much more sensitive to the fact that the concrete ordination of the present economy necessarily modifies the hypothetical possibilities of pure nature.

On the other hand, there is abundant support in Aquinas for the *intelligible* distinction between man's proportionate *natural* end and his disproportionate *supernatural* end. For example, he writes:

> Man by his nature is proportioned to a certain end for which he has a natural appetite, and which he can work to achieve by his natural powers. This end is a certain contemplation of the divine attributes, *in the measure in which this is possible for man through his natural powers*; and in this end even the philosophers placed the final happiness of man. But God has prepared man *for another end*, one that exceeds the proportionality of human nature. This end is eternal life, which consists in the vision of God in his essence, an end which exceeds the proportionality of any created nature, being connatural to God alone.[45]

Leaving aside the exegetical question, let us simply observe that such passages provided the pure-nature tradition with enough to go on for the next stage in its development, the key moment of which seems to have come when Tommaso de Vio (Cajetan) (1469–1534) expounded the rudiments of the pure-nature tradition in his commentary on St. Thomas' *Summa Theologiae*. The commentary venue certainly lent itself to the impression that Cajetan was merely expounding the teaching of the Angelic Doctor, no doubt bolstering the authority of the burgeoning pure-nature tradition.[46]

---

45. *De Veritate*, q. 27, a. 2, emphasis added.
46. De Lubac, *Augustinianism and Modern Theology*, 113: "His [Cajetan's] principal

According to de Lubac, by the time we get to the Jesuit Francisco Suárez (1548–1617), the pure-nature tradition had taken a "gigantic leap forward."[47] Indeed, by the seventeenth century, the codification of the pure-nature system seems to have been largely complete,[48] with the result that from Cajetan in the sixteenth century to Garrigou-Lagrange in the twentieth century, there seems to be a virtually unbroken lineage. In fact, the unanimity on this tradition appears to have been so strong that even Jesuit and Dominican alike were in fundamental accord, as Feingold writes here:

> Suárez completed the work of forming a classical synthesis con-
> cerning the interpretation of the natural desire to see God that
> remained basically unchanged for over three hundred years.
> . . . Later writers develop various points but add little that is sub-
> stantively new.[49]

At this juncture, we will turn to the controversy surrounding Michael Baius and its role in the development of the pure-nature tradition. Perhaps more than all else, it is this historical episode which spurred the rapid rise and enduring hegemony of the pure-nature tradition.

The Relation of Michael Baius to the Pure-Nature Tradition

As we discussed briefly in the first chapter, the condemnation of Michael Baius is central to the development of the pure-nature tradition.[50] The

---

originality . . . is that he puts forward his thesis as an explanation of the thought of St. Thomas." De Lubac does not fail to note the Humanist connection with Cajetan, citing his studies at Padua (a bastion of Italian humanism) from 1491–1496, and his subsequent teaching career there as well (ibid., 113). Published in French as De Lubac, *Augustinisme et théologie moderne*. The above citation in French is as follows: "Mais son originalité principale . . . c'est qu'il présente sa thèse comme une explication de la pensée de saint Thomas" (De Lubac, *Augustinianisme et Théologie Moderne*, 144).

47. De Lubac, *Augustinianism and Modern Theology*, 157; "Avec François Suárez . . . elle va faire pas de géant" (De Lubac, *Augustinianisme et Théologie Moderne*, 194).

48. For a brief but very good account of the historical rise of the doctrine of pure nature, see Voderholzer, *Meet Henri de Lubac*, 128–33.

49. Feingold, *Natural Desire to See God*, 276.

50. See for example, de Lubac, *Augustinianism and Modern Theology*, 162: "Without . . . going back any further than the time of Baius it is possible . . . to show that this idea of pure nature, as it is understood by modern theologians, is a systematic idea, quite legitimate . . . but *recent*." In French: "Sans remonter plus haut . . . que l'époque même de Baius, il est possible . . . de montrer que cette idée de 'pure nature', telle que l'entend la

concept of "pure nature," as a conceptual understanding of human nature distinct from grace, proved to be immediately useful in responding to Baius, as well as Cornelius Jansensius (1585–1638) who held to a similar anthropological doctrine. Both thinkers attempted to revive what they perceived to be the classic teaching of St. Augustine (354–430), and in so doing they exaggerated humanity's sinful (post-lapsarian) state to the point that the integrity of man's nature, *qua* nature, seemed to dissipate. For them, whatever pristine state man had been in before the Fall, the reality of sin had more or less destroyed the powers of human nature, making him virtually impotent to do any good, apart from the grace of Christ.

In this light, Henri Rondet describes the general thrust of Baius' teaching this way:

> His [Baius'] thought can be characterized quite simply. For the *primitive state* of man, Baius admits neo-Pelagianism which was seeking to take hold along with Renaissance ideas. But in regard to *fallen* man, he adopts a somewhat mitigated form of the Protestant theses.[51]

Therefore, after sin grace appears to be necessary; that is, man now seems to have a certain exigency for grace. On Baius' account, the pristine state of man before sin is one in which man could have quite literally "earned" salvation, as if by "right." But after sin, man now finds himself in such a state that his free will is incapable of good apart from Christ.[52]

The emerging theological problem was this: if man's nature stood in strict *need* of grace, then it would seem that grace would be *necessary*, on account of man's post-lapsarian depravity. And if grace were necessary to man's nature, then it would seem to be no longer gratuitous—no longer truly God's personal gift to which man is not entitled.

---

théologie moderne, est une idée systématique, légitime sans doute . . . mais recent" (De Lubac, *Augustinisme et théologie moderne*, 137).

51. Rondet, *The Grace of Christ*, 314, italics original in translation.

52. See Denzinger, *Enchiridion symbolorum*, DH 1901–1980. English translations of *Ex omnibus afflictionibus* will be drawn from Dupuis, *The Christian Faith*, unless otherwise noted. In the first proposition, Baius is condemned for holding the following: "One sins and even merits damnation in that which one does of necessity" (Dupuis, *The Christian Faith*, no. 1986/67). And after sin (without the grace of Christ), one sins of necessity: "It is a Pelagian error to say that free will is capable of avoiding any sin" (ibid., no. 1987/28).

But if grace is taken to be more or less necessary for the operation of post-lapsarian human nature, then grace could be construed as a necessary aspect of human nature—making it in a sense part and parcel of the *debitum naturae*, or at least, it could seem so with respect to man's post-lapsarian state. While this is certainly not the position of Baius or Jansenius, let us only stress that this is precisely how things would have looked to the pure-nature tradition.[53]

As we have seen, for the pure-nature tradition, human nature is self-contained and integral in its own right, and for that reason it has no strict exigency for anything beyond what is contained within the definition of its nature. In this light, it cannot be said that grace is necessary for the functioning of human nature, for such a statement would negate the gratuity of grace.

Accordingly, the possibility of *pure* nature follows straightforwardly from here: "pure nature" represents the coherent and hypothetical possibility that God could have ordained a purely natural order, an order which would not include any offer of grace or the beatific vision. In this purely natural order, man would have had a purely natural end, one which would have sufficed for man's natural beatitude, but which would be inferior to the beatific vision.[54]

According to the pure-nature tradition, the positing of this hypothetical possibility is necessary for the purpose of preserving the gratuity of supernatural grace and the beatific vision. In other words, grace must be *extrinsic* to man's nature, as such, which means that man's nature must be capable of existing without it—at least as a hypothetical possibility; otherwise, the gratuity of grace is forfeited.[55]

53. See Healey, *Jansenius' Critique of Pure Nature*, 68–69.

54. For pure-nature thinkers, natural beatitude would be "perfect" *secundum quid*, according to the proportionate good of human nature. The beatific vision, on the contrary, constitutes a "perfect" beatitude *absolutely speaking*, which is radically disproportionate to the human nature and proportionate only to God.

55. Accordingly, for these very reasons, Hans Urs von Balthasar (1905–1988)—certainly no apologist for the pure-nature doctrine—acknowledges the utility of the pure-nature tradition in the context of formulating a response to Baius: "To pose such a hypothesis, to maintain that a graceless order of nature or creation is at least *possible*, only became urgent for theology when a heretic wanted to make the fluid bond between nature and the supernatural a forced and juridical one. This happened when Baius chose to derive a *de jure* compulsory right to grace understood as a strict requirement (*debitum*) from nature based on the *de facto* configuration of both orders, which were linked because of grace, not necessity. The 'No' that the Church had to

With this backdrop in mind, let us note that when Pope Pius V condemned the teaching of Baius on 1 October 1567 in the bull *Ex omnibus afflictionibus*,[56] it easily seemed as though the pure-nature tradition was *ipso facto* receiving a papal approval.[57] Further, many of Baius' condemned propositions directly contradict the teaching of St. Thomas Aquinas, no doubt reinforcing the impression that the pure-nature tradition was itself of high theological pedigree.

For our purposes, the most important propositions of Baius concern his inability to consider man's nature in abstraction from his existential conditions, either pre- or post-lapsarian. As Rondet pointed out earlier, and as he states in the following, perhaps ironically, Baius seems to have held *too* high of a view of human nature *before* the Fall, only to be followed by *too* low of one *after* the Fall: "Baius grants *innocent* man the power of accomplishing his destiny all by himself, but he thinks that *fallen* man is incapable of any good whatsoever without Christ's grace."[58]

Related to this feature in Baius' thought is the fact that he views the role of grace almost entirely in *medicinal* terms, as ordered toward healing man's nature wounded from sin; that is, Baius does not have much place for *elevating* grace in his account, quite contrary to the teaching of St. Thomas on the matter.

In fact, this very theme is part of the backdrop for the Council of Trent's careful language used to describe man's original state, as one which was "constituted" in a state of grace,[59] as opposed to saying that man was "created" in a state of grace. This subtle nuance aims to preserve

---

pronounce against this sclerosis of the mystery of grace and of its laws and necessities must be understood within the confines of this intent" (Balthasar, *Theology of Karl Barth*, 269, emphasis original). Balthasar continues noting that this late-medieval/early-modern functional utility of the concept soon took on a life of its own: "In other words, the concept was functional, intended to preserve God's freedom *vis-à-vis* nature and the underivability of the Covenant from creation. But this conceptual hypothesis, which was not even necessary before Baius, soon managed to develop into a full system detached from its *theological* presuppositions, and on that basis it took on a life of its own" (ibid., 269–70).

56. Denzinger, *Enchiridion symbolorum*, DH 1901–1980.

57. See Pelikan, *The Christian Tradition*, 4:375: "These official proscriptions of extreme Augustinianism appeared to some to be putting the public doctrine of the church on the side of those whom Baius and Jansen had been attacking" (ibid., 4:376).

58. Rondet, *The Grace of Christ*, 319.

59. Denzinger, *Enchiridion symbolorum*, DH 1511, cited from Dupuis, *The Christian Faith*, no. 508.

the fact that man's original state was *not* one of pure nature, but one which included the gift of *grace*, as something over and above human nature.[60]

For Baius, on the contrary, man's pre-lapsarian gifts *are* in fact simply those of human nature. This is implied in the following proposition of Baius: "The sublimation and its elevation to participation with the divine nature was due to the integrity of the human being in its first state, and is therefore to be called *natural*, and *not supernatural*."[61] Likewise, Baius is quoted as stating: "It is absurd to hold that from the beginning the human being was raised above the natural human condition through a certain supernatural and gratuitous gift."[62]

Further, Baius is condemned for holding that pre-lapsarian man could have attained eternal life, *in virtue of his natural powers alone—* apart from grace: "The immortality of the first human being was not a gift of grace but a natural condition."[63] Indeed, in his view, as mentioned above, the merits of the first man are those of nature, not grace: "Neither the merits of an angel nor of the first man still in the state of integrity [the pre-lapsarian state] are called grace."[64] And again: "The merits of the first integral man were the gifts of the first creation, but according to the manner of speech in Sacred Scripture they are not rightly called grace; for this reason they should be called merits only, not grace."[65]

Such statements—especially as they would appear to the pure-nature tradition—would seem to imply that man's original state was

60. See Rondet, *The Grace of Christ*, 295–312. Similarly, regarding Aquinas, Rondet writes: "When Aquinas recalls that man could have been created *in naturalibus*, he means that Adam, who was in fact created with habitual grace and its accompanying virtues, could have been brought into being without these supernatural gifts" (ibid., 218).

61. Cited in Dupuis, *The Christian Faith*, no. 1984/21.

62. Cited ibid., no. 1984/23.

63. Cited in ibid., no. 1984/78. Similarly, the following is attributed to Baius: "By the natural law it has been ordained for man that, if he would persevere in obedience, he would attain to that life, in which he could not die." This proposition is cited from the translation of *Ex omnibus afflictionibus* found in *The Sources of Catholic Dogma*, 304-310, listed as prop. 6.

64. Cited in *The Sources of Catholic Dogma*, 304, prop. 1.

65. Cited in ibid., 305, prop. 7. Rondet puts this matter as follows for Baius: "In his [Baius'] view, man in a state of innocence had definite rights before God . . . For Adam, eternal life would actually have been a wage, a payment of good deeds" (Rondet, *Grace of Christ*, 314–15).

basically that of "pure nature." For this reason, Baius is condemned for the following: "The opinion of the doctors is wrong who hold that God could have created and constituted the human being without natural justice."[66] The pure-nature tradition would take Baius' statement here regarding "natural justice" as implying that *God could not have created man without the original grace with which he was originally constituted*— which in other words would be to say that this pre-lapsarian "grace" was merely *natural*—not supernatural—and hence, not gratuitous.

Accordingly, for the pure-nature tradition, Baius' account undermines the very gratuity of grace, precisely because man's original state was constituted by *grace*; it was not merely one of nature, as St. Thomas writes here: "The primitive subjection, by virtue of which reason was subject to God, *was not a merely natural gift, but a supernatural endowment of grace*."[67]

For St. Thomas and for the pure-nature tradition, neither man's pre-lapsarian, nor his post-lapsarian state is the equivalent of pure nature.[68] Both are *states* in which human nature either has existed or does

---

66. Cited in Dupuis, *The Christian Faith*, no. 1984/79.

67. *ST* I q. 95, a. 1, emphasis added.

68. Healey notes that Jansensius seems to have taken the pure-nature tradition to have equated post-lapsarian man with the state of pure nature. He describes Jansensius' thought this way: "In affirming . . . that *man's present* [post-lapsarian] *state is his natural* state the Scholastics deny the wound in man's liberty and the sickness which is for Jansensius the basis of the present economy of liberating and medicinal grace" (Healey, *Jansensius' Critique of Pure Nature*, 21, emphasis added; see also ibid., 39). Hence, on this account, the only ostensible role for grace is medicinal, *gratia sanans*, which must liberate a totally depraved post-lapsarian human nature, as seen here in Baius' account of post-lapsarian freedom: "It is a Pelagian error to say that free will is capable of avoiding any sin" (cited in Dupuis, *The Christian Faith*, no. 1987/28). Consider the following from St. Thomas: "In the state of perfect nature man referred the love of himself and of all other things to the love of God as to its end; and thus he loved God more than himself and above all things. But in the state of corrupt nature man falls short of this in the appetite of his rational will, which, unless it is cured by God's grace, follows its private good, on account of the corruption of nature. *And hence we must say that in the state of perfect nature man did not need the gift of grace added to his natural endowments, in order to love God above all things naturally,* although he needed God's help to move him to it; *but in the state of corrupt nature man needs even for this, the help of grace to heal his nature*" (*ST* I-IIae, q. 109, a. 3, emphasis added). Also: "When nature is perfect, it can be restored by itself to its befitting and proportionate condition; but without exterior help it cannot be restored to what surpasses its measure . . . But corrupted . . . [it] can [no longer] be restored, by itself, to its connatural good, much less to the supernatural good of justice" (*ST* I-IIae, q. 109, a. 6, ad 3).

exist, which—while necessarily modifying the existential *condition* of human nature—do not eradicate the objective intelligibility of human nature, as such.

For Baius, however, conceiving of man's original state as his natural state leads him to view grace as primarily *medicinal*, as we said above, and as Rondet puts it here: "Baius ignores elevating grace. . . . Grace intervenes only in order to give us back the natural powers that sin has destroyed in man."[69] In fact, when Rondet treats Aquinas, he draws out precisely this disparity between Baius and Aquinas, noting that St. Thomas' teaching emphasizes the role of *both* medicinal and elevating grace—and the latter pertains even to pre-lapsarian man: "In innocent man, grace . . . was only elevating. But in fallen man, and in general for man wounded by sin, grace is both elevating and medicinal."[70]

The underlying reason for this divergence between Baius and Aquinas is the absence in Baius' account of the distinction between man's *nature* and the *conditions* or *states* in which man's nature exists. As we have said, for the pure-nature tradition, the terms "pre-lapsarian" and "post-lapsarian" (or even "*pure nature*") refer to *states* or *conditions* in which human nature has existed or does exist (or could exist); importantly, man's *nature* is one and the same throughout each and every condition, as Aquinas states very clearly here: "Man's *nature* is the same before and after sin, but the *state* of his nature is not the same."[71]

This distinction presupposes the integral coherence of human nature, which then lends itself to the distinction between man's natural and proportionate end, as distinct from his supernatural and disproportionate end. In other words, as we will see later on, this very distinction between nature and condition quickly gives rise to the whole logical edifice of the pure-nature tradition.

For the pure-nature tradition, this logical edifice presupposes the coherence of nature—as distinct from any given existential condition—which in the mind of pure-nature advocates preserves the sublime transcendence and gratuity of grace. In a similar vein, St. Thomas states:

69. Rondet, *The Grace of Christ*, 314, 316.

70. Ibid., 226. A few pages later, Rondet anticipates his later treatment of Baius here in his treatment Aquinas, stating: "Baius ignores elevating grace, while Thomas place it at the center of his synthesis" (ibid., 229).

71. *ST* III, q. 61, a. 2, ad 2.

> Now no act of anything whatsoever is divinely ordained to any-
> thing exceeding the proportion of the powers which are the prin-
> ciples of its act; for it is the law of Divine providence that nothing
> shall act beyond its [proportionate natural] powers. Now ever-
> lasting life is a good exceeding the proportion of created nature.
> . . . And hence it is that no created nature is a sufficient principle
> of an act meritorious of eternal life, unless there is added a super-
> natural gift which we call grace.[72]

In closing, let us recall the earlier emphasis we placed upon
Aristotle's teaching that "nature" is a principle *in* things; it is not a thing
itself. This nuance is precisely what enables both St. Thomas and the
pure-nature tradition to hold that man's "nature" remains specifically
one and the same throughout each and every condition—despite the
obvious fact that some conditions presuppose important modifying factors (e.g., grace, sin).

For this reason, the claim that "nature" is intelligibly distinct from
its existential conditions need not be taken to mean that the intelligibility of "nature" implies the natural order's independent existence, as if
man could concretely exist in such a way so as to be devoid of any influence whatever, say, from sin or grace.

It is this very mode of abstraction—of human nature in precision
from its existential conditions—which enabled the pure-nature tradition to respond to Baius. Conversely, the Baius affair showed forth the
need for this very abstraction. Accordingly, perhaps more than all else,
it was this sixteenth-century controversy with Baius that provided the
pure-nature tradition with its *raison d'être*, a point drawn out by de
Lubac here:

---

72. *ST* I-IIae, q. 114, a. 2. Consider the juxtaposition between the following
proposition for which Baius is condemned and the teaching of St. Thomas: "The
distinction of a twofold love of God, namely a natural love whose object is God as the
author of nature, and a gratuitous love whose object is God as beatifying, is meaningless
and imaginary; it has been devised as a mockery of the sacred Scriptures and of the
numerous testimonies of ancient authors" (cited in Dupuis, *The Christian Faith*, no.
1988/34). But St. Thomas teaches directly to the contrary: "Charity loves God above all
things in a higher way than nature does. For nature loves God above all things inasmuch
as He is the beginning and the end of natural good; whereas charity loves Him, as He is
the object of beatitude, and inasmuch as man has a spiritual fellowship with God" (*ST*
I-IIae, q. 109, a. 3, ad 1). See Rondet where he states the following regarding Aquinas:
"The distinction between two last ends demands a distinction between natural and
supernatural virtues" (*Grace of Christ*, 221).

The principal motive that has pushed modern theology to forge its hypothesis of "pure nature" and to place it at the base of all its speculation on the final end . . . was the concern to assure, against the modern deviations of Augustinianism [i.e., Baius and Jansenius], the full gratuity of the supernatural gift.[73]

In the next section, we will turn to de Lubac's provocative charge that the pure-nature tradition abetted the rise of modern secularism; this allegation ultimately constitutes his principal case against the pure-nature tradition—a fact which should not be surprising, given his express intention of establishing a genuine Christian humanism. Hence, on de Lubac's account, while the pure-nature tradition may have offered a solution to the problems posed by Baius, it did so only to its own peril: for it played right into the hands of a much more formidable foe, namely, that of modern secularism—a point which Rondet alludes to here: "The great majority of theologians, who were concerned with teaching the opposite of what the Protestants or Baianists taught, preferred to construct an optimism of nature, giving nature extensive autonomy within a supernatural order."[74]

It is this very "autonomy" of the natural order that so worried de Lubac, making it necessary in his mind to push for a more intrinsic alignment of nature and grace, over against that which was put forth by the pure-nature tradition; and so to this issue, let us now turn.

The Relation of Modern Secularism to the Pure-Nature Tradition

The question to which de Lubac returns often is whether or not the theology of pure nature is the *only* way to preserve grace's essential gratu-

---

73. Henri de Lubac, "*Le Mystère du surnaturel*," 80–121 cited from "Mystery of the Supernatural" in *Theology in History*, 291. Hereafter, "The Mystery of the Supernatural" in *Theology in History*, in contrast to the abbreviated citation of his book with the same title: de Lubac, *The Mystery of the Supernatural*. As seen above, de Lubac again states that the affair with Baius lies behind the rapid unanimity and hegemony of the pure-nature tradition: "The two great rival schools, personified in some sort by the two great orders [Dominicans and Jesuits], had decided to form an alliance in this particular field, thus disposing . . . of the Baianist question" (de Lubac, *Augustinianism and Modern Theology*, 183); "Mais dès ce temps de la dispute *de auxiliis*, tout se passe déjà comme si les deux grandes écoles rivales, personnifiées en quelque sorte dans deux grands Ordres, avaient décidé de conclure une véritable alliance sur ce terrain, liquidant ainsi, pensaient-elles, la question baianiste . . ." (De Lubac, *Augustinisme et théologie moderne*, 222).

74. Rondet, *Grace of Christ*, 335.

ity. For if there are other ways to preserve grace's gratuity, these are to be preferred, since—for whatever problems the pure-nature tradition solved—it gave rise to others far more harmful in the long run. De Lubac writes:

> The new system [pure nature], therefore, was very useful; none-theless, its technique was inadequate and its very inspiration was not always sufficiently reliable. At the end of the day, its results often appear unfortunate. Did it not realize a separation of na-ture with reference to the supernatural which ultimately was to become murderous? . . . . Was it not a temptation to achieve independence? Did it not encourage, therefore, the movement of strict "laïcization" [secularism] from the Renaissance on? Was the dualism that it tended to establish merely conceptual? Was it quite sure that it had succeeded, at least in maintaining the idea of the supernatural in its integrity? Was it not too big a conces-sion to make to the adversary . . . ?[75]

In chapter 5, Long will address de Lubac's charge here. For now, let us simply note that de Lubac's conviction regarding the connection between the logic of the pure-nature tradition and modern secularism was itself enough for him to reject the pure-nature tradition.

However, de Lubac still had to account for the gratuity of grace—given his overall intrinsicist account of man's natural desire and its rela-tion to the order of grace; the crux of his explanation comes by way of his teaching on the importance of the category of paradox. For de Lubac's part, given the above connection between the pure-nature tradi-tion and secularism, as we mentioned, if there are other ways of correlat-ing nature and grace which do not reinforce secularism, and which can maintain the gratuity of grace, then these are to be preferred over the pure-nature tradition.

---

75. De Lubac, *Surnaturel*, 153–54: "Le nouveau système ne fut donc point sans rendre d'éminents services. Sa technique n'en était pas moins insuffisante et son inspiration même ne fut pas toujours assez sûre. Au bout du compte, ses résultants se révèlent souvent malheureux. N'a-t-il pas réalisé, de la nature au surnaturel, une séparation qui devait finalement être meurtrière? L'autonomie relative qu'il accordait à la nature n'était-elle pas, telle qu'il la définissait, une tentation d'indépendance? N'encourageait-il pas ainsi le mouvement de 'laïcization' déclenché dès la Renaissance? Le dualisme qu'il tendait à instituer était-il seulement pensable? Est-il bien certain qu'il ait réussi du moins à maintenir dans son intégrité l'idée du surnaturel? N'était-ce pas une concession déjà trop large faite à l'adversaire . . . ?"

For the pure-nature tradition, as we have seen, there is a mutually exclusive dilemma: if man's desire for the beatific vision is a *natural* desire, then its fulfillment is no longer *gratuitous*. But as de Lubac observes, if man no longer has a natural desire for his ultimate end, then this end appears only arbitrarily related to his nature, which subtly undermines man's inherent orientation to the supernatural, constituting a tacit acquiescence to secularism.

Accordingly, de Lubac's project is precisely the attempt to hold together the juxtaposition of man's *natural* desire for the beatific vision, along with the *gratuitous* character of its fulfillment—a juxtaposition which is made possible by way of his characteristic teaching on the category of paradox. And so to this important aspect of de Lubac's teaching, we will now turn.

Paradox and Mystery

For de Lubac, the theological category of paradox is the hermeneutical lens which enables a theologian to hold two essential truths together, especially when they may not appear to cohere easily together. Hence, the category of paradox allows the theologian to embrace the fullness of the ontological "mystery" of faith, in all its integral unity. On the other hand, without the deliberate employment of paradox, human reason naturally tends to emphasize one or other aspect of a given mystery, attempting to alleviate tension between various dimensions of a particular mystery of faith. For this reason, de Lubac cautions that, if left unrestrained, this movement of human reason invariably tends truncate a given mystery of faith.

The problem is not with theological distinctions *per se*, which will always be in order. Rather, his chief point is that the *separateness* of various aspects of a given mystery is something that pertains only to our side of the veil—not to the ontological mystery itself. Accordingly, the category of paradox allows one to move beyond the conceptual frailty of our finite intellectual faculties in order to behold the mystery as it truly is in itself, in all its unified integrity. Hence, de Lubac contends that the insistence upon paradox is the only way to retain the ontological unity and integrity of any given mystery of faith, not the least of which of course is nature and grace.

Accordingly, de Lubac has much to say regarding the dangers of doctrinal development in the heat of polemic, since such contexts tend to engender the very fragmented vision mentioned above. For the requisite clarity needed to adjudicate a given controversy makes the category of paradox less than expedient in the heat of the moment. Polemic usually results in the reaffirmation of some disputed point, but often to the neglect of other aspects of the integral mystery. For this reason, de Lubac writes: "It is a great misfortune to have learned the catechism *against* someone."[76] The necessary refinement in the heat of controversy creates a certain theological "impatience" on the part of the theologian, and so it is inevitably the heretic who frames the question and defines the issue at hand, setting forth the very terms of the debate.

In this context, both sides all too often end up *sharing* common assumptions in their approach to the question at hand—despite the fact that they may well come to opposite conclusions; moreover, the presence of this deeper commonality between the interlocutors usually goes unbeknownst to the orthodox protagonist. For de Lubac, in fact, such is precisely the case with regard to the development of the pure-nature tradition, as it strove to counter Baius first, and then subsequently the secularism of the Enlightenment. De Lubac writes:

> The very conflict between two doctrines nearly always implies certain presuppositions common to both. . . . [Thus there] arises another danger for the theologian who makes too many concessions to the demands of the controversy. *In his struggle against heresy he always sees the question, more or less, willingly or unwillingly, from the heretic's point of view.* He often accepts questions in the form in which the heretic propounds them, so that without sharing the error he may make implicit concessions to his opponent. . . . For about three centuries, faced by the naturalist trends of modern thought on the one hand, and the confusions of bastard Augustinianism on the other [i.e., Baius and Jansensius], *many could see salvation only in a complete severance between the natural and the supernatural.* Such a policy ran doubly counter to

---

76. De Lubac, *Catholicism*, 309, emphasis added; "C'est un grand malheur, a-t-on dit, d'avoir appris le catéchisme contre quelq'un" (De Lubac, *Catholicisme*, 267). On the next page, he continues noting that the pure-nature development in response to Baius is a case in point: "We have learned our catechism too much against Luther, against *Baius*, or even against Loisy" (De Lubac, *Catholicism*, 310, emphasis added): "Nous avons trop appris notre catéchisme contre Luther, contre Baius, ou même contre Loisy" (De Lubac, *Catholicisme*, 268).

> the end which they had in view. . . . Such dualism [i.e., extrinsi-
> cism], just when it imagined that it was most successfully op-
> posing the negations of naturalism, *was most strongly influenced
> by it,* and the transcendence in which it hoped to preserve the
> supernatural with such jealous care was, in fact, a banishment.
> *The most confirmed secularists found in it, in spite of itself, an ally.*[77]

Similarly, de Lubac illustrates his overall point by way of the
eleventh-century Eucharistic controversy with Berengarius (ca. 1010–
1088) which concerned the relationship between Christ's body and the
Eucharist. Here, again, on de Lubac's account, orthodoxy was safeguarded, but at the expense of a certain distortion in the integral understanding of the faith:

> It could be said that the ultra-orthodox party fell into the trap
> that had been set for them by the heretic, or again that they al-
> lied with him in mutilating the traditional teaching: one ground
> holding to symbolism, the other to the "truth." Against *mysti-
> cally, not truly,* was set, in no less exclusive a sense, *truly, not
> mystically.* Perhaps orthodoxy was safeguarded, but on the other
> hand, doctrine was certainly impoverished.[78]

77. De Lubac, *Catholicism,* 312–14, all emphases added; "L'opposition même entre
deux doctrines ne va guère sans impliquer certains présupposés communs. D'où, pour
le théologien qui sacrifie trop aux nécessités de la controverse, un autre danger. Dans sa
lutte contre l'hérésie il se place toujours plus ou moins, qu'il le veuille ou non, au point
de vue de l'hérétique. Il accepte souvent les questions telles que celui-ci les pose, en sorte
que sans partager ses erreurs il peut lui arriver de faire implicitement à son adversaire des
concessions d'autant plus graves qu'il le contredit plus explicitement. . . . Mais pendant
trois siècles environ, contre les courants naturalistes de la pensée moderne et contre les
confusions d'un augustinisme dévoyé, beaucoup n'avaient vu de salut que dans un fossé
creusé entre la nature et le surnaturel. Or, par cette tactique, ils allaient doublement à
l'encontre de la fin qu'ils se proposaient. . . . Au moment où il pensait s'opposer le plus
aux négations naturalistes, un tel dualisme en subissait donc fortement la poussé, et la
transcendance où il croyait maintenir jalousement le surnaturel se trouvait, en fait, un
exil. Les penseurs les plus résolument laïques trouvaient en lui, malgré lui, un allié" (De
Lubac, *Catholicisme,* 270–71).

78. De Lubac, *Corpus Mysticum,* 223, italics original; "On pourrait dire que ces
ultra-orthodoxes tombent dans le piège que l'hérétique leur avait dressé, ou encore
qu'ils s'entendent avec lui pour mutiler l'enseingement traditionnel: l'un retenant le
symbole, et les autres, la 'vérité'. Au *mystice, non vere* répond, non moins exclusif, un
vere, non mystice. L'orthodoxie est peut-être sauve, mais la doctrine, en revanche, est
sûrement appauvrie. Paschase Radbert était jadis mieux inspiré" (De Lubac, *Corpus
Mysticum: L'Eucharistie et l'Église au Moyen Âge,* 251, italics original).

The shortcoming of this "Christian rationalism," as de Lubac puts it,[79] is the loss of the integral *unity* of the mystery of faith—a unity which can only be retained by way of the category of paradox.[80] Accordingly, over-emphasizing theological distinctions leads first to a separation of the mystery's integral unity, and subsequently to a disregard for some or other aspect of the integral mystery of faith. For this reason, he exhorts theologians to "*unite* in order to distinguish."[81] For him, the theological category of paradox is simply a corollary of the virtue of humility; in short, it is the only proper response to God's revelation, and so he states:

> Antinomies loom everywhere, and always, to be faithful, we must begin again to hold in the night "the two ends of the chain." No mystery is a simple truth, and if we become attached with too narrow an attention to one of its aspects in order to establish the main part of it, we risk ending in many an absurdity or many a heresy. A mystery can never be . . . handled in the way a natural truth can; we will never have the right to apply the laws of our human logic to it univocally, without precautions and correctives.[82]

On this account, perhaps surprisingly, de Lubac sees an affinity between his theological hermeneutic of paradox here and the general epistemic stance of no less than the nineteenth-century atheist philosopher Friedrich Nietzsche (1844–1900). De Lubac cites with approval Nietzsche's antipathy for Socrates, stating that Socratic rationalism is essentially "myth-destroying" and mystery-reducing, and is therefore antithetical to the category of paradox.[83] Here the French Jesuit suggests a "third way," so to speak, that is neither Nietzschean, nor Socratic, and one which he takes to be embodied in Charles Péguy (1873–1914)— a French poet, socialist, and later in life, a devout Catholic: "In this sense, we shall side against him [Socrates]; against him but not, consequently, with Nietzsche; much rather with Péguy. Péguy will save us from Nietzsche."[84] Péguy's disposition as simultaneously poetic and

79. De Lubac, *Corpus Mysticum*, 238; "rationalisme chrétien" (De Lubac, *Corpus Mysticum: L'Eucharistie et l'Église au Moyen Âge*, 267).

80. De Lubac, *Corpus Mysticum*, 226.

81. De Lubac, *Catholicism*, 329, emphasis added; "unir pour distinguer" (De Lubac, *Catholicisme*, 286–287).

82. De Lubac, "Le problème du developpement du dogme," 130–60, cited in *Theology in History*, 265. Also see de Lubac, *At the Service of the Church*, 64.

83. De Lubac, *The Drama of Atheist Humanism*, 80, cf. 85, 91–92.

84. Ibid., 92; "En ce sens, nous serons contre lui. Contre lui, mais non pas pour

faithful, yet critical, represents for de Lubac the ideal temperament of the Christian theologian.[85] For de Lubac, the pure-nature tradition's estimation of philosophical reason was simply much too high,[86] and this divergence constitutes a sharp methodological divide between him and the pure-nature tradition, as we will see further in the following chapter.

For now, let us turn to the ebb and flow of de Lubac's fortunes, as his vision of nature and grace stirred controversy in the 1940s, only to be embraced by the Second Vatican Council some twenty years later. Indeed, his story is one of both exile and exaltation, only to end once more in isolation, though of a different sort in the latter years of his life.

From Exile to Peritus

It would certainly not be the whole story if we did not recount de Lubac's intellectual and spiritual suffering, coming as it did principally from those within the ranks of the Church. As we have seen, the critical event here of course is the publication of *Humani generis* in 1950 by Pope Pius XII which seemed to touch directly on de Lubac's cardinal thesis, as expressed in *Surnaturel*: "L'esprit est donc désir de Dieu."[87] This same thesis is found later in his 1965 work *Le Mystère du Surnaturel* where he states that anything less than the beatific vision necessarily results in man's "essential suffering."[88] This statement of course precludes the very possibility of a purely natural end.

The relevant passage once again from *Humani generis* is as follows: "Others [de Lubac?] destroy the gratuity of the supernatural order, since God, they say, *cannot* create intellectual beings *without ordering and call-*

---

autant avec Nietzsche. Avec Péguy bien plutôt. Péguy nous sauvera de Nietzsche" (De Lubac, *Le Drame de l'Humanisme athée*, 92–93).

85. Cf. de Lubac, *Corpus Mysticum*, 231–37.

86. For example, Nietzsche describes Plato as the "most dangerous" of philosophers precisely because of his "denial of *perspective*." Along these lines, Nietzsche states: "One should use 'cause' and 'effect' only as pure *conceptions*, that is to say, as convenient fictions . . . not for explanation" (Nietzsche, *Beyond Good and Evil*, 2, 30, emphases original).

87. De Lubac, *Surnaturel*, 483: "The spirit is desire for God."

88. De Lubac, *The Mystery of the Supernatural*, 54: "le 'désir de voir Dieu' ne saurait être éternellement frustré sans une souffrance essentielle. Je ne saurais nier cela sans faire une brèche à mon *Credo*" (De Lubac, *Le Mystère du Surnaturel*, 80).

ing them to the beatific vision."[89] Stated positively, this text seems to imply that God *could have created intellectual beings without ordering them to the beatific vision*—which is to say that God could have ordered man to a purely natural end. This natural beatitude, of course, could not result in "essential suffering," as described by de Lubac—or else it would not be a beatitude. Therefore, much like the effect of Pope Pius V's *Ex omnibus afflictionibus* of 1567, the alleged condemnation of de Lubac in *Humani generis* easily gave the impression that the official teaching of the Church was on the side of the pure-nature tradition.

In this context, we should make mention of de Lubac's distinction between man's "hypothetical" and "concrete" nature. De Lubac is here willing to concede some plausibility to the pure-nature teaching in virtue of man's "hypothetical" nature, but not with respect to his "concrete" nature. In this light, he can accommodate the teaching of *Humani generis* by acknowledging the possibility of a purely natural end in a *hypothetical* economy, while simultaneously denying its possibility in the *concrete* divine economy.

This distinction in de Lubac first appears in an article he published in 1949,[90] three years after the publication of *Surnaturel*, but still *before* the publication of *Humani generis* in 1950. For Feingold, this distinction marks a rupture in de Lubac's thought—a "significant development" which indicates a backing off from his 1946 thesis in *Surnaturel*. Feingold writes:

> There is a significant development in de Lubac's thought. In *Surnaturel*, spiritual nature is presented as if it intrinsically required the vision of God as its end. Thus the end of a spiritual creature necessarily exceeds its own level, and this necessary disproportion is presented as the paradox of the Christian view of the spirit. However, in the article of 1949, "Le mystère du surnaturel," and in the book of the same title of 1965, de Lubac allows the possibility that God could possibly create a rational creature which does not possess a natural desire to see God. . . . In this way, de Lubac could maintain that his thesis as presented in 1949

89. Pius XII, *Humani generis*, no. 26, DH 3875–99, emphasis added.

90. De Lubac, "Le Mystère du surnaturel," 80–121. See Feingold, *Natural Desire to See God*, 306. In English translation, the above-mentioned distinction can be found in: De Lubac, "The Mystery of the Supernatural," in *Theology in History*, 292.

and 1965 is not the same as the position condemned by Pius XII in 1950.[91]

However, de Lubac himself gives no indication of a radical development in his thought, and he certainly gives no indication that he has backed away from his original thesis. This point can be seen readily by the way in which he responds to critics of *Surnaturel* in the above-mentioned 1949 article which is where this development has supposedly taken place. De Lubac writes:

> Few precise objections, referring to what we have actually written, have been presented to us. As for the disparaging remarks and distortions of which our text has at times been the object, we will hope that they will be so obvious to the attentive reader that he will have no difficulty in noting them.[92]

Of course, the significance of Feingold's suggested development would be a bit stronger if de Lubac had written the 1949 article *after* the promulgation of *Humani generis* in 1950. But on the contrary, his memoirs stress the continuity of his thought on nature and grace; here, de Lubac recounts the circumstances and occasions surrounding all of his works; one would expect him to be forthright and honest in such a personal memoir at the end of his life, especially as it pertains to our topic at hand, since the controversy surrounding *Surnaturel* had almost entirely died down by the time he published his memoirs in 1989. For this reason, de Lubac's own appraisal of his work and the purported development therein should be our starting point.

In these memoirs, de Lubac indicates that his later works on nature and grace, *Augustinianism and Modern Theology* and *The Mystery of the Supernatural*, published in 1965, originated simply as a desire to publish a new edition of *Surnaturel*. That is, initially they were not intended to be *new* books at all, a fact which certainly suggests that no serious retraction had taken place in his mind from the earlier *Surnaturel*.[93] In fact, these later two works on nature and grace correspond in detail to *Surnaturel*, in terms of their plan and execution,[94] and presumably this

---

91. Feingold, *The Natural Desire*, 306–7.

92. De Lubac, "The Mystery of the Supernatural" in *Theology in History*, 290.

93. De Lubac, *At the Service of the Church*, 128–30.

94. By and large, *Augustinianism and Modern Theology* corresponds to *Surnaturel* up to the six "notes" (*Quatrième Partie Notes Historiques*); and *The Mystery of the*

is why *Surnaturel* has not yet been translated into English—since at least on the surface, the translation of the 1965 works (*Augustinianism and Modern Theology* and *The Mystery of the Supernatural*) has made translating *Surnaturel* superfluous to some extent.

However, there are those—such as John Milbank, the Anglican philosopher-theologian and founder of the postmodern-Augustinian movement known as Radical Orthodoxy—for whom *Humani generis* marks a point of radical departure in de Lubac's thought, a rupture to which Milbank alludes here: "In effect, the *Surnaturel* thesis *deconstructs* the possibility of dogmatical theology as previously understood in modern times, just as it equally deconstructs the possibility of philosophical theology or even of a clearly autonomous philosophy *tout court*."[95]

As is implicit in Milbank's comments here, this issue of development or rupture in de Lubac's thought is certainly influenced by the way in which one interprets *Surnaturel* in the first place; for Milbank, de Lubac's later works on ecclesiology contradict the bold trajectory of *Surnaturel*. But this purported rupture in de Lubac's thought may well be due to Milbank's importing something of his own postmodern theological vision into *Surnaturel*, an observation which Edward T. Oakes suggests here: "Milbank's admiration for de Lubac seems ultimately grounded . . . in his insistence that de Lubac was really the first advocate, *avant la lettre*, of Radical Orthodoxy."[96]

Further, the relationship between Pope Pius XII and de Lubac is a bit more complicated than either Feingold or Milbank make it sound. De Lubac was actually in Rome in 1946 from August through October when he met briefly with Pope Pius XII; he was there as a Jesuit delegate during the election of a new superior general (the election had been delayed due to the war).[97] These delegates were introduced by name to the

---

Supernatural represents an expansion upon the six notes (*Surnaturel*, 431–80), as well as especially the conclusion (*Surnaturel*, 483–94) where he summarizes and synthesizes his position on the matter—very much as he does in chapters 4 and 5 of *The Mystery of the Supernatural*, 53–100.

95. Milbank, *The Suspended Middle*, 11, emphasis original; also, see ibid., 7–8. See also McBrien, *The Church*, who writes: "Among the implied targets of the encyclical [*Humani Generis*] were two French theologians who *later took a decisive turn in a conservative direction and were created cardinals*: Henri de Lubac, S.J. (d. 1991) and Jean Daniélou (d. 1974)" (129, emphasis added).

96. Oakes, "The Paradox of Nature and Grace," 667–66, here 682.

97. Voderholzer, *Meet Henri de Lubac*, 65. The previous superior general, Father

Holy Father, and upon meeting de Lubac, Pope Pius XII said in a gentle and affirming voice: "Ah! I know your doctrine very well."[98]

At the time, de Lubac took the pope's remark unequivocally as a compliment. *Surnaturel* had already been published at the beginning of the summer of that same year, and the controversy surrounding it had already begun.[99] In this context, we should assume that the pope would have been very circumspect in his remarks to de Lubac, especially since much of the Catholic intellectual world eagerly awaited the Holy Father's verdict regarding *Surnaturel*. De Lubac's positive interpretation of the pope's remarks was confirmed by the newly-elected superior general of the Jesuit order, Father Jean-Baptiste Janssens: Janssens made a point to reassure de Lubac and to affirm his good standing with the Holy Father—and the superior general did this precisely because of the already-stirring controversy surrounding *Surnaturel*.[100]

Vladimir Ledochowski, had died in December of 1942.

98. De Lubac, *At the Service of the Church*, 61; "Ah! Je connais bien votre doctrine" (De Lubac, *Mémoir sur l'occasion de mes écrits*, 62).

99. See de Lubac, *At the Service of the Church*, 250–57.

100. Here is de Lubac's account of the matter: "At the end of the audience at Castelgondolfo, we had all filed before the Holy Father as the name of each was whispered to him by respective assistants; he had said to me, in a friendly tone: 'Ah! I know your doctrine very well'. His words, indistinctly heard by those closest to us, repeated, distorted, exaggerated, were commented upon in every possible sense. Several came to ask me the meaning of them. For some, it was, without a doubt, a commendation; for others, it was a reproach, or at least a warning; for others, it was even the designation of the sacrificial victim. . . . In town, commentaries quickly made the rounds. At Saint-Louis-des-Française, Abbé Monchanin, who had come from India to accompany his bishop on his *ad limina* visit, heard me denounced in the middle of dinner as a heretic to be overcome. Yet, at the end of the General Congregation Janssens [the newly elected Superior General of the Jesuits] took the initiative to call me. He had been obliged, he told me, to forgo receiving many of the Fathers, Provincials and Superiors from distant missions who had asked him for an appointment before leaving Rome, but he insisted on seeing me in order to tell me this (and I report his remarks very faithfully): 'You have heard many rumors here; *I am anxious to reassure you; in the misgivings that have been manifested, you are not in question; I speak to you in full knowledge of the case, after having been well informed by a good source: I have seen the secretary of the Holy Office and the Holy Father himself. You can affirm it with certainty: know that you have the entire confidence of the Father General, and do not be concerned about anything'* (De Lubac, *At the Service of the Church*, 61, emphasis added); "A la fin de l'audience à Castel-Gandolfo, nous avions tous défilé devant le Saint-Père, le nom de chacun lui étant soufflé par nos assistants respectifs; il m'avait dit, d'un ton aimable: 'Ah! Je connais bien votre doctrine'. Le mot, vaguement perçu par les plus proches, répété, déformé, amplifié, fut commenté dans tous les sens. Plusieurs venaient m'en demander

Sometime later, however, Janssens must have changed his mind—for the aftermath of *Humani generis* saw de Lubac stripped of his faculties for teaching Catholic theology, as well as the removal from the shelves of Jesuit libraries of *Surnaturel*, *Corpus Mysticum*, *Discovery of God*, and the 1949 article, "Le Mystère du Surnaturel."[101] This, as we have seen, constitutes the beginning of de Lubac's nearly decade-long exile.

Fortunately, by the late 1950s things had taken a turn for the better, marking a new springtime for de Lubac's priestly and academic vocation.[102] He—along with another controversy-beset theologian, the Dominican Yves Congar—was invited to be a *peritus* at the Second Vatican Council at the request of the newly-elected Holy Father, St. Pope John XXIII.[103] Arguably, no pair of theologians influenced the Council more so than de Lubac and Congar.[104] Their presence at the Council was

---

la signification. Pour les uns, c'était un reproche, ou du moins un avertissement; pour quelques-uns, c'était même la désignation de la victime expiatoire . . . En ville, les commentaires allaient bon train. A Saint-Louis-des-Française, l'abbé Monchanin, venu de l'Inde pour accompagner son évêque dans sa visite ad limina, m'entendait dénoncer en pleine table comme l'hérétique à abattre. Cependant, sur la fin de la Congrégation générale, le Père Janssens prit l'initiative de m'appler. Il avait dû renoncer, me dit-il, à recevoir bien des Pères, Provinciaux ou Supérieurs des missions lointaines, qui lui demandaient audience avant de quitter Rome, mais il tenait à me voir, pour me dire ceci (je rapporte très fidèlement ses propos): Vous avez pu entendre ici bien des bruits; je tiens à vous rassurer; dans les inquiétudes qui se sont manifestées, il n'était pas question de vous; je vous parle en connaissance de cause, après m'être renseigné à bonne source: j'ai vu le secrétaire du Saint-Office, et le Saint-Père lui même. Vous pouvez l'affirmer avec assurance: sachez que vous avez la confiance entière du Père général, et ne vous inquiétez de rien" (De Lubac, *Mémorie sur l'occasion de mes écrits*, 62–63).

101. Voderholzer, *Meet Henri de Lubac*, 71–72.

102. By 1953, things had a relaxed a little, and de Lubac was able to return to Lyons and teach sporadically; he was even able to publish *Méditation sur l'Église* (English title: *Splendor of the Church*). Lest anyone think this is some sort of Lubacian retraction, this book emerged out of talks given between the years 1946–49; thus this 1953 text on the Church manifests no rupture in de Lubac's thought (see Voderholzer, *Meet Henri de Lubac*, 76).

103. Voderholzer, *Meet Henri de Lubac*, 83–84. *Peritus* (singular) and *periti* (plural) refer to a theological "expert" invited to assist the bishops at a council, synod, or similar gathering, such as the Second Vatican Council. De Lubac discovered this invitation, oddly enough, by surprise while looking through a newspaper, only to see his name listed with the other esteemed *periti* (see ibid.).

104. See Alberigo and Komonchak, *History of Vatican II*, 460. As Komonchak notes, the plight of de Lubac and the *Ressourcement* school of theology is nothing short of a "dress rehearsal" for the drama of Vatican II: "Vatican II is unintelligible without an understanding of the controversy over '*la nouvelle théologie*'" (Komonchak, "Theology

undoubtedly symbolic of a new era, one which included among other things the Church's shift in its understanding of nature and grace—*from* extrinsicism, *toward* intrinisicism. By this point, the hegemony of the pure-nature tradition had undeniably come to an end.

In fact, at the end of Pope Pius XII's life, in the last year of his pontificate in March of 1958, four of de Lubac's books were sent to the Holy Father, along with a personal dedicatory letter. De Lubac-scholar, Rudolf Voderholzler, recounts the pope's warm response to this guesture as follows:

> Pius XII promptly sent cordial words of thanks and encouraged de Lubac. The Jesuit General, Father Janssens, unsure of what to do, was unwilling to look at the letter because it was not official. Janssens, incorrectly informed about de Lubac's real specialty, thought that with permission to give lectures on Hinduism and Buddhism the original *status quo ante* had been restored. De Lubac had to set him right and point out that he had also taught fundamental theology on the Faculty of Theology. Finally, a conciliatory letter from the General arrived, which spoke of misunderstandings and of the fact that God turns all things to the good for those who love him.[105]

Much of de Lubac's very own teaching would be adopted by the Second Vatican Council, sometimes appearing almost verbatim, as if transcribed from his earlier works. For example, in his 1938 work *Catholicism*, he wrote a passage eerily reminiscent of a very famous text from *Gaudium et Spes*, and one which was echoed many times over by Pope John Paul II: "By revealing the Father and by being revealed by him, *Christ completes the revelation of man to himself.*"[106] And as is well known, *Gaudium et Spes* teaches: "It is only in the mystery of the Word made flesh that the mystery of humanity truly becomes clear. . . . *Christ . . . fully reveals humanity to itself.*"[107]

---

and Culture at Mid-Century," 580). Here Komonchak uses *"nouvelle théologie"* to refer to the *Ressourcement* movement in theology; the former is usually a more pejorative designation, though such is not the case in this passage of Komonchak here. For what is likely the origin of the term *nouvelle théologie* and its pejorative connotations, see Garrigou-Lagrange, "La nouvelle théologie, où va-t-elle?," 126–45.

105. Voderholzer, *Meet Henri de Lubac*, 79–80.

106. De Lubac, *Catholicism*, 339; "En révélant le Père et en étant révélé par lui, le Christ achève de révéler l'homme à lui-même" (De Lubac, *Catholicisme*, 295).

107. *Gaudium et Spes*, no. 22 in *Vatican Council II: Constitutions, Decrees,*

Perhaps of lesser importance (since the idea is not uniquely de Lubac's), there is another point of contact between de Lubac and the Council, and again one which becomes something of a leitmotif in the pontificate of John Paul II: namely, that the "gift of self" is man's fundamental human vocation. In the same 1938 work cited above, de Lubac writes: "To find himself man must lose himself."[108] And Vatican II likewise states: "Human beings can fully discover their true selves only in sincere self-giving."[109] St. John Paul II follows suit here as well: "The fullest, the most uncompromising form of love consists precisely in self-giving, in making one's inalienable and non-transferrable 'I' someone else's property."[110] And later as pope, in his important moral encyclical, John Paul II states: "Perfection demands that maturity in self-giving to which human freedom is called."[111]

The link between de Lubac, Vatican II, and Pope John Paul II demonstrates that the trajectory of the Church's development on nature and grace after the Council follows that set forth by de Lubac at mid-century. This congruence is no accident since de Lubac and Wojtyla actually collaborated together at the Council, and they did so on the very document where de Lubac's influence on nature and grace is most apparent, *Gaudium et Spes*. In what follows, de Lubac comments on his impression of the young Wojtyla and their work together at the Council:

> I had known Bishop Wojtyla in Rome, at the time of the Council. We worked side by side at the time of the arduous birth of the

Declarations. It is worth recalling here that it was this very document that affirmed de Lubac's specific thesis regarding the *single* final end for man: "all are in fact called to one and the same destiny, which is divine" (ibid.).

108. De Lubac, *Catholicism*, 368; "L'humanisme n'est pat spontément chrétien. L'humanisme chrétien doit être un humanisme *converti*. D'aucun amour naturel on ne passe de plain-pied à l'amour surnaturel. *Il faut se perdre pour se trouver*" (De Lubac, *Catholicisme*, 323, first italics are original, second italics are added for emphasis). Also: "There is no solitary person: each one in his being receives all, of his very being must give back to all" (De Lubac, *Catholicism*, 333); "Point de personne isolée: chacune, en son être même, reçoit de toutes, et de son être même doit rendre à toutes" (De Lubac, *Catholicisme*, 289).

109. *Gaudium et Spes*, no. 24 in *Vatican Council II: Constitutions, Decrees, Declarations*. The third pillar of the Catechism even begins along these lines (see *Catechism of the Catholic Church*, nos. 1701–1702).

110. Wojtyla, *Love and Responsibility*, 97; originally published in Polish as *Miłość I Odpowiedzialność*.

111. John Paul II, *Veritatis Splendor*, no. 17.

famous Schema 13, which, after a number of hasty modifications, became the Constitution *Gaudium et Spes*. It did not take long observation to discover in him a person of the very highest qualities. He knew my works, and we were soon on good terms.[112]

Let us conclude here by noting that the final vindication of de Lubac came when Pope John Paul II created him a cardinal in 1983. Though isolated by dominant strains of postconciliar theology, de Lubac's legacy was definitively restored; the Church would forever be in debt to his important contribution, not the least of which concerns the issue of nature and grace.

Conclusion

As we noted above, though de Lubac's formal exile was behind him, he was similarly isolated from the 1970s onward until his death in 1991—this time not from the hierarchy, but from the more progressive wing of theologians after the Council. Perhaps ironically against this new set of interlocutors, de Lubac set out to defend positions on nature and grace that were oddly reminiscent of those he had criticized some forty years earlier. De Lubac seems to have noticed a different imbalance after the Council—this time one marked by an exaggerated *intrinsicism*; this concern lies behind the following statement he made at St. Louis University in 1969, upon receiving an honorary doctorate:

> Does not such an "openness" [to the world] become a forgetfulness of salvation and of the gospel, a tending toward secularism, a loosening of faith and morals? Finally, this "openness" becomes for others a loss of identity, in a word, the betrayal of our obligation toward the world. Because the Council, following the desire of John XXIII, did not wish either to define new dogmas or to pronounce anathemas, many conclude that the church no longer has the right to judge anything or anyone; they recommend a "pluralism" which is not the pluralism of the theological schools

---

112. De Lubac, *At the Service of the Church*, 171; "J'avais connu Mgr. Wojtyla à Rome, au temps du Concile. Nous avions travaillé côte, lors de l'enfantement pénible du fameux schéma 13, devenu après nombre de remaniements précipités la Constitution *Gaudium et Spes*. Pas n'était besoin de longues observations pour découvrir en lui une personnalité de tout premier plan. Il connaissait mes ouvrages, et nous avions vite sympathisé" (De Lubac, *Mémoire sur l'occasion de mes écrits*, 175).

but that of entirely different beliefs from those of the normative
faith. . . . The "renewal" can cover a multitude of abuses![113]

Accordingly, after the Council de Lubac saw that what was at stake
was the supernatural transcendence of the faith. For this reason, in his
1980 work *A Brief Catechesis on Nature and Grace*, he ardently defends
the real *distinction* between nature and grace, a point to which his pre-
conciliar pure-nature counterparts would have warmly agreed:

> The supernatural . . . is that divine element which man's effort
> cannot reach (no self-divinization!) but which unites itself to
> man, "elevating" him as our classical theology used to put it, and
> as Vatican II still says (*Lumen Gentium*, 2), penetrating him in
> order to divinize him, and thus becoming as it were an attribute
> of the "new man" described by St. Paul. While it remains forever
> "un-naturalizable," it profoundly penetrates the depths of man's
> being. In short, it is what the old Scholastics and especially St.
> Thomas Aquinas called . . . an "*accidental form*" or an "*accident*."
> Call it an accident, or call it a *habitus*, or "created grace": these are
> all different ways of saying . . . that man becomes in truth a sharer
> in the divine nature.[114]

113. De Lubac, "The Church in Crisis," 312–25; here 319. A revised version of this
address was published in *Nouvelle Revue Théologique* 91 (1969): 580–96.

114. De Lubac, *A Brief Catechesis on Nature and Grace*, 41–42, emphasis added;
"Le surnaturel . . . cet élément divin, inaccessible à l'effort de l'homme (pas d'auto-
divinisation!), mais s'unissant à l'homme, l'élevant', comme disait notre théologie
classique et comme dit encore Vatican II (*Lumen Gentium*, 2), le pénétrant pour le
diviniser, devenant ainsi comme un attribut de 'l'homme nouveau' tel que nous le
décrit saint Paul. Quoique toujours 'innaturalisable', il est profondément inviscéré en
lui. Bref, il est ce que les anciens scholastiques, et particulièrement Thomas d'Aquin,
appelaient, d'un mot venu d'Aristote et sur lequel on a fait bien des contresens, une
'forme accidentelle', un 'accident'. Accident, ou encore *habitus*, 'grâce créé': ce sont
là manières de dire (même si on les estime sujettes à maintes précisions ou à maints
correctifs) que l'homme devient réellement participant de la Nature divine ('*divinae
cosortes naturae*', 'théias koinônoi phuseôs': 2 Petr. 1, 4)" (De Lubac, *Petite Catéchèse sur
Nature et Grâce*, 31–32). Oakes comments on the shift in de Lubac's emphasis based on
the changing context: "This [shift to a greater sympathy with the extrinsicist tradition]
becomes particularly evident in de Lubac's critique of trends following in the wake
of Vatican II. For in the postconciliar years he spotted an error at work, which, for
him, was the mirror-opposite of the extrinsicism he fought before the Council: the
opposite but twin, error of intrinsicism. Intrinsicism comes to the opposite conclusion
as extrinsicism but uses the same logic" (Oakes, "The Paradox of Nature and Grace,"
693, emphasis original).

Though the emphasis is perhaps more striking in his later works, we should note that de Lubac made similar statements already in his 1965 work *The Mystery of the Supernatural* when he clearly distinguished between nature and grace: "The gifts of grace and of glory . . . could never be confused with the gifts of nature."[115] In fact, the following passage from this same work is actually cited favorably by none other than contemporary pure-nature advocate, Lawrence Feingold:

> The desire [for God] itself is by no means a "perfect appetite." It does not constitute as yet even the slightest positive "ordering" to the supernatural. Again, it is sanctifying grace, with its train of theological virtues, which must order the subject to his last end; at least, it alone can order him "sufficiently" or "perfectly" or "directly." This grace is a certain "form," a certain "supernatural perfection" which must be "added over and above human nature" in order that man "may be ordered appropriately to his end."[116]

It is difficult to pin de Lubac down on these issues because he wishes to affirm the principal theses of all sides of the debate; and he claims he can do so by recourse to his teaching on paradox. For this reason, it must be said that his teaching on paradox forms the centerpiece of his overall position; and the assessment of his thought on nature and grace really comes down to the legitimacy of his use of paradox. For this reason, we must ask whether this category of paradox is sufficient to hold together all the elements of his thought—or whether it is merely a case of special pleading, a sort of intellectual panacea, against which no serious objection can ever really be brought.

Since this is really *the* issue in the assessment of de Lubac, the next chapter is devoted entirely to his underlying methodological hermeneutic, of which his teaching on paradox no doubt forms the fulcrum. Indeed, the divergence between him and the pure-nature tradition occurs at just this juncture, and so the *prolegomena* treated in the following

115. De Lubac, *The Mystery of the Supernatural*, 89: "Les *dona gratiae et gloriae* ne sauraient jamais être confondus avec les *dona naturae*" (De Lubac, *Le Mystère du Surnaturel*, 121).

116. De Lubac, *The Mystery of the Supernatural*, 85; "Le désir lui-même n'est point un 'appétit parfait'. Il ne constitue pas encore la moindre 'ordination' positive au surnaturel. C'est encore la grâce sanctifiante, avec son cortège de vertus théologales, qui droit 'ordonner' le sujet à sa fin dernière; du moins peut-elle seule l'y ordonner 'suffisamment', qui doit être 'surajoutée à la nature humaine', pour que l'homme 'convenienter ordinetur finem'" (De Lubac, *Le Mystère du Surnaturel*, 117).

chapter greatly enhances our understanding of the specific reasoning employed by each side of the debate. And so to this next phase of Part One, we now turn.

3

Foundations for Nature and Grace

As we have seen, for Henri de Lubac, the most constructive way to deal with the issues surrounding nature and grace is by way of the theological category of paradox. Anything less inevitably brings about distortions in one direction or another, as the emphasis upon one aspect of a certain mystery often results in the diminishing significance of another. De Lubac's teaching here is but one of several methodological divergences which distance him from the pure-nature tradition. Accordingly, this chapter will survey these basic hermeneutical differences in order to elucidate how they inform the nature-grace debate more generally.

We will proceed as follows: (1) we will treat de Lubac's teaching on fundamental theology, over against Neoscholastic apologetics; (2) we will revisit de Lubac's teaching on man's natural desire and the beatific vision, noting especially the emphasis he places upon man as a "created spirit," as opposed to treating him as an Aristotelian "nature." Similarly, (3) we will discuss his preference for treating man in accord with the *imago Dei*, again, as opposed to allowing Aristotelian natural philosophy to govern one's theological anthropology—a tendency which he identifies as problematic in the pure-nature tradition. Finally, (4) we will treat de Lubac's account of why he has not forfeited grace's gratuity, despite his insistence that man has a *natural* desire for the beatific vision.

Let us now turn to his teaching on fundamental theology.

Fundamental Theology

De Lubac gave his inaugural lecture on apologetics and fundamental theology in 1929, his first year as a professor at Lyon; it was published the following year as an article entitled "Apologétique et théologie."[1] This lecture marks a general shift in the Church's thinking on apologetics—specifically a move *away* from Neoscholastic apologetics, and *toward* fundamental theology.[2] In this inaugural lecture, he argued that the Church's mode of apologetics must seek to show the inherent connections between the human condition and the mysteries of faith. That is, one should attempt to draw a more *intrinsic* alignment between natural reason's assessment of the human condition and the perspective afforded by Christian faith.

Accordingly, the divide between Neoscholastic (pure-nature) apologetics and de Lubac's teaching on fundamental theology is nothing other than the epistemological expression of their respective orientations toward either extrinsicism or intrinsicism, as de Lubac himself acknowledges here:

> The [Neoscholastic] error consists in conceiving of dogma as a kind of "thing in itself," as a block of revealed truth *with no relationship whatsoever to natural man*, as a transcendent object whose demonstration (as well as the greater part of its content) has been determined by the *arbitrary nature of a "divine decree."*[3]

1. De Lubac, "Apologétique et théologie," 361–78. It can be found in English in De Lubac, *Theological Fragments*, 91–104.

2. Körner, "Henri de Lubac and Fundamental Theology," 710–23, here 714–15. Rudolf Voderholzer likewise states: "De Lubac's inaugural lecture in 1929 marked a turning point in the history of theology from apologetics to fundamental theology, as it is widely understood today" (*Meet Henri de Lubac*, 46).

3. De Lubac, "Apologetics and Theology" in *Theological Fragments*, 93, emphases added. Cf. Körner, "Henri de Lubac and Fundamental Theology," 711. Körner states: "Precisely this revolution in terminology and substance [fundamental theology versus apologetics] is also evident in Henri de Lubac's inaugural lecture. Whereas the title still speaks of apologetics, by which is meant above all the extrinsicist apologetics of neo-scholasticism, de Lubac suggests the name 'fundamental theology' for that part of apologetics whose argumentation is to be content-relative (intrinsicist), hence, not apologetic in the former sense, but theological" (ibid., 715). Likewise, the German de Lubac-scholar Voderholzer writes: "Taking as its point of departure man, as a being that is ordered to the divine transcendence, the kind of apologetics that Henri de Lubac has in mind should demonstrate how the Gospel message addresses the real questions of the human spirit" (Voderholzer, *Meet Henri de Lubac*, 46).

Neoscholastic apologetics aimed to demonstrate the preambles of faith (e.g., God's existence) and to establish motives of credibility for accepting the divine founding of Christianity and the Church; as typically understood, it did so with very little emphasis upon the actual *content* of dogma, the chief apologetic aim being largely negative—often simply an effort to demonstrate the *absence* of contradiction, say, with respect to some particular dogma.[4]

In the Neoscholastic scheme, the realm of faith correlates with the realm of grace; the result is that there can be no direct or inherent link between human nature and the supernatural mysteries of faith. The two cannot be related intrinsically to one another—only extrinsically—so that the faith (as well as grace) will be seen to come to man "from without," so to speak. Rudolf Voderholzer explains this basic difference between the two schools of thought when he describes the Neoscholastic procedure this way:

> While the business of theology is the exhibition of the internal consistency of the Church's doctrines, which are to be believed as mysteries either revealed by God or deduced from his revelation, apologetics, operating in the forecourt of faith and prescinding to a large extent from its contents, seeks to demonstrate the credibility of revelation on the basis of signs and miracles that confirm *it as revelation*.[5]

This discussion undoubtedly relates to the overall issue at hand—especially de Lubac's overarching aim of grounding a Christian humanism—because the manner in which the Church seeks to engage the culture is directly affected by its adoption of either an extrinsicist or intrinsicist nature-grace framework. It is no coincidence that extrinsicism correlates with Neoscholastic apologetics—and de Lubac's push toward intrinsicism goes hand in hand with his teaching on fundamental theology. For de Lubac's part, as Joseph Komonchak suggests in the following, an overly extrinsicist framework will in the end have great difficulty engaging secularism. Komonchak writes:

> [In Neoscholasticism] all encounter between faith and the world outside the Church was assigned to apologetics, while theology itself was considered "the science of revealed truths," for which an understanding of faith was a matter of drawing ever more nu-

4. See Kerr, *Twentieth-Century Catholic Theologians*, 1–16.
5. Voderholzer, "Dogma and History," 652, italics original.

merous and ever more remote conclusions, but was no longer an understanding of all reality *through the faith*. To suggest [as did de Lubac] that theology and apologetics were integrally related, that theology must seek to display its inner intelligibility and beauty of Christian doctrine and its ability to interpret all of reality, was to risk being accused [by Neo-Scholastics] of naturalism and of confusing the natural and the supernatural.[6]

For de Lubac, as he recounts in a letter dated 5 May 1961, the "sole passion" of his life was always simply the defense of the faith.[7] This sentiment is present already in his inaugural lecture in 1929 when he states: "*A Theology that does not constantly maintain apologetical considerations becomes deficient and distorted*, while, on the other hand, *all apologetics that wishes to be fully effective must end up in theology*."[8] Hence, in his mind, theology must always seek to engage the culture; and conversely, this apologetic stance must always root itself in the faith of the Church, a point which Bernard Körner makes here, as he explains de Lubac's teaching on this very point: "Just as a rightly understood apologetics may not prescind from the content of the faith, so too theology must not ensconce itself in faith's inner sanctum without bearing in mind the age and the conditions in which men live."[9]

This hermeneutic of de Lubac has been rightly referred to as a "suspended middle,"[10] which runs throughout his thought. This term was first coined by his student and long-time friend, Hans Urs von Balthsar (1905–1988), and it refers to de Lubac's refusal to separate in a mutually exclusive manner conventional dichotomies such as faith and reason,

6. Komonchak, "Theology and Culture at Mid-Century," 582–83, emphasis original. See De Lubac, "Apologetics and Theology" in *Theological Fragments*, 94–95.

7. De Lubac, *At the Service of the Church*, 324; "La seule passion de ma vue est la défense de notre foi" (De Lubac, *Mémoire sur l'occasion de mes écrits*, 325).

8. De Lubac, "Apologetics and Theology" in *Theological Fragments*, 96, emphasis original in translation.

9. Körner, "Henri de Lubac and Fundamental Theology," 717. Likewise, Gianfranco Coffele describes the missionary *élan* of de Lubac's theological program: Coffele, "De Lubac and the theological foundation of the missions," 757–75, here 758, 768, 772.

10. Balthasar, *Theology of Henri de Lubac*, 11, 15. Balthasar states: "In *Surnaturel* de Lubac defends the suspended middle without any compromise against all attempts on the part of philosophers and theologians to bracket the other side" (ibid., 17). Balthasar's use of "suspended middle" seems to be the origin of the title of Milbanks' work mentioned in the previous chapter (Milbank, *The Suspended Middle*). See also Voderholzer, *Meet Henri de Lubac*, 110–11.

theology and philosophy, or even theology and apologetics. In this light, de Lubac would undoubtedly delight in Pope John Paul II's approval of "Christian philosophy," which is but another indication of the general shift that has taken place in the Church toward intrinsicism. The late Holy Father writes:

> The philosopher who learns humility will also find courage to tackle questions which are difficult to resolve if the data of revelation are ignored—for example, the problem of evil and suffering, the personal nature of God and the question of the meaning of life or, more directly, the radical metaphysical question, "Why is there something rather than nothing?"[11]

Let us turn now more specifically to man's natural desire for God and the beatific vision, noting especially its relation to the distinctive methodological *prolegomena* of de Lubac. As we have said, in his mind, the notion of man as "created spirit" is absolutely central, and his emphasis here in fact significantly alters the very contours of the debate.

Natural Desire and the Beatific Vision

For de Lubac, all created spirits naturally desire the beatific vision as their final end—without exception—a point which we have seen him make already: "L'esprit est donc désir de Dieu."[12] In 1932, he wrote to the French philosopher, Maurice Blondel (1861–1949), expressing the same conviction as follows: "This concept of a pure nature runs into great difficulties, the principal one of which seems to me to be the following: *How can a conscious spirit be anything other than an absolute desire of God*?"[13] Man quite simply has embedded in his very nature an

11. John Paul II, *Fides et Ratio*, 1998, no. 76.

12. De Lubac, *Surnaturel*, 483: "The spirit is desire for God." Elsewhere de Lubac writes: "The laws of the 'dynamism proper to the spirit' are not calculated on the laws of the 'dynamism of natural forms'" (De Lubac, "Mystery of the Supernatural" in *Theology in History*, 303).

13. De Lubac, *At the Service of the Church*, 184, emphasis added; "Cette conception d'une pure nature se heurte à de grosses difficultés, don't la principale me paraît être celle-ci: comment un esprit conscient peut-il être autre chose qu'un désir absolu de Dieu?" (De Lubac, *Mémoire sur l'occasion de mes écrits*, 188). Indeed, this is where he and Blondel strike such a chord of affinity, since Blondel's dissertation *L'action*, defended in 1893, sought to show that the dynamism of man's natural willing leads inexorably to the supernatural—thereby establishing the *inherent* connection between the orders of nature and grace. Blondel, *L'action: Essay on a Critique of Life and a Science of Action*;

inexorable desire for this supernatural union with God, a desire which necessarily precludes the possibility of a purely natural beatitude. For anything short of the vision of God leaves the created spirit in a state of longing and frustration. And so de Lubac writes:

> In me, a real and personal human being, in my concrete nature—that nature I have in common with all real men, to judge by what my faith teaches me, and regardless of what is or is not revealed to me either by reflective analysis or by reasoning—the "desire to see God" cannot be permanently frustrated without an *essential suffering*. To deny this is to undermine my entire Credo. For is not this, in effect, the definition of the "pain of the damned?" And consequently—at least in appearance—a good and just God could hardly frustrate me, unless I, through my own fault, turn away from Him by choice. The infinite importance of the desire implanted in me by my Creator is what constitutes the infinite importance of the drama of human existence.[14]

---

in French published as Blondel, *L'Action*, vol. 1, *Le Problème des Causes Secondes et Le pur Agir* and Blondel, *L'Action*, vol. 2, *L'Action Humaine et Les Conditions de son Aboutissement*. See also Blanchette, *Maurice Blondel*, 681. De Lubac is clear regarding his debt to Blondel on this issue, especially as it pertains to his thesis in *Surnaturel*. In the same letter to Blondel cited above, de Lubac writes: "You see, Monsieur, how I let myself speak to you with all the freedom of a disciple. *It is in fact the study of your work that made me begin*, some eleven years ago, to reflect on these problems [cf. *Surnaturel*], and I believe that I have remained faithful to its inspiration" (cited in De Lubac, *At the Service of the Church*, 184–85, emphasis added); "Vous le voyez, Monsieur, je me laisse aller à parler devant vous avec l'abandon d'un disciple. C'est en effet l'étude de votre œuvre qui m'a fait, voici onze ans, commencer de réléchir à ces problèmes, et je crois être resté fidèle à son inspiration" (De Lubac, *Mémoire sur l'occasion de mes écrits*, 189). For the influence of Blondel upon de Lubac, see Russo, *Henri de Lubac*, 289–92. See also Blondel's works, *Letter on Apologetics* (1896) and *History and Dogma* (1904) which bear an affinity to de Lubac's teaching on fundamental theology. For the essential kinship between these works of Blondel and de Lubac, see also Coffele, "De Lubac and the Theological Foundation," 766. Also: Voderholzer, "Dogma and History," 653–54.

14. De Lubac, *The Mystery of the Supernatural*, 54, emphasis added. In French: "En moi, être humain réel et personnel, en ma nature concrète, dans cette nature que j'ai en commun avec tous les hommes réels si j'en juge à partir de ce que a foi m'enseigne, et quoi qu'il en soit de ce que peut ou non me reveler soit une analyse reflexive soit un raisonnement quelconnue, le 'désir de voir Dieu' ne saurait être éternellement frustré sans une souffrance essentielle. Je ne saurais nier cela sans faire une brèche à mon *Credo*. N'est-ce pas là, en effet, la définition même de la peine 'du dam'? Et par consequent – au moins à ce qu'il semble – comment le Dieu juste et bon pourrait-il m'en frustrer, si ce n'est pas moi qui, par ma propre faute, me détourne librement de Lui? Le sérieux infini du drame de l'existence humaine" (De Lubac, *Le Mystère du Surnaturel*, 80).

This desire is constitutive of man's very being as a created spirit, and is therefore his *specifying* feature, as it were; in short, for de Lubac, it is what ultimately makes man a *man*:

> For this desire is not some "accident" in me. It does not result from some peculiarity, possibly alterable, of my individual being, or from some historical contingency whose effects are more or less transitory. *A fortiori* it does not in any sense depend upon my deliberate will. *It is in me as a result of my belonging to humanity, as it is, that humanity which is, as we say, "called." For God's call is constitutive.* My finality, which is expressed by this desire, is inscribed upon my very being as it has been put into this universe by God. And, by God's will, *I now have no other genuine end, no end really assigned to my nature or presented for my free acceptance under any guise, except that of "seeing God."*[15]

Hence, man's orientation to the beatific vision is not something extrinsic or extraneous to his nature; that is, it is not *accidental* to his nature. Rather, this desire constitutes his ontological fabric—such that man's nature cannot be abstracted from this most basic desire for the beatific vision. For this reason, on de Lubac's account, man's nature cannot be considered coherently on the hypothesis of a purely natural end, for to do so would be to consider a different nature altogether.[16]

Of course, this position directly undermines the logic of the pure-nature tradition which is predicated upon the assumption that we can indeed abstract man's nature from his existential conditions—since man's nature always remains *specifically the same across each and every condition*, whether or not man is called to the beatific vision. Therefore,

---

15. De Lubac, *Mystery of the Supernatural*, 54–55, emphasis added. In French: "C'est que ce désir n'est pas en moi un 'accident' quelconque. Il ne me vient pas de quelque particularité, peut-être modifiable, de mon être individuel, ou de quelque contingence historique aux effets plus ou moins transitoires. A plus forte raison ne depend-il aucunement de mon vouloir délibéré. Il est en moi du fait de mon appurtenance à l'humanité actuelle, à cette humanité qui est, comme on dit, 'appelée'. Car l'appel de Dieu est constitutif. Ma finalité, dont ce désir est l'expression, est inscrite en mon être meme, tel qu'il est posé par Dieu dans cet univers. Et, de par la volonté de Dieu, je n'ai pas aujourd'hui d'autre fin réelle, c'est-à-dire réellement assignée à ma nature et offerte sous quelques espèces que ce soit, à mon adhesion libre, que de 'voir Dieu'" (De Lubac, *Le Mystère du Surnaturel*, 81). Also: De Lubac, *The Mystery of the Supernatural*, 167; cf. De Lubac, "The Mystery of the Supernatural" in *Theology in History*, 292–93.

16. De Lubac, *The Mystery of the Supernatural*, 54–55, 59–60, 62.

the principles employed by de Lubac here remove the foundational un-
derpinnings of the most basic reasoning of the pure-nature tradition.

Imago Dei or Aristotelian Physis?

Similar to his preference for treating man as a "created spirit," the revelation of man as created in the *imago Dei* is also likewise privileged as a
starting point for de Lubac.[17] Let us begin here by considering the mystery of man as expressed by the Psalmist, as he reflects upon the opening
chapter of Genesis:

> What is man that you are mindful of him, and the son of man
> that you care for him? Yet you have made him little less than the
> angels, and you have crowned him with glory [וְכָבוֹד] and honor.
> You have given him dominion over the works of your hands; you
> have put all things under his feet, all sheep and oxen, and also
> the beasts of the field, the birds of the air, and the fish of the sea.
> (Ps 8:4–8a)

The coming of Christ further elevates the grandeur of this anthropological mystery—the fullness of which must include man's participation in the glory and work of the New Adam whose victory is described
here: "The last enemy to be destroyed is death. For God has put all things
in subjection under his feet" (1 Cor 15:26–27; cf. Ps 8:6). This victory of
the New Adam is also described in the most oft-cited psalm in the New
Testament: "Sit at my right, till I make your enemies your footstool" (Ps
110:1b).

For this reason, de Lubac strongly criticizes what he refers to as
Cajetan's "*naturalization* of the soul,"[18] by which de Lubac means the for-
feiture of man's *sui generis* uniqueness—the penchant of the pure-nature
tradition to treat man just like any other natural thing. On de Lubac's

---

17. Cf. Gen 1:26–27: "Then God said, 'Let us make man in our image [בְּצַלְמֵנוּ]
[LXX, εἰκόνα] and our likeness [כִּדְמוּתֵנוּ] [LXX, ὁμοίωσιν] and let them have dominion
over the fish . . . birds . . . cattle . . . every creeping thing. . . . So God created man in
his own image, in the image of God he created him; male and female he created them
[וַיִּבְרָא אֱלֹהִים אֶת-הָאָדָם בְּצַלְמוֹ בְּצֶלֶם אֱלֹהִים בָּרָא אֹתוֹ זָכָר וּנְקֵבָה בָּרָא אֹתָם]." In the Vulgate,
for "image and likeness" is "*imaginem et similitudinem.*" Only after the sixth day, the
day on which God made man, is creation then pronounced "very good" [טוֹב מְאֹד]
(Gen 1:31).

18. De Lubac, *The Mystery of the Supernatural*, 140, emphasis added: "C'est à cette
naturalisation de l'âme, ou de l'être humain, qu'il faut attribuer la doctrine soutenue
par Cajetan sur puissance obédientielle" (De Lubac, *Le Mystère du Surnaturel*, 179–80).

account, Cajetan has neglected the unique grandeur of the mystery of man, and the reason is due to the fact that the pure-nature tradition is simply too beholden to Aristotle. De Lubac writes:

> We shall not agree with him [Aristotle] in determining the laws of spirit according to the laws of the stars. We shall reply that though Aristotle may have been right about the stars, the analogy could not in any circumstances apply to men. We shall not be misled by an apparent induction which is really begging the question. We shall take exception to any arguments based on so deceptive a method.[19]

When de Lubac earlier described the pure-nature tradition's "gigantic leap forward,"[20] taking place at the time of Suárez (1548–1617), he was referring to this very transposition of Aristotelian philosophy onto Christian anthropology—especially as it pertains to man's natural desire. The key to this development, as we have seen, is the concept of the *debitum naturae* which is drawn from the Aristotelian principle that *nature does nothing in vain*, and which is then applied to man and his natural desire. This move by itself secures the codification of man's twofold end, creating the necessity of positing man's purely natural end, therefore more or less securing the logical structure of the pure-nature tradition—a point which Lawrence Feingold implies here: "Once the notion of the *debitum naturae* is clarified, Suárez's argument for the possibility of a connatural final end for man is relatively straightforward; for it rests on the distinction between what is gratuitous and what is due."[21] De Lubac, too, sees this logical development along the very same lines:

19. De Lubac, *The Mystery of the Supernatural*, 156–57: "Nous n'accepterons pas de déterminer comme lui les lois de l'esprit d'après les lois des astres. Nous lui répondrons qu'Aristote pouvait bien, dans sa Physique, avoir raison pour les astres, mais que, en tout cas, l'analogie ne vaut pas pour les hommes. Nous ne serons pas dupes d'une induction qui n'est en réalité q'une pétition de principe. A tous les raisonnements qui se fondet sur une méthode aussi trompeuse, nous opposerons une fin de non-recevoir" (De Lubac, *Le Mystère du Surnaturel*, 197–98).

20. De Lubac, *Augustinianism and Modern Theology*, 157: "Avec François Suárez (1548–1617), elle va faire un pas de géant" (De Lubac, *Augustinisme et Théologie Moderne*, 194).

21. Feingold, *Natural Desire to See God*, 230. Cf. De Lubac, "*Duplex Hominis Beatitudo* (Saint Thomas, Ia 2ae, q. 62, a. I)," 290–99; translated by Aaron Riches and Peter M. Candler Jr. as "Duplex hominis beatitudo" in *Communio* 35 (2008): 599–612. For a discussion of Suárez and Réginald Garrigou-Lagrange on this matter, see ibid., 600–601.

Suárez starts from the idea that man, being a natural being, must normally have an end within the limits of his nature. . . . It is therefore contradictory to envisage an end which would be . . . "natural with respect to appetite, supernatural with respect to attainment." Long before Fr. Garrigou-Lagrange, Suárez decisively rejects this venerable maxim.[22]

This methodological divergence between de Lubac and the pure-nature tradition is front and center in the following from de Lubac:

The end of a natural being is always in strict proportion to its means. For Suárez this is an absolute principle and its application to the case of man is no less absolute, no less undeniable. By virtue of his creation man is therefore made for an essentially natural beatitude. If we suppose that in fact he is called to some higher end, strictly speaking this could only be superadded. The first, by right, was sufficient; alone therefore it remains naturally knowable and alone it can come to a definition of man. If it is objected that there is a desire for this higher beatitude, *Suárez, before even examining the objection, answers that it is impossible, because, still according to Aristotle, the natural appetite follows the natural power.*[23]

---

22. De Lubac, *Augustinianism and Modern Theology*, 158–59. De Lubac's citation is referencing this maxim as found in Domingo de Soto (1494–1560) and Robert Bellarmine (1542–1621). This pithy expression represents de Lubac's position. In French, the above citation is as follows: "Suárez part de l'idée que l'homme, étant un être de la nature, doit normalement avoir une fin dans les limites de la nature. . . . Il est donc contradictoire d'envisager une fin qui serait . . . *naturalis quoad appetitionem, supernaturalis vero quoad adsecutionem.* Bien avant le R. R. Garrigou-Lagrange, Suárez réprouve avec decision ce vénérable adage" (De Lubac, *Augustinisme et théologie moderne*, 195–96). Likewise, de Lubac elsewhere writes: "According to a principle received from Aristotle, all natural beings must have an end that is proportionate to them" (De Lubac, *Surnaturel*, 114): "selon un principe reçu d'Aristote, tous les êtres de la nature doivent avoir un fin qui leur soit proportionée."

23. De Lubac, *Augustinianism and Modern Theology*, 158, emphasis added: "La fin d'un être naturel est toujours rigoureusement mesurée à ses moyens. C'est là pour Suárez un principe absolu, et non moins absolue, non moins indiscutable est l'application de ce principe au cas de l'homme. En vertu de sa creation, l'homme est donc fait pour une beatitude d'essence naturelle. A supposer qu'en fait il se trouve appelé à quelque fin plus haute, celle-ci ne pourra être que proprement surajoutée. La première, en droit, suffisait; seule, donc, elle rest naturellement connaissable et seule elle peut entrer dans une définition de l'homme. Que si l'on objecte qu'il y a dans homme un désir naturel de cette beatitude supérieure, Suárez, avant même de l'examiner, répond que cela est impossible, parceque, toujours suivant Aristote, l'appétit de la nature suit la puissance de la nature" (De Lubac, *Augustinisme et théologie moderne*, 195–96).

In fact, according to de Lubac, *even* St. Thomas fell into this very problem; that is, by striving to give Aristotle his due, de Lubac suggests that Aquinas conceded far too much and actually created the very space within which later distortions could emerge. Accordingly, de Lubac writes:

> To come back to the very expression "natural desire," it is still true that Saint Thomas, transposing the traditional doctrine into Aristotelian terms, was to contribute, more than anyone else, to making the fundamental objection arise one day.[24]

Hence, despite the fact that de Lubac calls forth Aquinas as witnessing to his own twentieth-century teaching on man's natural desire and his unitary final end in the beatific vision, nonetheless, he criticizes St. Thomas here for much the same reasons as he does the pure-nature tradition:

> For the nature to which he [Aquinas] was referring, completely spiritual as it was, did not essentially differ from the other natures from which his universe was composed. It was that "philosophic" nature, as the ancients had conceived it (who did not believe in a creator God at all). Although extrinsically [*du dehors*] to the intervention of the idea of creation, it was no longer exactly that image of God, whose features the Fathers of the Church had so intensely developed, being inspired less by Plato, than by the Bible. . . . For the Fathers, there was no *nous* [Gk. "mind"] without an ever-gratuitous and ever-precarious participation in advance in the unique *pneuma* [Gk. "spirit"]. . . . [But] for Aristotle, nature was a center of properties and a source of activity, strictly delimited and enclosed within its own order.[25]

Here de Lubac is most explicit: Aquinas allowed the Aristotelian philosophical framework and the patristic inheritance of faith to stand side by side, never making it entirely clear which was ultimately architectonic over which. This dueling juxtaposition resulted in an uneasy Thomistic "synthesis," which resulted in the tensions that later devolved into the very problems that de Lubac saw in the pure-nature tradition. For this reason, de Lubac contends that Aquinas represents a crucial stage in this anthropological deviation—one certainly not unrelated to the problems he sees in Cajetan:

24. De Lubac, *Surnaturel*, 434–35. Full French citation will be given below.
25. Ibid.

> *Now everywhere in Saint Thomas, these two conceptions of Aristo-*
> *telian nature and the Patristic image are mixed up without ever*
> *being able to say whether they are truly combined, or whether*
> *they collide, nor which of the two finally succeeds in controlling*
> *the other.* As powerful as his spirit of synthesis was, he did not
> always succeed at fusing the received elements from two diverse
> traditions into a perfect unity.[26]

Echoing the language of the previous section, de Lubac's vantage
point is summed up by Edward T. Oakes this way: "Spirit . . . demands its
own logic."[27] Oakes continues with the same point regarding de Lubac's
teaching here:

> The presence of spirit in the cosmos requires a revision in the
> standard terms under which debates on grace and nature [take]
> place. In other words, spirit is a *different kind of nature* from the
> natural forms found in the rest of the natural world, and thus
> requires a different kind of ontology.[28]

In this light, let us note that no objection can be brought against de Lubac
on nature and grace—not if its premises draw from an Aristotelian philosophical framework. For this reason, one's assessment of de Lubac here
in terms of his overarching methodological framework is absolutely

---

26. Ibid: "Pour en revenir au mot même de désir naturel, il est encore vrai que
saint Thomas, transposant la doctrine traditionelle en termes aristotéliciennes, devait
contribuer plus que tout autre à faire surgir un jour l'objection fondamentale que lui-
même n'apercevait point encore. Car la nature à laquelle il se référait, toute spirituelle
qu'elle était, ne différait pas essentiellement des autres natures dont se composait son
univers. C'était cette nature philosophique telle que l'avaient conçue les Anciens qui ne
croyaient point en un Dieu créateur, quoique corrigée du dehors par l'intervention de
l'idée de création. Ce n'était plus tout à fait cette image de Dieu, dont les Pères de l'Eglise
avaient si fortement buriné les traits en s'inspirant moins de Platon que de la Bible.
. . . Pour les Pères, il n'y avait point de *nous* sans une participation anticipée, toujours
gratuite et toujours précaire, à l'unique *pneuma*. Pour Aristote, la nature était un centre
de propriétés et une source d'activité strictement délimitée et enfermée dans son ordre.
Or partout, chez saint Thomas, ces deux conceptions de la *nature* aristotélicienne et de
l'*image* patristique se mêlent, sans qu'on puisse dire si ells s'y combinent vraiment ou si
elles s'y heurtent, ni laquelle des deux finalement réussit à dompter l'autre. Si vigoureux
que soit son esprit de synthèse, il ne réussit pas toujours à fonder les elements reçus
de deux traditions diverses en une parfait unité." See also Komonchak, "Theology and
Culture at Mid-Century," 579–602.

27. Oakes, "The Paradox of Nature and Grace," 674.

28. Ibid., 673. Cf. De Lubac, "Mystery of the Supernatural" in *Theology in History*,
298.

crucial for one's overall assessment of his position. Indeed, the debate between him and the pure-nature tradition stands or falls on this very issue. With de Lubac's hermeneutic in place, his position becomes virtually impregnable.

Let us now turn to de Lubac's account of grace's gratuity in light of his earlier teaching on man's natural desire, where this methodological divide between him and the pure-nature tradition will again become quite evident.

Paradox and Gratuity

For de Lubac, the Christian tradition presents us with two unimpeachable truths, both of which must be taken as non-negotiable: "Man cannot live except by the vision of God . . . and that the vision of God depends totally on God's good pleasure."[29] As we have seen, on de Lubac's account, the Christian intellectual ought to strive to maintain the unified integrity of a mystery of faith, rather than to seek at all costs to alleviate whatever tension which may arise from the juxtaposition of various aspects of a given mystery. In this light, de Lubac writes:

> All too often there remains the same timidity, the same impatient anxiety to eliminate every paradox from the human situation and arrive at a positive and clearly understandable result; so much so that this "natural desire" to see God which they [pure-nature theologians] have been trying to re-establish is twisted almost at once into a vague "wish," a wholly Platonic "prayer" quite inadequate for the work it should be doing [that is, quite "inadequate" to make for an inherent bridge between man's nature and the gift of the beatific vision].[30]

For this reason, where others accuse him of contradiction,[31] de Lubac unfailingly sees paradox, and nowhere is this divergence more

---

29. De Lubac, *Mystery of the Supernatural*, 179; "L'homme ne peut vivre que par la vue de Dieu—et cette vue de Dieu dépend absolument du bon plaisir divin" (De Lubac, *Le Mystère du Surnaturel*, 223).

30. De Lubac, *Mystery of the Supernatural*, 180; "Trop souvent une même timidité de pensée les inspire encore, un même souci impatient d'éliminer de la réalité humaine tout paradoxe et d'aboutir à un résultat positif entièrement clair à l'entendement; si bein que ce 'désir naturel' de voir Dieu qu'on avait entrepris de rétablir s'infléchit. Presque aussitôt en un vague 'souhait', en un 'voeu' tout platonique, inapte au service qu'il devait render" (De Lubac, *Le Mystère du Surnaturel*, 224).

31. See Feingold, *Natural Desire to See God*, 310: "De Lubac holds that it is possible

manifest than on the issue of man's natural desire and its relation to grace's gratuity. De Lubac writes:

> The desire to see him [God] is in us, it constitutes us, and yet it comes to us as a completely free gift. Such paradoxes should not surprise us, for they arise in every mystery; they are the hall-mark of a truth that is beyond our depth. "Faith embraces several truths which appear to contradict one another." It "is always a harmony of two opposing truths."[32]

For de Lubac's part, without a steadfast insistence upon the herme-neutic of paradox, orthodoxy may well be safeguarded but all too often at the price of a certain rationalistic reduction in the mystery of faith. Defended in this manner, de Lubac contends that the integrity of the faith will be adversely affected in the long run. And so he writes:

> When it is between two truths of faith that positive conciliation is not visible, the choice of one of the two to the exclusion of the other constitutes, properly speaking, heresy. . . . *Without leaving the bounds of orthodoxy, a theology overly concerned about tangible conciliations and definitive explanations always risks compromising the balance of the synthesis by taking away something.*[33]

For de Lubac, the fact that theologians gave excessive attention to the question of grace's gratuity is itself symptomatic of the problem at hand. The anxiety caused over this purported "problem" of grace's gratu-

---

to maintain simultaneously without contradiction that God would not be unjust if He were to deprive the innocent rational creature of the vision of God, and that the vision of God is man's *only possible* final end. This is seen not as a contradiction, but as the 'paradox of human nature' (or of the created spirit), although an Aristotelian philosophical framework, badly adapted to the Christian tradition, may make it appear contradictory. It should be noted that this contradiction results only when it is held that man (or the created spirit) has only *one possible beatitude*, which nevertheless is *not due* him. If, on the contrary, one admits with St. Thomas a twofold beatitude for the rational creature—connatural and supernatural—then this apparent contradiction totally vanishes."

32. De Lubac, *Mystery of the Supernatural*, 167. De Lubac does not cite the source of the quotation. In French: "Le désir de Le voir est en nous, il est nous-mêmes, et il n'est pourtant comblé que par un pur bienfait. Ne nous étonnons pas de telles antinomies. Elles surgissent de tout mystère. Elles sont le signe de toute vérité qui nous dépayse. 'La foi embrasse plusieurs verités qui semblent se contredire'. Elle 'est toujours accord de deux verités opposées." (De Lubac, *Le Mystère du Surnaturel*, 209).

33. De Lubac, "Mystery of the Supernatural" in *Theology in History*, 311, emphasis added.

ity led theologians to neglect the more basic fact that creation itself is already gratuitous—which for de Lubac implies the absolute gratuity of all else, *a fortiori*. Thus, the only "problem," on de Lubac's account, regarding the gratuity of grace lay precisely in the fact that so many theologians bewitched themselves into thinking that there was such a "problem" at all. For him, the matter is really quite simple: "God is in no way governed by our desire. . . . There can be no question of anything being *due* to the creature."[34] God simply *owes* nothing to the creature no matter what, and so the whole notion of the *debitum naturae* is wrongheaded from the start, a point which de Lubac makes emphatically here:

> God could have refused to give himself to his creatures, just as he could have, and has, given himself. The gratuitousness of the supernatural order is true individually and totally. It is gratuitous in itself. It is gratuitous as far as each one of us is concerned. It is gratuitous in regard to what we see as preceding it, whether in time or in logic. Further—and this is what some of the explanations I have contested seem to me not to make clear—its gratuitousness remains always complete. *It remains gratuitous in every hypothesis.* It is forever new. It remains gratuitous at every stage of preparation for the gift, and at every stage of giving of it. *No "disposition" in creatures can ever, in any way, bind the Creator.*[35]

Hence, for de Lubac, God is not obliged on any account. No exigency on the part of the creature can ever "force God's hand," as it were, no matter how much human nature might be said to stand in *need* of grace; the gift of such grace remains gratuitous on *any* hypothesis—regardless of whether man's nature has an exigency for grace, and whether or not the beatific vision is man's only possible end. Therefore, in de

34. De Lubac, *Mystery of the Supernatural*, 207, emphasis added; "Dieu ne se règle pas sur notre désir!. . . . Toute question d'exigence de la part de la créature est bannie" (De Lubac, *Le Mystère du Surnaturel*, 257).

35. De Lubac, *Mystery of the Supernatural*, 236–37, emphasis added; "Dieu aurait pu se refuser à sa créature, tout comme Il a pu et voulu se donner. La gratuité de l'ordre surnaturel est particulière et totale. Elle l'est en elle-même. Elle l'est pour chacun de nous. Elle l'est par rapport à ce qui pour nous, temporellement ou logiquement, le precédé. Bien plus—et c'est ce que certaines explications que nous avons discutées nous ont paru ne pas assez laisser voir—cette gratuité est toujours intacte. Elle le demeure ên toute hypothèse. Elle est toujours nouvelle. Elle le demeure à toutes les étapes de la preparation du Don, à toutes les étapes du Don lui-mêmes. Aucune 'disposition' dans la créature ne pourra jamais, en aucune manière, lier le Créateur" (De Lubac, *Le Mystère du Surnaturel*, 289–90).

Lubac's mind, the notion of the debt of nature—and the appropriation of the Aristotelian axiom that *natural desires cannot be in vain*—actually created this purported theological problem whole cloth. For this reason, he states:

> In no sense and on no account, neither natural nor moral, do we have any rights over God. *God is a debtor to no one in any way whatsoever.* This dictum of Ockham is the echo of the whole tradition. It is one of the first axioms of the Christian faith.[36]

We will discuss this passage further in the subsequent chapter, but for now let us simply observe that what de Lubac attributes to Ockham as the "first principle of Christian faith" is precisely what Aquinas *denies*, placing this very position in the mouth of the objector (*ST* I, q. 21, a. 1, obj. 3). As we mentioned in the opening chapter, St. Thomas teaches that the question of justice does indeed apply to God in relation to creatures: God is just toward His creatures when He gives them their *due*, in accordance with their "nature and condition."[37] This point of contact establishes clearly that—at least on this issue—the teaching of the pure-nature tradition aligns with that of St. Thomas, despite the claims of de Lubac.

Ultimately for de Lubac, everything God does is gratuitous—from creation to the new creation in Christ, if only we had the eyes to see (cf. Isa 6:9–10). For him, the theological "phantom" of gratuity and the supposed problem following thereof is simply a "false problem," arising only on account of the infelicitous insistence on the part of theologians to frame the issue in Aristotelian categories. Accordingly, de Lubac writes:

> The monster of exigency was only a *phantom*. The attempt was made to resolve a *false problem*. In reality, the question of exigency *does not come up*. As pressing, in effect, as is the desire for the supernatural, as strict as is the spirit's need, which the desire manifests, how can one speak of something in man which would weigh on God, putting Him in dependence on man, since such a

---

36. De Lubac, *Surnaturel*, 487–88: "Tout de même, en comblant notre désir de nature, il répond à son propre appel. Comme tout être créé, l'esprit humain a ses limites, naturellement infranchissables. En aucun sens et à aucun titre, ni naturel, ni moral, nous n'avons de droits sur Dieu. *Deus nulli debitor est quocumque modo*: cette d'Occam est l'écho de toute la tradition. Elle est un des premiers axiomes de la foi chrétienne."

37. *ST* I, q. 21, a. 3.

desire or such a need—if it is in man—is not from him? It is first
entirely willed by God.[38]

Conclusion

For de Lubac, the theologian must always be cognizant of the creature's
"ontological humility" [d'une humilité ontologique], as he states here:
"The I who aspires is not the I who requires."[39] For this reason, he reso-
lutely rejects engaging the question of nature and grace with categories
such as "need" and "debt," opting to frame the issue instead in terms of
"love" and "gift."[40] Though seemingly subtle, this recasting of the debate
significantly changes the discussion, and decisively in de Lubac's favor.

However, as we have noted, in recent years there has been a significant resurgence in the pure-nature tradition.[41] While the pure-nature

38. De Lubac, *Surnaturel*, 487, emphases added: "Le monster de l'exigence n'était
donc qu'un fantôme. On s'évertuait à résoudre un faux problème. En réalité, la question
de l'exigence *ne se pose pas*. Si pressant, en effet, que soit le désir du surnaturel, si strict
que soit dans l'esprit le besoin qu'il traduit, comment pourrait-on parler à son sujet de
quelque chose de l'homme qui pèserait sur Dieu, mettant Dieu sous la dependence de
l'homme, puisqu'un tel désir ou qu'un tel besoin, s'il est dans l'homme, n'est pas de lui?
Il est tout entire d'abord voulu par Dieu."

39. Ibid., 484: "Le 'moi qui aspire' n'est pas un 'moi qui réclame.'" See also "Mystery
of the Supernatural" in *Theology in History*, 315–16.

40. De Lubac, *Mystery of the Supernatural*, 207: "There can be no question of
anything being due to the creature. But one may perhaps say, it remains true nonetheless
that once such a desire exists in the creature it becomes the sign, not merely of a possible
gift from God, but of a certain gift." In French: "Toute question d'exigence de la part de
la créature est bannie. Mais il n'en reste pas moins, dira-t-on peut-être, qu'un tel désir
existant dans la créature devient alors le signe, non seulement d'un don possible de la
part de Dieu, mais d'un don certain" (De Lubac, *Le Mystère du Surnaturel*, 257).

41. Feingold, *Natural Desire to See God*. See also Long, *Natura Pura*. Also: Long, "On
the Possibility of a Purely Natural End for Man," 211–37; Long, "Obediential Potency,
Human Knowledge, and the Natural Desire for God," 45–63; Hütter, "Desiderium
Naturale Visionis Dei," 81–131; Hütter, "Aquinas on the Natural Desire for the Vision
of God," 523–51; White, "The 'Pure Nature' of Christology," 283–22; Mansini, "The
Abiding Theological Significance of Henri de Lubac's *Surnaturel*," 593–619. See also
Nichols, "Thomism and the Nouvelle Théologie," 1–19. Happily, we should note that
the vitriol of this debate has certainly subsided from its mid-twentieth-century form:
"The fact that I come to disagree . . . with the interpretation made famous by Henri de
Lubac in his works *Surnaturel* and *The Mystery of the Supernatural* does not mean that
I disapprove of his works on other subjects or that I am blind to his contributions. On
the contrary, I think that many of his works are classics, such as *Catholicism: Christ
and the Common Destiny of Man*; *The Splendor of the Church*; *The Motherhood of the*

tradition held sway for centuries, that trend was definitively reversed at the Second Vatican Council. But the vigor of this shift has given rise to the perception that perhaps the pendulum has moved *too* far in the direction of intrinsicism. It is this postconciliar context—and the perception that the transcendent and supernatural character of grace has been lost—that has given rise to this renewal of the pure-nature tradition.

As we saw at the conclusion of the previous chapter, even Lubac seems to have felt the need to defend extrinsicist aspects of the nature-grace relation after the Council, seeing that this aspect had now fallen into neglect. Accordingly, it is worth considering the contemporary re-articulation of the pure-nature tradition, and it is particularly opportune to do so now since the polemical context of this debate is now far behind us; perhaps now more than ever is the time to take up this most important issue of nature and grace once again.

Let us begin the next stage of this project, turning to the pure-nature tradition in its contemporary form, taking up first the thought of Lawrence Feingold.

Church; and *Medieval Exegesis*, among others. I do not think that the particular stance taken by de Lubac on the question of natural desire is intrinsically implied in these and other works dealing with questions of ecclesiology and patristic exegesis, and so forth. . . . De Lubac was a key contributor to the movement of *ressourcement*: a return to the primary sources of Christian faith and theology" (Feingold, *Natural Desire to See God*, xxxiv–xxxv). Similarly, Steve Long aptly notes that there simply are "two sets of texts" in Aquinas' corpus, some of which support the pure-nature position and some of which support de Lubac (*Natura Pura*, 13–14). This is a significant concession and one which would have been rare at mid-century on the part of the pure-nature tradition.

PART TWO

The Contemporary Resurgence
of the Pure-Nature Tradition

4

Lawrence Feingold and the Defense
of the Pure-Nature Tradition

While de Lubac's intrinsicism captures the Christocentric aspect of nature and grace, the pure-nature tradition capitalizes on the need to distinguish between nature and grace for the purpose of preserving the sublime transcendence and gratuity of divine grace. For if nature is not distinguished from grace, one can piously say, "all is grace"; but at the same time, is this not tantamount to saying that "all is nature?" In other words, if the specific meaning of supernatural grace is indefinitely extended to include all of creation, then the uniqueness of what is meant by "grace" loses its specificity, as Edward Oakes writes here:

> Either one can say that "it's all the same God anyway," and thus each religion is ineluctably moving toward some Transcendent Meaning, however defined; or one can say that these various religions are making incomplete truth claims that have to be adjudicated on terms other than the naïve positing of a transcendent element in human beings that provides a more or less direct access to God. A moment's reflection will show that both options help to determine, and are determined by, one's view on the relationship of nature and grace. If all men are *naturally* religious . . . and if all religions . . . give equal access to the transcendent, *then this must imply that there is a more or less seamless transition from (man's) nature to (God's) grace.* But if one religion (Christianity, say) raises a truth claim over all the others that can be shown on its own grounds to be true over against the truth claims of all the

other religions . . . *then this too must imply that grace is somehow radically distinct from man's religious nature.*[1]

In what follows, we will focus on three pivotal concepts for the pure-nature tradition: obediential potency, *debitum naturae*, and the possibility of a purely natural end. As we will see, the underlying logic of all three concepts is very similar and they align for the purpose of maintaining the independent integrity of the natural order—which in turn preserves the distinctively supernatural character of divine grace.

And so we turn first to the concept of obediential potency.

Obediential Potency

Obediential potency refers to man's *capacity* for the beatific vision, and as such this concept attempts to describe the precise relationship between human nature and the beatific vision. Henri de Lubac had little patience for this concept because he saw in it the very "naturalization of the soul," of which he charged Cajetan in the previous chapter. In opposition to *obediential* potency stands *natural* potency, which is closely related to the notion of natural desire; and as we have seen, de Lubac's teaching on man's natural desire connects man's nature directly to the beatific vision in an *intrinsic* way. In de Lubac's mind, obediential potency establishes a far too extrinsic relation between human nature and

1. Oakes, "The Paradox of Nature and Grace," 668, emphasis added. Oakes continues with a methodological point as to which is logically prior and decisive for the other: one's position on nature and grace, or one's position on pluralism? His point here is that either way the two are related: "Now whether theologians first decide to solve the problem of pluralism in religion and then develop a theology of grace to justify that position, or first work out a theology of grace and nature and then draw out the implications of that theology when taking up the question of pluralism, is itself an intriguing methodological question . . . *For the real point is simply that the two issues are inextricably linked . . . One's position regarding pluralism in religion both determines and is determined by the position one adopts regarding the relationship of nature and grace.* The closer the line between nature and grace, the easier it will be to detect signs of grace in all religions of the world without exception . . ." (ibid., 669, emphasis added). In an email correspondence, Feingold emphasized that he thought that the exaggerated intrinsicism mentioned above came from de Lubac *through* Karl Rahner, and on into the postconciliar situation (see Feingold, *Natural Desire to See God*, 331–35). See Herman-Emiel Mertens who states: "Rahner's vision of 'the free self-communication of God as supernatural existential' has to be situated in the whole of his 'anthropologically-oriented theology'. . . and [in his] existential anthropology. . . . Moreover, his perception of grace is completely in keeping with his strongly ecumenically-oriented doctrine of anonymous Christianity" (Mertens, "Nature and Grace," 256).

the beatific vision—a relation which then appears somewhat arbitrary, having God's decree as its only basis, and not anything inherent in man's fundamental nature, as such.

As we will see in a moment, de Lubac flattens out the concept of obediential potency down to its generic signification alone, showing virtually no awareness of the distinction that "specific" obediential potency entails. This fact goes a long way in explaining his harsh criticism of Cajetan; and conversely, the clarification of the nuance entailed in the notion of *specific* obediential potency is crucial for the response of the pure-nature tradition to de Lubac on this very point.

Let us begin by noting that the concept of obediential potency does find expression in Aquinas, as seen here in his treatment of the Incarnation, and which we will explain below:

> A double capability may be remarked in human nature: one, in respect to the order of natural power, and this is always fulfilled by God, Who apportions to each according to its natural capability; the other in respect to the order of the Divine power, which all creatures implicitly obey.[2]

Similarly, in his treatment on prophecy, St. Thomas writes:

> It belongs to man's mode and dignity that he be uplifted to divine things, from the very fact that he is made to God's image. And since a divine good infinitely surpasses the faculty of man in order to attain that good, he needs the divine assistance which is bestowed on him in every gift of grace. Hence it is not contrary to nature, but above the faculty of nature that man's mind be thus uplifted in rapture by God.[3]

As we will see, this language of a divine elevation which is "not contrary to nature, but above nature" is precisely what is signified by the notion of specific obediential potency; but first let us begin with the "generic" meaning of obediential potency.

Generic obediential potency refers to the capacity of a creature simply to "obey" the Creator (hence the name "obediential"). In this sense, it is a purely passive capacity of the creature to receive a miracle from God and has virtually nothing to do with the particular nature of the creature, as such; in this light, it can also be described as a "negative"

---

2. *ST* III, q. 1, a. 3, ad 3.
3. *ST* II-IIae, q. 175, a. 1, ad 2.

capacity, since generic obediential potency refers to nothing "positive" in the creature. Understood in this light, the relation between human nature and the beatific vision would be exceedingly extrinisicist—just as de Lubac alleges against the pure-nature tradition. Thus, if the pure-nature tradition employed obediential potency in this sense to describe man's capacity for the beatific vision, de Lubac's criticisms would be quite appropriate—since man would stand in no different relation to the beatific vision than would any other creature.

However, as we will see, this is not exactly the case when all is said and done: while de Lubac's charge is appropriate with respect to generic obediential potency, it does not have any force against specific obediential potency, and it is ultimately the latter that the pure-nature tradition employs for the purpose of understanding the relation of human nature to the beatific vision.

First, let us provide illustrations of both types of obediential potency, beginning with generic obediential potency; our first example is taken from the biblical episode of Balaam and his "talking" donkey. When Balaak, the Moabite King solicited the services of the prophet "near the River" (i.e., Balaam, Num 22:5), Balaam proceeded to strike his donkey, which provoked the following response from the Lord:

> Then the Lord *opened the mouth of the donkey, and she said to Balaam,* "What have I done to you, that you have struck me these three times?" And Balaam said to the donkey, "Because you have made sport of me. I wish I had a sword in my hand, for then I would kill you." *And the donkey said to Balaam,* "Am I not your donkey, upon which you have ridden all your life long to this day? Was I ever accustomed to do so to you?" And he said, "No." (Num 22:28–30, emphasis added)

In order to adjudicate whether we have here a generic or a specific obediential potency, we need only ask the following set of questions: is there anything in the *nature* of the donkey that lends itself to such oratorical elevation? In other words, does the elevated action of the donkey have anything to do with its nature, *as* donkey? Or, on the other hand, is it the case that such an action more or less *contradicts* the specific dynamism of the donkey's nature, as such? In other words, is it the case that the action of speaking has virtually *nothing* to do with being a donkey *per se*?

An affirmative answer to the first two questions is indicative of a specific obediential potency, whereas an affirmative answer to the second two questions indicates a generic obediential potency. Since this elevation has nothing to do with the donkey's nature as such, we have here an example of a *generic* obediential potency.

Accordingly, the litmus test for obediential potency is non-contradiction; that is, all things are possible for God, except for a genuine contradiction (which is not *really* possible in the first place). But "non-contradiction" can be said in two ways, corresponding to the two types of obediential potency, generic and specific: generic obediential potency must obey the law of non-contradiction most generally, absolutely speaking, while specific obediential potential must obey the law of non-contradiction in a much more narrowly defined sense—namely, that the elevation of the creature cannot contradict the *specific nature* of the creature in question. Balaam's talking donkey passes the test of non-contradiction in the first sense, but not in the second—making the example of a talking donkey an instance of generic obediential potency, as we have said above.

Another example of generic obediential potency (which we mentioned in the introductory chapter) is taken from John the Baptist's words: "God is able from these stones to raise up children of God" (Matt 3:8–9). Supposing that God transformed these stones into human beings, and supposing that those human beings then received the beatific vision, would it then follow that these stones were susceptible to being elevated to the beatific vision all along, in virtue of their *lithic* nature? The answer of course is "no" because these hypothetical stones, now-turned-human, could not attain the beatific vision *as* stones; rather, they would have to be first transformed into knowing and loving agents—in which case, they would no longer be *stones*. For this reason, *only* knowing and loving agents have the kind of nature that can be elevated to the beatific vision—which is to say that only such spiritual creatures have a *specific* obediential potency for the beatific vision.

In order to have the presence of a specific obediential potency, the elevation of the creature must not result in a change in the fundamental nature of the thing; that is, the elevation must be *perfective* of the very nature in question—albeit in a way that transcends the powers of its nature, simply speaking.

For this reason, specific obediential potency *does* indeed signify something *positive* in the creature—something which is in fact rooted in the very nature of the creature in question. In this light, specific obediential potency is best understood as a *relation* between divine omnipotence and the dynamism of a particular nature.

For the pure-nature tradition, the reason for designating this potency as obediential—*as opposed to natural*—is for one reason and one reason only: because the creature cannot actualize this potency on its own, whereas a creature *can* actualize a natural potency on its own. However, a specific obediential potency *is* "natural"—if all that is meant by this term is some positive foundation for this potency in the specific nature of the creature.

Therefore, de Lubac's neglect of this nuance shows his criticisms here to be largely unfounded, as they pertain only to generic obediential potency.

Let us now offer illustrations of specific obediential potency in order to elucidate this point. The first example, taken from Steven A. Long (whom we will treat more fully in the subsequent chapter), is of a stained-glass window illumined by the sun. Taking the window by itself, apart from the sun's illumination, the window is a piece of art which participates in the perfection of beauty in its own right. This natural perfection of the window (without the sun) corresponds to the window's natural potency, accessible by way of the creature's own natural powers. However, the stained-glass window has the potential for a greater perfection which goes beyond the powers of its nature taken by itself, but which does not contradict its specific nature as window—but which is in fact perfective of its nature, *as* window. If the sun were to enhance the window's beauty by enabling the colors of the stained-glass to shine with greater refulgence, the resultant beauty would be greater than that of the window taken by itself without the sun. Moreover, the sun's illumination does not contradict the specific nature and beauty of the window, but rather enhances it—and precisely *as a stained-glass window*.

For this reason, the illumination of the stained-glass window by the sun corresponds to a specific obediential potency.[4] And in fact, St. Thomas uses a similar analogy, one which may in fact lie behind Long's example:

---

4. Long, "Obediential Potency," 45–63, here, 51: "Obediential pontency is simply the potency of a creature toward acts achievable only with the assistance of divine causality. As a stained-glass window can irradiate colored light only with the assistance of light, so the human soul can directly contemplate God only with the assistance of God."

> Whatever is received within a subject is received according to the
> subject's capacity. . . . As variously colored glass derives its splen-
> dor from the sun's radiance, according to the mode of color . . .
> [even though] it can be seen in its color without its brightness.[5]

This last phrase from Aquinas here, "[even though] it can be seen in its
color *without* its brightness," corresponds to a thing's natural perfection,
apart from its elevation by God (which would then actualize a specific
obediential potency). Accordingly, as we suggested above, the sun's radi-
ance makes possible a disproportionate perfection in the colored glass,
allowing the glass to reach an elevation above and beyond the capacity
of its own nature taken by itself.

Analogously, the supernatural perfection which actualizes a specific obediential potency in man and raises him to the beatific vision is
such that human nature cannot reach this end by its own natural powers; but man can be so elevated by God's direct supernatural action, and
precisely *as* man. Therefore, though not capable of being actualized by
his natural powers alone, this elevation is not contrary to human nature
but is actually supernaturally perfective of it.

As we have said, the elevation by grace to the beatific vision is indeed a possibility which finds its root *in* human nature itself, but it is a
specific *obediential* potency precisely because man cannot actualize this
end by way of his natural powers alone.

In this sense, specific obediential potency is simply the application
of the Thomistic principle: "*the received is in the receiver according to
the mode of the receiver.*"[6] The "mode" of the receiver in this case is the
fundamental nature of the creature which then constricts the ways in
which God can elevate that particular creature, in accordance with its
particular nature. For this reason, specific obediential potency is decidedly *not* the same for every creature: on the contrary, the diversity of
specific obediential potencies flows from the diversity of the *natures* of
various creatures—which then "contract" the ways in which God can
elevate any one particular creature in a manner truly perfective of its
particular kind.

St. Thomas employs this very reasoning in his treatment on the
mystical visions of St. Paul, which the Angelic Doctor takes to be nothing short of the vision of God, as he writes here: "It is more becoming

---

5. *ST* III, q. 54, a. 2, ad 1.
6. *ST* I, q. 84, a. 1.

to hold that he [Paul] saw God in His essence."[7] The biblical episode to which Aquinas is referring is recounted here as follows:

> I will go on to the visions and revelations of the Lord. I know a man in Christ [i.e., Paul] who fourteen years ago was caught up to the third heaven—whether in the body or out of the body I do not know, God knows. And I know that this man was caught up into Paradise—whether in the body or out of the body I do not know, God knows—and he heard things that cannot be told which man may not utter. On behalf of this man I will boast, but on my own behalf I will not boast, except of my weaknesses. Though if I wish to boast, I shall not be a fool, for I shall be speaking the truth. But I refrain from it, so that no one may think more of me than he sees in me or hears from me. And to keep me from being too elated by the abundance of revelations, a thorn was given me in the flesh, a messenger of Satan, to harass me, to keep me from being too elated. Three times I begged the Lord about this, that it should leave me; but he said to me, "My grace is sufficient for you, for my power is made perfect in weakness." (2 Cor 12:1b–9b)

St. Paul remained human throughout these elevated experiences, which makes this once again another example of specific obediential potency; and without using the specific term, Aquinas says as much when he writes:

> It belongs to man's mode and dignity that he be uplifted to divine things, from the very fact that he is made to God's image. And since a divine good infinitely surpasses the faculty of man in order to attain that good, he needs the divine assistance which is bestowed on him in every gift of grace. Hence it is not *contrary* to nature, but *above* the faculty of nature that man's mind be thus uplifted in rapture by God.[8]

St. Thomas' reference to this elevation as not being "contrary" to St. Paul's human nature refers to the way in which the criterion of non-contradiction applies to specific obediential potency—which as we have seen, requires that the divine elevation of a particular creature cannot contradict the specific nature of the creature in question. If it did, then such a potency would thereby be a generic obediential potency. Accordingly, Feingold summarizes our discussion in the following:

7. *ST* II-IIae, q. 175, a. 3.

8. *ST* II-IIae, q. 175, a. 1, ad 2, emphasis added.

> We distinguish obediential potency in the generic sense, and [an-other] *specific obediential potency* that is proper to the spiritual creature. The former simply refers to the capacity that is to be changed in obedience to the omnipotent will of God. The latter refers to the capacity to be elevated to share in some preroga-tives of the divine nature *without losing one's specific nature and personal identity*.
> In other words, this criterion of non-contradiction can be considered in two ways: (1) with regard to any possible nature, or (2) with regard to the *specific* nature of the rational creature. *If non-contradiction is taken in the former sense, then any nature has an obediential potency to be changed into any other nature. . . . If, however, non-contradiction is taken in the latter sense, then it indeed poses a very significant limitation on obediential potency.*[9]

Consequently, as we have stated, de Lubac's criticism of Cajetan and the pure-nature tradition on this score is misguided. Before we turn to Cajetan directly, let us observe de Lubac's allegation in his own words:

> For Cajetan, the idea of obediential potency is adequate. . . . [He] . . . reduces the case of the supernatural destiny of created spirit to a particular instance of *miracle*. The fundamental reason for this reversal is that he has first reduced human nature itself to a case merely of one species among others in his consider-ation of natural beings. And this double mistake has very grave consequences.[10]

De Lubac's statement clearly indicates that he takes Cajetan's use of obediential potency in its generic sense, as indicated especially here by de Lubac's use of the word "miracle." Indeed, this seems to be the only sense of obediential potency that de Lubac takes as being relevant to the discussion at hand, and so again he states:

9. Feingold, *Natural Desire to See God*, 113, all emphases original. See also Lawrence Feingold, "Man as *Imago Dei* and *Capax Dei*" in Thompson and Long, *Reason and the Rule of Faith*, 197–211.

10. De Lubac, *The Mystery of the Supernatural*, 143, emphasis added; "Pour Cajetan, elle y suffit . . . '*Statuit (Cajetanus) quod potentia nobis ad videndum Deum est oboedientalis dumtaxat*'. Autrement dit, Cajetan repousse le principe de saint Thomas: '*naturaliter anima est gratiae capax*'; prenant le contrepied de l'opposition formulée par saint Thomas, il réduit le cas de la destinée surnaturelle de l'esprit créé à un cas particulier de miracle. La raison fondamentale de ce renversement est qu'il a commencé par réduire le cas de la nature humaine à un simple cas d'espèce dans sa considération des êtres naturels. Et cette double réduction est de portée très grave" (De Lubac, *Le Mystère du Surnaturel*, 182–83).

> For St. Thomas, the simple idea of obediential potency [was] con-
> ceived not "to express the condition in which God's gift places us
> of being able to become children of God," but to account *for the
> possibility of miracle*, [which] is not adequate as a definition of
> the relationship of human nature to the supernatural: [because]
> it *does not lay sufficient stress on the "absolutely special case of
> spirit."*[11]

Here we see de Lubac's charge that Cajetan has lost sight of man's *sui
generis* uniqueness, an implication which is only true if Cajetan's employs obediential potency in its *generic* sense. But if Cajetan and the
pure-nature tradition utilize obediential potency in its *specific* sense, the
situation is of course very different. Nonetheless, de Lubac writes:

> In this new system [i.e., pure-nature] the only remaining link
> of the created spirit with the end which God has promised
> will be no more henceforward than that of a sheer "obediential
> power"; in other words, the idea that the Fathers and the early
> Scholastics had worked out to account for *miracles*, will in the
> future be applied to the problem of the last end. . . . Every link
> will be broken *since this "obediential power" is something not only
> purely passive . . . but purely negative*: a mere word to denote the
> *"non-repugnance,"* the non-resistance of every creature to divine
> omnipotence.[12]

11. De Lubac, *The Mystery of the Supernatural*, 143, emphases added; "Pour
saint Thomas la seule idée de 'puissance obédientielle' [was] n'a pas été conçue 'pour
exprimer la condition où le don de Dieu nous met de pouvoir devenir enfants de Dieu',
mias pour rendre compte de la possibilité du miracle, [which] ne suffit point à définir
le rapport de la nature humaine au surnaturel. Elle ne fait pas ressortir, comme il le
faudrait, 'le cas absolument original de l'esprit'" (De Lubac, *Le Mystère du Surnaturel*,
182). De Lubac mentions the notion of "specific obediential power" on this page, but
does not come near grasping its real meaning and importance for the pure-nature
tradition. The passages below from Cajetan, Báñez, and Sylvester of Ferrara all bear out
this point very clearly.

12. De Lubac, *Augustinianism and Modern Theology*, 199–200, emphasis added;
"En tout cas, dans ce nouveau système, le seul lien qui demeure de l'esprit créé à la
fin que Dieu nous a promise ne sera plus désormais que celui d'une pure 'puissance
obédientielle', c'est-à-dire qu'on appliquera désormais au problème de la fin dernière la
notion que les Pères et les anciens Scolastiques avaient élaborée pour render compte
du miracle. Autant dire que tout lien sera rompu, cette 'puissance obédientielle' étant
quelque chose, non seulement de purement passif,—les anciens ne parlaient pas
dans notre problème d'une autre puissance que passive,—mais du purement negative:
simple mot pour exprimer la 'non-répugnace', la non-résistance de toute creature à
l'Omnipotence divine" (De Lubac, *Augustinisme et théologie moderne*, 242).

And in de Lubac's mind, it is principally Cajetan who receives the lion's share of the blame:

> It was left to Cajetan . . . to place natural potency decidedly in opposition to obediential potency in the soul, declaring that the potency of the soul for grace "is not natural, but obediential." . . . We have here a further indication of that "naturalization" or "materialization" of the spirit which we have already seen to be at work. It is a new application of the principle according to which each thing should find its end—corresponding to its natural appetite and its natural potency—within the limits of its own nature. The case of the spirit should then enter entirely within the more general case of natural beings.[13]

Let us also note that this lack of awareness of the particular meaning and nuance of specific obediential potency seems to have been particularly widespread in the twentieth century. For example, even the great twentieth-century French philosopher Etienne Gilson (1884–1978) also shares in this mistaken view of the matter:

> I don't think either of us has ever found a set of terms adequate to define the Thomist position, and that's quite to be expected, since he himself could not find one either. In fact, his terminology is somewhat loose, because he never throws away an expression if it is possible to justify it in some sense. Potentiality subject to obedience is an instructive example of what I'm talking about. He came upon the term ready-made; strictly speaking, it is applicable only to miracles, where nothing in matter either prepares for, expects, or makes the phenomenon possible. . . . [A]ll nature is in a state of potentiality subject to obedience to whatever it may please God to do with it, provided that this is not, in itself, contradictory or impossible.[14]

---

13. De Lubac, *Surnaturel*, 137: "Mais il était réservé à Cajetan . . . d'opposer décidément puissance naturelle et puissance obédientielle dans l'âme, en déclarent que la puissance de l'âme à la grâce '*non est naturalis oboedientialis*'. . . . Nous tenons ici un nouvel indice de cette 'naturalisation' ou de cette 'matérialisation' de l'esprit que nous avons déjà saisie à l'œuvre. C'est une nouvelle application du principe selon lequel tout être doit trouver sa fin, correspondant à son appétit naturel et à sa puissance naturelle, dans les limites de sa propre nature. Le cas de l'esprit doit renrer en tout dans le cas plus généeral de l'être naturel."

14. Gilson, *Letters of Etienne Gilson*, 81–82.

Likewise, the eminent Jesuit theologian Karl Rahner (1904–1984) follows suit here, referring to obediential potency only in its generic sense:

> The orientation of "nature" to grace is conceived of in as negative a way as possible. . . . But of itself nature has only a "*potentia oboedientialis*" to such an end, and this capacity is thought of as negatively as possible. It is no more than non-repugnance to such an elevation.[15]

Let us now turn to Cajetan directly in order to observe that he clearly makes use of obediential potency in its *specific* sense—quite contrary to de Lubac's allegations. In Cajetan's own words, he writes: "That obediential potency to [receive] faith and charity is *in the nature of man* because he is intellectual. *It is not in the nature of a lion, because [such perfections] are repugnant to it [i.e., its nature].*"[16]

Feingold comments on the legacy of Cajetan's teaching here, suggesting in fact that—had de Lubac fully understood the meaning of specific obediential potency—he may well have *embraced* the concept as his very own:

> It seems that the fundamental reason Cajetan's position has been so severely attacked, particularly by de Lubac, *is that his assertion of obediential potency has been misinterpreted*. . . . This would make Cajetan's position (and that of subsequent Thomists for the following four centuries) appear radically deficient, implicitly denying that human nature as such is immeasurably perfected by grace and glory.[17]

Cajetan is not alone among the pure-nature tradition in utilizing obediential potency in its specific sense. His successor as master general of the Dominicans Sylvester of Ferrara (Ferrariensis) (1474–1528) teaches in the exact same fashion, stating that no other creature besides

15. Rahner, "Nature and Grace" in *Theological Investigations IV*, 165–88, here 168.

16. Cajetan, Commentary on *Summa theologiae* I, q. 1, a. 1, n. 10, emphasis added: "Potentia siquidem illa oboedientialis ad fidem et caritatem, est in natura hominum, quia intellectiva est: non autem in natura leonina, quoniam sibi repugnat." I would like to thank Father Cajetan Cuddy, O.P., for his help in translating the Latin texts here and in what follows.

17. Feingold, *Natural Desire to See God*, 181, emphasis added. "De Lubac comes to this conclusion because he identifies obediential potency with the capacity for miracles, and seems to be unaware of the notion of specific obediential potency, proper to the rational creature" (ibid., 116).

man has such a positive capacity for the supernatural life of grace and the beatific vision. Sylvester states: "To have faith or charity is not contrary to the nature of man, *as [it would be] to the nature of a rock.*"[18]

Likewise, the Spanish Dominican Domingo Báñez (1528–1604) is in complete accord with his fellow Dominicans on this point. He is especially clear on the *sui generis* character of man, especially as it pertains to man's specific capacity for the beatific vision—which means that he, too, understands obediential potency in its specific sense. Báñez states:

> In man there is a *capacity and aptitude of nature according to obediential potency* that he is able to be elevated to the vision of God [*ad videndum Deum*]. This is proved first [as follows]. *A rock cannot be elevated to this [talem] operation, nor [can] any irrational creature.* Man, however, can [be elevated]. Therefore, there is a *natural capacity in man for this dignity which is not in other creatures.*[19]

As Feingold mentioned, it may well be the case that had de Lubac understood the pure-nature tradition's teaching on this point, he likely would not have been so critical. For specific obediential potency undoubtedly affirms the fundamental uniqueness of man, over against all other natural creatures; and for this reason, the charge against Cajetan's "naturalization" of man is inaccurate, as Feingold writes here:

> The notion of a specifically spiritual obediential potency does not treat the spiritual creature as if it were no different from any other natural thing. This was de Lubac's most serious charge against the Thomistic commentators. On the contrary, the Thomistic

18. Sylvester of Ferrara, "Commentary on *Summa*" I, ch. 5, n. 5, 4, emphasis added: "Non enim repugnat naturae hominis habere fidem et caritatem, sicut naturae lapidis." See Feingold, *Natural Desire to See God*, 183.

19. Báñez, *Scholastica commentaria in primam partem*, q. 12, a. 1, emphasis added: "In homine est capacitas naturae et aptitudo secundum potentiam oboedientialem ut possit elevari ad videndum Deum. Probatur primo. Lapis non potest elevari ad talem operationem, neque aliqua creatura irrationalis, homo vero potest; ergo in homine est capacitas naturalis hujus dignitatis, quae non est in aliis creaturis." Similarly, Long writes: "Man may be elevated to the higher life of grace and divine friendship, because the spiritual nature is such that with divine aid it may be so uplifted, *whereas a rock cannot be uplifted to acts of supernatural knowledge and love precisely because it lacks rational nature. If a rock were uplifted to the divine friendship in knowledge and love of God, it would by that fact cease to be a rock* . . . Indeed, properly understood, this doctrine of obediential potency involves the realization that human nature is *itself* elevated and perfected by God . . ." (Long, *Natura Pura*, 32–33, emphasis added).

tradition consistently recognizes that the spiritual creature has sublime obediential potencies rooted in the nature of the spirit, and not shared by any lower nature. . . . The ironic thing is that one would have thought that the notion of specifically spiritual obediential potency should have been attractive to de Lubac, because it underlines the unique capacity of a spiritual creature for the supernatural extension of his natural privilege to God by means of his own acts.[20]

Let us now turn to our next concept, which is perhaps the most central of all in this entire debate, namely, the notion of the *debitum naturae*.

Debitum Naturae

As we will see, the *debitum naturae* is not as impious as it might at first sound. It certainly has a *prima facie* difficulty in that it appears to suggest that God *owes* something to the creature. And as we have seen, de Lubac dismissed it for this very reason, since it seems not to recognize the basic fact of the gratuity of creation. In de Lubac's words, he writes:

> The monster of exigency was only a phantom. The attempt was made to resolve a false problem. In reality, the question of exigency does not come up. . . . How can one speak of something in man which would weigh on God, putting Him in dependence on man?[21]

However, as we will see in a moment, he is wrong to suggest here that the notion of the *debitum naturae* makes God *dependent* upon the creature, and he is likewise incorrect to allege that the notion of the debt of nature undermines the basic gratuity of creation. For de Lubac, the question of "gratuity" and the issue of "dependency" are one and the same—and since God cannot be dependent upon the creature, nothing can ever be *due* to the creature, in which case everything is always gratuitous no matter what. However, this view fails to take into account the sense in which something can be *due* to the creature on the one hand, while still maintaining the absolute gratuity of creation, on the other hand. Perhaps

20. Feingold, *Natural Desire to See God*, 120.

21. De Lubac, *Surnaturel*, 487: "Le monstre de l'exigence n'était donc qu'un fantôme. On s'évertuait à résoudre un faux problème. En réalité, la question de l'exigence *ne se pose pas*. . . . comment pourrait-on parler à son sujet de quelque chose de l'homme qui pèserait sur Dieu, mettant Dieu sous la dependence de l'homme?"

as a bit of irony, then, it is Feingold and the pure-nature tradition—not de Lubac—who advocate for holding these two theses together which at first glance appear to be in opposition. Accordingly, Feingold states:

> It is indeed unquestionable that God is never dependent on the creature. If something is due to nature in the Thomistic sense, it does not make God dependent on the exigency of the creature. God is never debtor to the creature, *but only to Himself* and *to the order which He Himself has freely willed to establish.*[22]

In order to understand Feingold's point here, we need to take note of the fact that presupposed in the very notion of the *debitum naturae* is a strong metaphysical realism, a realism which holds that the intelligible natures of things are objectively real and are ultimately rooted in the Divine Essence. For this reason, Feingold can maintain the above juxtaposition (debt of nature, alongside creation's gratuity) because the intelligibility of the natural order—which is the very source of the *debitum naturae*—derives ultimately from God Himself. Hence, the debt of nature implies not so much God's "debt" to the creature, as it does God's "debt" to Himself and to the natural order which He has freely willed into existence. Accordingly, the *debitum naturae* simply signifies the natural order, with the additional nuance that the natural order is seen as an expression and manifestation of divine wisdom, which is to say, it is an expression of divine providence.[23]

The notion of this metaphysical intelligibility of the natural order allows us to see God's natural teleology, that is, the ordination of divine providence in and through the order of nature;[24] this natural order of creation constitutes an order which God has willed for His creatures;

22. Feingold, *Natural Desire to See God*, 378, emphasis added. He writes further: "God is not a debtor to anyone, except, in a metaphorical sense, to Himself. The order of nature established by God, with the manifold subordination that it entails, is ordered to the rule of the divine wisdom, and so it is ultimately nature that is debtor to the wisdom of God . . . Something is due to the nature of a creature not because God must submit to the exigency of the creature, but because God wills the creature to submit to the order established by divine wisdom. Thus the problem of 'dependence' is indeed a false problem" (ibid., 379).

23. See Hütter, "Desiderium Naturale Visionis Dei," 81–132: "Feingold insists on engaging de Lubac's own account by *metaphysical realism* and its rigorous discourse in which the Thomist commentators conducted their interpretation and enquiry . . ." (ibid., 93–94, emphasis added).

24. By "teleology" I simply mean the natural order, which can then be taken as an expression of divine providence.

and the very acknowledgement and recognition of this natural order and its relation to divine wisdom is precisely what is signified by the *debitum naturae*. This debt of nature, therefore, is entirely dependent upon God's wisdom and His free decision to create—it simply recognizes this natural order as an expression of divine wisdom.

As we saw in chapter 1, this notion is not foreign to St. Thomas, as he states again here: "It suffices for the perfection of the universe that the creature be ordained in a natural manner to God as to an end. But that a creature should be united to God in person exceeds the limits of the perfection of nature."[25] When Aquinas discusses God's justice, he finds a way to affirm simultaneously: (1) that God is not dependent upon any creature (i.e., creation is gratuitous); and (2) that God *is* just toward creation by giving creatures their *due*, in accordance with their nature (i.e., the *debitum naturae*). Accordingly, as we have seen, it is the objector in the *Summa Theologiae* who states: "God is no man's debtor"[26]— a sentiment which de Lubac made his own, as we have seen: "*Deus nulli debitor est quocumque modo*."[27] And as we have seen, the source of this pithy statement, de Lubac tells us, is none other than William of Ockham: "*Deus nulli debitor est quocumque modo*: cette parole d'Occam est l'écho de toute la tradition. Elle est un des premiers axiomes de la foi chrétienne."[28] But of course, St. Thomas teaches directly to the contrary:

> It is due to God that there should be fulfilled in creatures what His will and wisdom require, and what manifests His goodness. In this respect God's justice regards what befits Him; inasmuch as He renders to Himself what is due to Himself. *It is also due to a created thing that it should possess what is ordered to it*. . . . Thus also God exercises justice, *when He gives to each thing what is due to it by its nature and condition*.[29]

25. *ST* III, q. 1, a. 3, ad 2.

26. *ST* I, q. 21, a. 1, obj. 3.

27. De Lubac, *Surnaturel*, 488.

28. Ibid. "*God is a debtor to no one in any way whatsoever*: this phrase of Ockham echoes the entire tradition. It is one of the first axioms of the Christian faith."

29. *ST* I, q. 21, a. 1, ad 3, emphasis added. Feingold states: "The creation of any creature does not pertain to justice, but once a creature with a particular nature has been created, it pertains to distributive justice that the creature be given what belongs to its nature. . . . In other words, grace is distinguished from what is natural, because what is natural cannot be witheld without injustice with regard to the rule of God's own wisdom . . ." (Feingold, *Natural Desire to See God*, 225).

What Ockham and de Lubac have in common here is a shared rejection of the *debitum naturae,* a point which is seen in the following from Ockham:

> As God creates any creature according to his mere will, so likewise according to His mere will he can do with the creature whatever pleases Him. Just as God could annihilate, without any injustice, someone who always loved God and did every work acceptable to Him, likewise after such works He could give, not life eternal, but eternal damnation, without any injury. . . . *God is not a debtor to anyone,* but whatever He does to us is done from mere grace. And therefore from the very fact that God does something, it is done justly.[30]

Pope Benedict Emeritus, in his famous Regensburg lecture criticizes another Franciscan Bl. John duns Scotus for a very similar view, one he describes as being "opposed to . . . the faith of the Church." The emeritus pope writes:

> In contrast with the so-called intellectualism of Augustine and Thomas, there arose with Duns Scotus a voluntarism which, in its later developments, led to the claim that we can only know God's

30. Ockham, *Quaestiones in librum quartum Sententiarum (Reportatio),* q. 5, "De effectibus Baptismi," in *Opera philosophica et theologica,* vol. 7: "Ad secundum dico quod poena debetur quia Deus sic ordinavit, quia sicut Deus creat creaturam quamlibet ex mera voluntate sua, ita ex mera voluntate sua potest facere de creatura sua quidquid sibi placet. Sicut enim si aliquis semper diligeret Deum et faceret omnia opera Deo accepta, posset eum Deus annihilare sine aliqua iniuria, ita sibi post talia opera potest non dare vitam aeternam sed poenam aeternam sine iniuria. Et ideo eo ipso quod *Deus nullius est debitor,* sed quidquid nobis facit, ex mera gratia facit. Et ideo eo ipso quod Deus aliquid facit, iuste factum est. Patet enim quo Christus numquam peccavit, et tamen fuit punitus gravissime usque ad mortem" (emphasis added). Feingold states: "De Lubac does not cite St. Thomas's response [*ST* I, q. 21, a. 1, ad 3], nor does he resolve the sense in which something can be due to nature without making God a debtor. Instead he cites Ockham: 'In no sense and by no title, whether natural or moral, can we have any rights over God. God is not a debtor to anyone in any way; this phrase of Ockham is the echo of the entire tradition' [de Lubac, *Surnaturel,* 488]. De Lubac has cited the principle used by St. Thomas in the more absolute form given by Ockham, who adds the qualification in that nothing can ever really be due to the creature by God *in any way* (*quocumque modo*), so that the beatific vision will not be due even if it is the only end possible for man. Here de Lubac is much closer to Ockham than to St. Thomas, without pointing out the abyss between the two!. . . . The point of similarity, which I presume is the reason why de Lubac cited Ockham, is that both reject the notion of *debitum naturae* as a means to distinguish the natural from the gratuitous, and to delineate the coherence of the natural order" (Feingold, *Natural Desire to See God,* 380–81, emphasis added).

voluntas ordinata. Beyond this is the realm of God's freedom, in virtue of which he could have done the opposite of everything he has actually done. This gives rise to positions which clearly approach those of Ibn Hazm and might even lead to the image of a capricious God, who is not even bound to truth and goodness. God's transcendence and otherness are so exalted that our reason, our sense of the true and good, are no longer an authentic mirror of God, whose deepest possibilities remain eternally unattainable and hidden behind his actual decisions. As opposed to this, the faith of the Church has always insisted that between God and us, between his eternal Creator Spirit and our created reason, there exists a real analogy, in which—as the Fourth Lateran Council in 1215 stated—unlikeness remains infinitely greater than likeness, yet not to the point of abolishing analogy and its language. God does not become more divine when we push him away from us in a sheer, impenetrable voluntarism; rather, the truly divine God is the God who has revealed himself as *logos*.[31]

Such is the result if we lose sight of the objective intelligibility of the natural order and the metaphysical realism which secures this objective intelligibility. In other words, there is a short leap from Nominalism to Voluntarism: if the natures of things are not objectively grounded (as in Nominalism), then Voluntarism is surely the result because the divine will is portrayed as free in an arbitrary and capricious manner— unbounded by any "natural order."[32] Servais Pinckaers summarizes well the issues involved here:

For him [Ockham], the divine will was totally free; it governed morality itself and all the laws of creation. What God willed was necessarily just and good precisely because he willed it. Law, and all moral value or qualification, flowed from this will. Determined in the establishment of good and evil by nothing other than itself, the divine will could at any instant change what we considered to be permitted or forbidden according to the commandments, notably the Decalogue. . . . Similarly, hatred of neighbor, theft, and adultery could become meritorious if God had commanded them. Ockham did not recognize in human nature any law or order whatsoever that might determine the divine freedom and omnipotence.[33]

31. Cited in Schall, *The Regensburg Lecture.*

32. See Pinckaers, *Sources of Christian Ethics*, 241–53. Originally published in French as *Les sources de la morale chrétienne.*

33. Ibid., 246–47.

In contrast, metaphysical realism precludes such Voluntarism, and to be more specific, the *debitum naturae* precludes Voluntarism—not because God is dependent upon the creature or upon the categories of natural reason—but because He is the *source* of these very categories themselves. For the pure-nature tradition, rather than "restricting" God's freedom, the debt of nature actually *manifests* it and *recognizes* it—as a free expression of His own divine wisdom. The *debitum naturae* is again nothing other than the intelligibility of the natural order, a natural order which derives its ontological source from God and owes its existence entirely to Him. Hence, as we have said, God is "bound" to this order of nature insofar as He is "bound" by His own divine wisdom and His own divine nature. In virtue of His willing an intelligible natural order, the *debitum naturae* is merely an expression of His nature and His divine providence, as the French Dominican J. H. Nicolas explains here:

> There is a certain justice of God towards his creature. Admittedly God was completely free to create or not to create such a creature: it is clear that what does not exist has no claim to put forward. Once he has created, however, God, through this very act of liberality, commits himself in a certain way not to abandon this creature which he has called into being: to be more precise, it is towards himself that he is committed not to leave the work which he has begun unfinished. What is the meaning of: not abandoning his creature? This means providing him with the things he needs in order to attain the destiny inscribed in his nature . . .[34]

In conclusion here, let us note that though de Lubac is well-intended in his assessment of the *debitum naturae*, his fears and criticisms are largely unfounded and ultimately based on a misunderstanding—in this case, the mistaken notion that the *debitum naturae* entails God's *dependence* upon the creature, thereby undermining the basic gratuity of creation.

Such is not the case, and as we noted at the outset, the *debitum naturae* simply seeks to distinguish between two levels of gratuity: namely, the gratuity of creation on the one hand, and the gratuity of supernatural grace, on the other. It is only through Aquinas' teaching here—that God gives creatures their due, in accordance with their "nature and condition"—that provides the necessary contrast by which we can see the sur-

---

34. Nicolas, *Mystery of God's Grace*, 88–89; originally published in French as *Le Mystère de la Grâce*.

passing transcendence of supernatural grace. What God grants to man that is "over and above" his "nature and condition" must be understood to be gratuitous in a sense wholly surpassing the primordial gratuity of creation. This twofold gratuity is reinforced and articulated by the notion of the *debitum naturae*. For this reason, the *debitum naturae* need not detract in the least from the gratuity of creation.

But once in place, the *debitum naturae* helps to preserve the supernatural grandeur of divine grace. This is the sense in which Aquinas makes ready use of the concept, as seen for example here:

> Grace, inasmuch as it is gratuitously given, excludes the notion of debt. Now debt may be taken in two ways: first as arising from merit. . . . The second debt regards the *condition of nature*. Thus we say it is due to a man to have reason, and whatever else belongs to human nature. . . . *And hence natural endowments are not a debt in the first sense but in the second. But supernatural gifts are due in neither sense.* Hence they especially merit the name of grace.[35]

The next question that arises is whether or not God could have willed a purely natural order—namely, an order which would include all that is contained within the *debitum naturae* but nothing more. Such is the consideration of the possibility of a pure nature, to which we now turn.

The Possibility of Pure Nature

Let us begin by reiterating the point made above that the notions of the *debitum naturae*, the independent intelligibility of the natural order, and here the possibility of pure nature all amount to more or less the same thing. These terms all stem from the abstraction of the *nature* of a thing, in precision from its existential *conditions* (or states). As we have seen, for the pure-nature tradition, the *nature* of a thing is *specifically* the same across any and all conditions in which it may exist, which means that the conditions for example of sin and grace or even the offer of the beatific vision do not nullify the intelligibility of human nature, as such. In other words, contrary to de Lubac, the ordination to the beatific vision is *not* the constitutive element of man's nature, since human nature can be intelligibly considered apart from this supernatural end; only man's natural end is necessarily entailed by his nature. The result is that a hypothetical

---

35. *ST* I-IIae, q. 111, a. 1, ad 2, emphasis added.

order of pure nature could exist without absurdity or contradiction, in which case man would have had a purely natural end.

In the following, we can see Aquinas' clear acceptance of the distinction between the nature of man and the existential condition in which he exists when he states: "Man's *nature* is the same before and after sin, but the *state* of his nature is not the same."[36] Similarly, Christ's human nature is specifically the same as our human nature, though its condition is of course very different on account of the Hypostatic Union. St. Thomas writes: "The nature assumed by Christ may be viewed in two ways. First, in its specific nature [i.e., nature abstractly considered]. . . . Secondly, it may be considered with regard to what it has from its union with the Divine hypostasis" [i.e., its existential condition].[37] In this first respect (namely, that of "nature") Christ's human nature is the same as ours, but this is not the case in the second respect (namely, that of existential condition)—a point which Aquinas also makes again here: "Christ's body in the Resurrection was of the same nature, but differed in glory."[38]

The hypothetical possibility of pure nature flows from this very same reasoning: if we can abstract the definition of human nature from its existential conditions, it follows that we can consider the possibility of human nature existing in a hypothetical *condition* of pure nature. This hypothetical order of pure nature includes no more than that which is entailed in the definition of human nature as such, in abstraction from the present economy. Since the beatific vision surpasses the nature of *any* creature, the beatific vision must be excluded from this hypothetical order of pure nature.[39] And so again, the hypothetical possibility of pure nature implies the possibility of a purely natural end for man, as Feingold describes here:

> This thesis has come to be referred to as the possibility of a "state of pure nature." Here we are not interested in the details of this thesis, but only with the assertion of the *possibility* (i.e.,

36. *ST* III, q. 61, a. 2, ad 2.

37. *ST* III, q. 15, a. 3, ad 1.

38. *ST* III, q. 54, a. 3.

39. *ST* II-IIae, q. 175, a. 3, ad 2: "The Divine essence cannot be seen by a created intellect save through the light of glory." Also: "Because grace is above human nature, it cannot be a substance or a substantial form, but is an accidental form of the soul" (*ST* I-IIae, q. 110, a. 2, ad 2).

non-absurdity) of a natural happiness for the intellectual creature short of the vision of God. The "state of pure nature" is normally understood by Scholastic theologians to refer to a state in which God would give to man only what belongs to or follows from the constitutive principles of human nature, together with those aids of God's providence that are due to human nature so that it may reach its proportionate and connatural final end.[40]

For Suárez (1548–1617), this is likewise very straightforward. Given the justice of God, He cannot thwart the *debitum naturae*, since it flows from His wisdom and His own divine nature. Given the supernatural character of the beatific vision, God must supply a purely natural end which correlates with man's natural desire, and which is therefore attainable by man's natural powers alone; all of this is implied by the *debitum naturae*, as Suárez writes here:

> We have shown that there is a natural beatitude for man other than this supernatural beatitude. Consequently, this will be desired by an innate appetite [i.e., natural desire]. It will be desired as a final [natural] perfection. . . . No further beatitude will be desired by this [natural] appetite. . . . [The] natural felicity of a creature does not consist in the clear vision of God . . . especially because otherwise the ordination to that end would be due to the intellectual creature through proportionate and sufficient means. . . . Nothing pertains more to the providence due to each nature than its ordination to its connatural end through fitting means.[41]

---

40. Feingold, *Natural Desire to See God*, 224. See also Long, "On the Possibility of a Purely Natural End for Man," 211–37, here 233. Feingold's comments here regarding the "aids of God's providence that are due to human nature" raises an interesting question regarding, for example, prevenient grace. At a recent *Nova et Vetera* conference in Denver (April 1–2, 2011), Reinhard Hütter mentioned another category which perhaps would be worth considering, namely, that of *auxilium naturalis*. Such a category draws from the distinction between God's providence in the order of nature and His providence in the order of grace—which in other words is to say that not all divine aid is "grace" in the same sense. On a related note, one might also say that not all spirituality or mysticism is the same *just because it is mysticism*. Perhaps, there is room to speak of a "natural mysticism." See Cottier, "On Natural Mysticism" in Bonino, *Surnaturel*, 273–94. Cottier speaks of a "pansupernaturalism" that "if pushed, leads to the tragic effacement of the specificity of grace and of theologal [sic] life" (ibid., 284). Cottier's reference to "theologal" life here draws from the French Dominican tradition which distinguishes between "théologique" and "théologal"; the former refers to theological study, while the latter refers to divinized life. For this distinction, see also Cessario, *Christian Faith and The Theological Life*, 1.

41. Suárez, *De ultimo fine hominis*, disp. 16, sect. 1. n. 10; disp. 30, n. 37: "Ostendimus

Insofar as the pure-nature hypothesis implies only the conceptual coherence and possibility of a purely natural order and a purely natural end, it can find support in *Humani generis*, as we have already mentioned: "Others destroy the gratuity of the supernatural order, since God, they say, cannot create intellectual beings without ordering and calling them to the beatific vision."[42] As we have noted, this statement seems to imply its unstated converse, namely, that God *could* have created an order wherein He did not offer the beatific vision, which is tantamount to acknowledging the hypothetical possibility of an order of pure nature.

It also seems that de Lubac's account of natural desire cannot accommodate even this hypothetical possibility, since for him anything less than the beatific vision entails "essential suffering."[43] This is further seen to be the case on account of the fact that he takes man's natural desire for the beatific vision to be the "ontological"[44] and "constitutive"[45] feature of his nature; for de Lubac, man can have "no other genuine end . . . except that of seeing God."[46]

---

esse in homine aliam naturalem beatitudinem praeter hanc supernaturalem et consequenter illam appetere appetitu innato: appetit ergo illam quasi ultimam perfectionem suam, alias non appeteret tanquam beatitudinem: ergo illo appetitu non appetit ulteriorem perfectionem, quia sicut impossibilis est dari duos ultimos fines respectu ejusdem: ita impossibilis est naturaliter appetere duas perfectiones tanquam ultimas, seu quod idem est, per modum beatitudinis. . . . Naturalem felicitatem creaturae non consistere in clara Dei visione . . . maxime, quia alias debita esset intellectuali creaturae ordinatio in talem finem, per proportionata ac sufficientia media neque aliter cum illa agi posset, nisi providentiam naturae illius debitae ei denegando: hoc autem censeo esse magnum absurdum in Theologia, et perniciosum fundamentum ad materiam de gratia explicandam. Sequela vero est manifesta, quia nihil magis pertinet ad providentiam unicuique naturae debitam, quam ordinatio ejus in connaturalem finem per convenientia media. Quod si felicitas illa nullo modo naturalis est, nec naturalis et innatus appetitus ad illam esse potest, quia . . . hic appetitus solum est ad ea quae naturalia sunt."

42. Pius XII, *Humani generis*, n. 26, DH 3875–99.

43. De Lubac, *The Mystery of the Supernatural*, 54; "souffrance essentielle" (De Lubac, *Le Mystère du Surnaturel*, 80).

44. De Lubac, *The Mystery of the Supernatural*, 62; "ontologique" (De Lubac, *Le Mystère du Surnaturel*, 90).

45. De Lubac, *The Mystery of the Supernatural*, 55; "constitutive" (De Lubac, *Le Mystère du Surnaturel*, 81).

46. De Lubac, *The Msytery of the Supernatural*, 55; "Ma finalité, donc ce désir est l'expression, est inscrite en mon être même, tel qu'il est posé par Dieu dans cet univers. Et, de par la volonté de Dieu, je n'ai pas aujourd'hui d'autre fin réelle, c'est-à-dire réellement assignée à ma nature et offerte sous quelques espèces que ce soit, à mon

In this sense, de Lubac cannot account—even *hypothetically*—for the possibility of a human being who is not called to the beatific vision. For him, such a supposed "human being" would seem not to be even *human*—since this creature would lack the "ontological" and "constitutive" feature of human nature itself. For him, all men are *human* precisely because, as he puts it: "we all have the same essential finality [i.e., the beatific vision]."[47] In short, his thought seems to imply that the term "man" cannot be equally predicated of both (a) the hypothetical man of pure nature and (b) man as he actually exists in the present divine economy.

There are two serious philosophical problems underlying de Lubac's account here: (1) his claim that a purely natural man would not have the same *nature* as the man who exists in the present divine economy; and (2) his claim that man's *de facto* supernatural end is determinative or "constitutive" of his nature. The two difficulties are related, but the following illustrates well the first in de Lubac's thought:

> Mankind is a reality. Human nature is, in its way, a reality. But the fact that we all share in it precisely, at least in part, *because we all have the same essential finality*. If someone then tells me of another nature that might exist, with another finality, in another universe—and this is in fact what is being done by those who speak of . . . "pure nature"—I can feel only the most abstract link with it, however much they may describe it as being like ours.[48]

There is a latent Nominalism here in that he expressly denies the *sameness* of human nature across each and every condition—contrary to Aquinas and the pure-nature tradition, as we have seen.[49]

---

adhésion libre, que de 'voir Dieu'" (De Lubac, *Le Mystère du Surnaturel*, 81).

47. De Lubac, *The Mystery of the Supernatural*, 63.

48. Ibid., emphasis added: " L'humanité est une réalité. La nature humaine est, à sa manière, une réalité. Mais précisément, si nous y participons tous, c'est, au moins en partie, parceque nous avons tous la même essentielle finalité. Si l'on vient ensuite me parler d'une autre nature hypothétique-ment réalisable avec une autre finalité dans un autre univers—et c'est bien de cela que l'on parle lorsqu'on évoque ce 'futurible' que serait la 'pure nature'—je ne me sens plus avec elle qu'un lien purement abstrait, quoi qu'il en soit des traits de ressemblance qu'on lui confère, peut-être d'ailleurs arbitrairement, avec la nôtre" (De Lubac, *Le Mystère du Surnaturel*, 90–91).

49. Cf. *ST* III, q. 61, a. 2, ad 2: "Man's nature is the same before and after sin, but the state of his nature is not the same."

The following statement illustrates both difficulties in de Lubac, but let us take special note of the second, namely, again his claim that man's *de facto* end is determinative of his nature:

> By putting forward the hypothesis of another order of things, one cannot help by that very fact supposing another humanity, a different human being, and thus a different "me." In this "purely natural" universe which some have imagined, or have at least declared to be possible, "my nature," they say, would be included. We may perhaps agree—though it cannot be as certain as they think, except in the most abstract sense, since it must be said at the same time that this nature would be "materially" different. But even then it would not be the same "me." You may put into this hypothetical world a man as like me as you can, but you cannot put *me* into it. Between that man who, by hypothesis, is not destined to see God, and the man I am in fact, between that futurable and this existing being, there remains only a theoretical, abstract identity, without the one really becoming the other at all. *For the difference between them is not merely one of individuation, but of nature itself.*[50]

At least for a Thomist, differing "materially" is precisely a matter of "individuation,"[51] contrary to what de Lubac states here. Differing "for-

---

50. De Lubac, *The Mystery of the Supernatural*, 59–60, emphases added; "C'est qu'en effet, pour maintenir la gratuité du surnaturel par le seul recours à une autre finalité possible, il ne suffirait pas de dire—nous venons de la voir—que la même nature humaine eût pu être constituée, dans un autre ordre de choses, avec cette autre finalité. Ce ne serait pas serrer la question d'assez près. Il faudrait encore pouvoir affirmer cela de la même humanité, du même être humain; finalement, du même moi. Or, à la réflexion, c'est ce qui n'offre aucun sens. Car, en posant l'hypothèse d'un autre ordre de choses, on pose du même coup, qu'on le veille ou non, une autre humanité, un autre être humain, et, si l'on peut dire encore, un autre moi. Dans cet univers 'purement naturel' qu'on imagine ou du moins qu'on affirme possible, 'ma nature', dit-on, aurait trouvé place. Admettons-le—encore que cela ne soit pas aussi assuré qu'on le croit, sinon dans un sens bien abstrait, puisqu'on doit dire en même temps que cette nature eût été 'physiquement' autre. Mais en tout cas ce n'eût pas été le même moi. Qu'on place dans ce monde hypothétique un homme aussi parfaitement semblable à moi que l'on voudra; on ne m'y place pas, moi. Entre cet homme qui, par hypothèse, n'est pas destiné à voir Dieu et l'homme que je suis en réalité, entre ce futurible et cet existant, il n'y a encore qu'une identité tout idéale, tout abstraite, sans passage réel de l'un à l'autre. Peut-être même est-ce là déjà trop concéder. Car la différance entre l'un et l'autre n'affecte pas seulement l'individualité: elle ne peut manquer d'affecter la nature meme" (De Lubac, *Le Mystère du Surnaturel*, 86–87).

51. Aquinas writes: "Now individual matter, with all the individualizing accidents, is not included in the definition of the species. For this particular flesh, these bones, this

mally," on the other hand, implies a difference in nature or species. De Lubac seems to have taken a contingent aspect of the current economy, that is, a particular aspect of the present *condition* in which human nature exists—namely, man's supernatural calling to the beatific vision—and made it into the *sine qua non* of human nature itself. Without the beatific vision, on his account, we would no longer have human nature. And so in response, Feingold writes:

> [The] very distinction between "abstract" and "concrete" nature is out of place and incompatible with the Aristotelian-Thomistic tradition. For St. Thomas, a nature is necessarily the same in all individuals that participate in that nature. It is the *individual* that is historical and concrete, and not the nature or essence itself. The nature includes only what is expressed by the definition of the species. A given man has in himself things (individuated matter and accidental forms) not contained in "humanity." However, the nature itself of man cannot contain something not contained in "abstract" nature, so as to make the nature itself concrete.[52]

Here, Feingold is referring to the fact that the nature of a thing is necessarily abstract. In Thomistic-Aristotelian philosophy, any individual is comprised of not just form (abstract nature), but (individuating) matter as well. The form, or *nature*, of man is specifically the same in all instances (that is, across all conditions); if such were not the case, as we have said above, the word "man" could not be predicated univocally of all such purportedly "human" entities.

As to the second philosophical problem noted above, let us observe that St. Thomas' position differs from de Lubac here: for Aquinas, while a thing's *natural* end specifies its nature, such is not the case with regard to a thing's *supernatural* end. In other words, a thing's final end determines its nature—*if* we are speaking of a thing's *natural* end, which is not necessarily the same as a thing's *de facto* end. In fact, in the following,

---

blackness or whiteness, etc., are not included in the definition of a man. Therefore this flesh, these bones, and the accidental qualities distinguishing this particular matter, are not included in humanity; and yet they are included in the thing which is a man. Hence the thing which is a man has something more in it than . . . humanity. Consequently humanity and a man are not wholly identical; but humanity is taken to mean the formal part of a man, because the principles whereby a thing is defined are regarded as the formal constituent in regard to the individualizing matter" (*ST* I, q. 3, a. 3).

52. Feingold, *Natural Desire to See God*, 335. See also Long, *Natura Pura*, 83–91.

it is the *objector* who once again makes more or less the same argument as de Lubac:

> It would seem that the soul is of the same species as an angel. For each thing is ordained to its proper end by the nature of its species, whence is derived its inclination for that end. *But the end of the soul is the same as that of an angel*—namely, *eternal happiness.* Therefore they are of the same species.[53]

St. Thomas' response is as follows: "This argument proceeds from the proximate and natural end. Eternal happiness is the ultimate and supernatural end."[54] In other words, *if* the argument proceeded from man's natural or proportionate end, then the objector's argument (and de Lubac's) would have force; but since the argument proceeds from man's supernatural end, *it does not follow.* Long explains the same point this way:

> The question is in essence simple: Does human nature receive its proper definition from the ordering to supernatural beatitude? No. For it shares the last supernatural beatific end with all the innumerable distinct species of angels. Rather, it receives its species from the *proportionate*, proximate natural end . . .[55]

53. *ST* I q. 75, a. 7, obj. 1, emphasis added.

54. *ST* I q. 75, a. 7 ad 1.

55. Long, *Natura Pura*, 91, emphasis added. Similarly, Feingold writes that de Lubac's "thesis seems to derive from an over-extension of the philosophical principle that 'the end determines the nature'. . . . De Lubac presupposes that the actual or *de facto* end must necessarily be the natural end, inscribed in the nature" (Feingold, *Natural Desire to See God*, 320–21). Likewise, Feingold again writes: "De Lubac's argument makes the assumption that God's intention to elevate us to a supernatural end essentially *determines the constitution of our nature, making it necessarily different from that of another hypothetical man not destined by God for a supernatural end*" (ibid., 387, emphasis added). On a related note, Reinhard Hütter states: "Another order of providence seems for St. Thomas hypothetically entertainable in a perfectly legitimate way, and under such an order the non-attainability of the divine vision seems also to be perfectly thinkable. What seems, by entailment . . . is *the continuity of the self-same human nature under different orders of providence. . . . For different orders of providence do not entail an ontological transmutation of the human being*" (Hütter, "Desiderium Naturale Visionis Dei," 100–101, emphasis added). Hütter is drawing from *De Malo*, q. 5, a. 15, ad 2 where Aquinas states: "*Man endowed with only natural powers* would be without the divine vision if he were to die in this state, but nevertheless the debt of not having it would not be applicable to him. For it is one thing not to be bound to have, *which does not have the nature of punishment* but of defect only, and it is another thing to be bound not to have, which does have the nature of punishment" (cited in *On Evil*, 214, emphasis added).

At this point, we can see that there is nothing impossible about the hypothetical possibility of pure nature. What remains to be seen, however, is the extent to which this notion of a purely natural end can be realized in the present divine economy, given that God has in fact ordered man to the beatific vision. And so to this issue, we now turn.

A Purely Natural End in *this* Economy

Feingold goes further than merely entertaining the conceptual possibility of pure nature, for he argues in favor of the actual possibility of a purely natural end in *this* economy. In support of this notion, he appeals to limbo as a final (natural) state:

> There can be an imperfect happiness in this life both in the natural and in the supernatural orders. Likewise, happiness in heaven includes both natural and supernatural beatitude (with the natural ordered to the supernatural), since grace does not destroy nature. Furthermore, *St. Thomas holds that a purely natural happiness after this life is also possible and corresponds to the state of the souls in limbo.*[56]

While it is perhaps noteworthy on historical grounds that Aquinas may have had no problem with limbo,[57] as far as the contemporary magisterium goes—and as it has a bearing on the speculative truth of the matter—this premise is less viable now than it used to be. At least by way of theological consensus, the days of limbo as a customary teaching of the Church seem to be long past, and so Feingold's premise here is not likely to be a cogent one at the present time. For this reason, Edward Oakes writes: "Unfortunately for Feingold's thesis, once the hypothesis of limbo is abandoned for other reasons, it only begs the question to appeal to the authority of the medieval doctors for its restitution."[58]

---

56. Feingold, *Natural Desire to See God*, 235, emphasis added. Similarly: "De Lubac neglects to consider the fundamental importance of the Thomistic thesis that there is no spiritual suffering in limbo—*a thesis which provides powerful illustration of the possibility of a natural beatitude after this life*" (ibid., 250, emphasis added).

57. Cf. *ST* III, q. 52, a. 7 and q. 52, a. 1, ad 1.

58. Oakes, "The *Surnaturel* Controversy," 635–36, 641. As St. Thomas states: the argument "from authority is the weakest form of proof" (*ST* I, q. 1, a. 8, ad, 2). See also Oakes, "Catholic Eschatology and the Development of Doctrine," 419–46. See also Ratzinger, *The Ratzinger Report*, 147.

Moreover, the concrete instantiation of pure nature, *as* pure nature, in this economy is fraught with at least one insurmountable difficulty: namely, the fact that pure nature has *never* actually existed. This is due to the fact that the first man was constituted in a state of grace, *not* one of pure nature—a point witnessed here in St. Thomas: "The primitive subjection, by virtue of which reason was subject to God, *was not a merely natural gift, but a supernatural endowment of grace.*"[59] Long describes Cajetan's thought on the matter likewise: "Of course, Cajetan did not hold that the hypothetical state of pure nature had ever existed, knowing full well St. Thomas's teaching that man is created [or perhaps better, "constituted"] in sanctifying grace."[60]

Consequently, Adam's progeny receives—not a *pure* nature—but a *fallen* nature; humanity now lacks the grace with which it was originally constituted. In other words, post-lapsarian man now has a void which grace previously filled, *and which grace was meant to fill.* Though we will treat him more extensively in chapter 6, let us observe how Matthias Scheeben captures this very point: "Original sin . . . is the *privation* of the supernatural quality that *ought* to be present in nature."[61] The notion of "privation" here implies not just an absence, but an absence which ought to be filled—and herein lies the subtle but very profound difference between post-lapsarian man and the hypothetical man of pure nature.

We will treat the implications of Scheeben's teaching here further in chapter 6, but for now let us note that the *hypothetical* possibility of pure nature differs vastly from the prospects of its *concrete* realization in the present divine economy. In conclusion, let us note that Feingold establishes well the grounds of the former, but his venture into the latter tends to take away from the overall persuasiveness of his account.

In this respect, as we will see in the next chapter, Long adds to Feingold's analysis by emphasizing the fact that since the eternal law governing this economy orders man to grace, the actual possibility of man's purely natural end cannot remain unaffected thereby. Ultimately, Long argues that a purely natural end in *this* economy is precluded for

59. *ST* I q. 95, a. 1, emphasis added.

60. Long, *Natura Pura*, 229 n. 17.

61. Scheeben, *The Mysteries of Christianity*, 301, emphasis added: "Was die Erbsünde eigentlich ausmacht und an der Natur haftet, ist die Privation der übernatürlichen Beschaffenheit, die an der Natur haften sollte" (Scheeben, *Die Mysterien Christentums*, 251).

two reasons: (1) man is subject to the providential ordering of the eternal law as manifest in the concrete divine economy; and (2) the condition of sin is such that healing grace is now necessary, even for the attainment of man's natural good.

With this in mind, let us now turn to Long's contribution to the contemporary renewal of the pure-nature tradition.

5

Steven A. Long on Natural and Eternal Law

While Feingold seeks to show the organic continuity between St. Thomas and the pure-nature tradition, Long is more concerned with articulating the speculative superiority of the pure-nature tradition in the contemporary debate. Accordingly, Edward Oakes comments on the two, noting that Long supplements Feingold's treatment "with more directly theological arguments, which means less reliance on the argument from authority."[1] To this end, Long makes use of St. Thomas' teaching on eternal and natural law in order to elucidate the pure-nature account; and in fact, this recourse to Aquinas' legal treatment is largely new to the debate, as Edward T. Oakes oberves here:

> One of the great merits in Long's book is the way he transposes this debate to a discussion of the moral law, both natural and divinely promulgated, a dimension long missing from this debate. As is conceded by all sides, St. Thomas recognizes both forms of law; but rarely has it been noted that his discussion on the inter-relationship of these two versions of law has direct bearing on the nature-grace relationship.[2]

1. Oakes, "The *Surnaturel* Controversy," 644.
2. Ibid., 645. Oakes continues: "In my opinion, Long scored a bull's-eye when he demonstrates . . . the existence of the natural law and its continued validity. . . after the promulgation of divine law . . ." (ibid., 652). And again: "no one has ever claimed that St. Thomas considered the natural law to be a mere 'hypothesis', meant only to guarantee the gratuity of the divine law" (646). Long sets the tone of his book early on along similar lines: "The following chapters converge on one central point; the crucial need to return to the actual teaching of St. Thomas Aquinas with respect to the *distinction* within *unity* of nature and grace. Never has the phrase of Jacques Maritain, 'distinguish in order to unite', been more necessary, yet seemingly more desolate and forgotten" (Long, *Natura Pura*, 1).

In this chapter, we will proceed as follows: (1) we will treat Long's general assessment of nature and grace, including his appraisal of de Lubac; (2) we will once again take up the importance of the distinction between a man's *nature* and the *conditions* of his nature; (3) we will explore St. Thomas' teaching on natural and eternal law and its implications for the nature-grace debate. Finally, (4) we will take up the issue of how the pure-nature tradition's emphasis upon the distinction between nature and grace can be reconciled with the Christocentricism with which we began in our opening chapter; this concluding section anticipates to some extent the way in which Scheeben will bring about this reconciliation of extrinsicism and intrinsicism in the following chapter.

Long on the Recovery of the Theonomic Character of the Natural Order

Long believes that de Lubac was more or less *right*, at least in terms of his instincts regarding nature and grace, but for some of the "wrong" reasons. For example, Long admires de Lubac's focus on teleology in the face of "anti-theistic" sentiments of the day (e.g., Marx, Nietzsche),[3] and given the intellectual context of the 1940s, he readily concedes that de Lubac's solution may well have been the only one viable at the time. In Long's mind, (for reasons to be considered below) a sharp distinction in this context between nature and grace easily lent itself to becoming a charter for secularism—which was no doubt chief among de Lubac's concerns. Accordingly, Long writes:

> One grants that at the moment of the composition of *Surnaturel*, it must have seemed . . . unlikely that Thomism would prove up to the challenge posed by the cultural confluence of Catholic and secular tendencies promoting the *autonomy of nature and of human agency* from God. . . . The distinction of nature and grace might then be construed simply as formalizing the evacuation of God from creation: a wall of demarcation excluding God from the world.[4]

3. By "teleology" here and throughout I simply mean the "ends" which God has ordained; most often I am referring to man: hence, de Lubac's use of teleology is his use of man's natural desire, as *teleologically* inclining man to his final end.

4. Long, *Natura Pura*, 45, emphasis added. As with Feingold, Long's presentation is indicative that the polemical context of this debate is behind us; he describes de Lubac as a "great scholar and lover of the Church" (ibid., 36–37). And further: "The need

For Long, the underlying problem in context is a weakened notion of "nature," one which ultimately tarnishes de Lubac's otherwise worthy efforts. Since all parties, in Long's mind, by mid-twentieth century had inherited a conception of nature that was no longer "theonomic," de Lubac's solution was likewise marred by this deficiency. For this reason, Long states:

> [De Lubac] drew unmistakable attention to the elements nec-essary to a true solution to the problem. Unlike so many other minds in the twentieth century, he affirms the critical impor-tance of teleology, *erring only in a deficient confidence in natural teleology* [due to the] . . . fear of the distortions of naturalism and to a theological[ly] problem[atic] situation that had already too decisively separated itself from the metaphysical realism neces-sary to vindicate nature as a theonomic principle.[5]

Hence, for Long, the real problem afflicting the nature-grace dis-cussion in de Lubac's day is the loss of this "theonomic" conception of the natural order, by which Long means the entire Thomistic edifice of creation, providence, and law. This robust notion of the natural order as taught by Aquinas is witnessed in the following, where St. Thomas distinguishes between man's *natural* and supernatural love of God:

> Charity loves God above all things in a higher way than nature does. For nature loves God above all things inasmuch as He is the beginning and the end of natural good; whereas charity loves Him, as He is the object of beatitude, and inasmuch as man has a spiritual fellowship with God.[6]

---

to safeguard a profound theological intention *in an inhospitable intellectual climate* seemed to point toward the argument [made by de Lubac] that the object of the natural desire for God must be intrinsically supernatural beatific vision" (ibid., emphasis added.). Likewise, he praises de Lubac's general theological orientation: "The nature of this animating intention requires greater consideration. No theologian worthy of the name should fail to affirm the theocentric character of reality as such" (ibid.). For this reason, Long cautions against a reactionary assessment of de Lubac: "It is perhaps the final salute that a Thomist owes to the efforts of de Lubac on this score to see to it that the chief effect of emending his error about the natural desire for God is not merely to throw us back to the status quo ante. For that status quo ante already was deeply marred and impaired by the grievous attrition of the tradition's emphasis upon *nature as a normative principle in theology*—a *theonomic* principle" (ibid., 51, emphasis original).

5. Long, *Natura Pura*, 203, emphasis added.

6. *ST* I-IIae, q. 109, a. 3, ad 1. Similarly, he writes: "God, in so far as He is the universal good, from Whom every natural good depends, is loved by everything with *natural love*. So far as He is the good which of its very nature beatifies all with

Understood in this light, the natural order is hardly one of secular autonomy, and here is precisely where Long takes issue with de Lubac's charge that the pure-nature tradition is somehow conceptually connected to the rise of modern secularism. Long writes:

> One must ask: who said the realm of pure nature is self-sufficient? Does it not proceed from, and depend upon, the Creator?. . . . Does not all of created nature, and every natural motion, presuppose God not only remotely and indirectly but even with respect to the application of natural motion to particular acts?[7]

According to Long, this misunderstanding of the natural order as purportedly self-sufficient is the result of two historical factors: (1) the view

---

supernatural beatitude, He is loved with the love of *charity*" (*ST* I, q. 60, a. 5, ad 4, emphasis added). Further he states: "The good we receive from God is *twofold*, the good of nature, and the good of grace. Now the fellowship of natural goods bestowed on us by God is the foundation of *natural love*, in virtue of which . . . [man] loves God above all things. . . . Wherefore much more is this realized with regard to the fellowship of the gifts of grace . . . [by] *charity*" (*ST* II-IIae, q. 26, a. 3, emphasis added). Long of course concurs: "Distinct from supernatural charity is natural love, and Thomas rightly affirms that man *by natural love* loves God above himself . . . (Long, *Natura Pura*, 45, emphasis original). Long continues: "For if it is *naturally knowable* that God, our Creator and Lord, exists, *then* it would seem that we *know* that all public and private goods flow from God, and *this* implies *natural duties in justice*" (Long, *Natura Pura*, 69, all emphases are Long's). Religion, for St. Thomas, is a *natural* virtue: "Religion is neither a theological nor an intellectual, but a moral virtue since it is a part of justice . . ." (*ST* II-IIae, q. 81, a. 5, ad 3). Further, Aquinas states: "It belongs to the dictate of natural reason that man should do something through reverence for God" (*ST* II-IIae, q. 81, a. 2, ad 3). And similarly: "It belongs to religion to show reverence to the one God . . . as the first principle of creation and government of things" (*ST* II-IIae, q. 81, a. 3). This includes even the notion of sacrifice as part of the natural law: "Natural reason tells man that he is subject to a higher being. . . . Hence it is a dictate of natural reason that man should use certain sensibles, by offering them to God. . . . Now this is what we mean by a sacrifice, and *consequently the offering of sacrifice is of the natural law*" (*ST* II-IIae, q. 85, a. 1, emphasis added). Similarly: "The offering of sacrifice belongs generically to the natural law . . . but the determination of sacrifices is established by God or by man . . ." (*ST* II-IIae, q. 85, a. 1, ad 1). For this reason, Long concludes: "*As Aquinas shows with masterful orthodoxy, public worship and prayer is owed to the Creator from whom every public and private benefit is derived, and the virtue of religion falls under the natural good of justice*" (Long, *Natura Pura*, 69, emphasis original).

7. Long, *Natura Pura*, 75, emphasis added. To hold that the natural realm is self-sufficient (according to natural reason) is, for Long, to hold that: "the truth of divine creation and of providence [is] available solely through divine revelation" (ibid., 208–9). But Long, of course, takes strong exception here: "The doctrine of creation and of God's providence over contingent singular effects is not only received in faith but is demonstrable by reason" (ibid., 209).

of human freedom put forth by the Jesuit Luis de Molina (1535–1600); and (2) the post-Enlightenment inheritance of the natural order as a causally-closed system. Both factors seem to give the impression that the natural order is somehow independent of God's overarching providence. Regarding Molina, Long writes:

> Apart from the question of Molina's full theological position, his negative treatment of the dependence of human freedom on divine causality seems in historical terms to be one large stride in the direction of undifferentiated libertarianism of a sort that implies that the created will is a being *a se* [i.e., self-sufficient].[8]

For Long's part, de Lubac's alleged connection between the pure-nature tradition and secularism fails to take into account the *theonomic* conception of the natural order. In other words, if one removes the full theonomic conception of the natural order—and *then* attempts to utilize the pure-nature system of theology—*then* one will end up reinforcing secularism. But Long's point is that this has nothing to do with the genuine pure-nature tradition, but only a deviant form of it. For this reason, he states: "The emphasis in this work has been to insist that the thesis of *natura pura* has no necessary entailment of secularist minimalism in cultural and public life."[9] For Long, in fact, the case is just the opposite: it is precisely the *loss* of the theonomic conception of the natural order that has given rise to modern secularism and thereby the depreciation of the supernatural. He writes:

> Far from natural truth constituting a metaphysical Berlin Wall keeping man in, and God out of man's world, such truth is by its own character essentially ordered toward God. *By its own charac-*

---

8. Ibid., 40–41. For Aquinas, on the contrary: "All things inasmuch as they participate [in] existence, must likewise be subject to divine providence" (*ST* I, q. 22, a. 2); and also: "Natural things . . . are not outside the order of . . . the First Cause, i.e., God, from Whose providence nothing can escape" (*ST* I-IIae, q. 93, a. 5, ad 3). For Aquinas, free will is of course no exception: "The very act of free will is traced to God as to a cause [and so] it necessarily follows that everything that happens from the exercise of free will must be subject to divine providence" (*ST* I, q. 22, a. 2, ad 4); and further: "We have free-will with respect to what we will not of necessity, nor by natural instinct. For our will to be happy does not appertain to free-will, but to natural instinct" (*ST* I, q. 19, a. 10). Similarly, he writes: "Although our intellect moves itself to some things, yet others are supplied by nature, as are first principles, which it cannot doubt; and the *last end, which it cannot but will*" (*ST* I, q. 18, a. 3, emphasis added).

9. Long, *Natura Pura*, 208.

ter—that is, as *naturally* ordered toward God . . . [which] means that nature is essentially ordered toward God . . .[10]

Moreover, Long contends that certain perils have followed for the Church, precisely because of this diminishing sense of the coherence and integrity of the natural order. For example, the inheritance of the Enlightenment is undoubtedly with us whenever we stipulate that human reason cannot transcend the measurable and quantifiable, a point made by none other than Pope Benedict Emeritus in his well known Regensburg address:

> Behind this thinking lies the modern self-limitation of reason, classically expressed in Kant's "Critiques," but in the meantime further radicalized by the impact of the natural sciences. . . . This gives rise to two principles which are crucial for the issue we have raised. First, only the kind of certainty resulting from the interplay of mathematical and empirical elements can be considered scientific. . . . A second point . . . is that by its very nature this method excludes the question of God, making it appear an unscientific or pre-scientific question. Consequently, we are faced with a *reduction of the radius of science and reason*, one which needs to be questioned. . . . The intention here is not one of retrenchment or negative criticism, but of *broadening our concept of reason*.[11]

The emeritus pope's point here is the same as Long's: if reason is arbitrarily restricted to the measurable and quantifiable, then certain matters will *a priori* be excluded from the purview of rational consideration—not the least of which are matters pertaining to God, the soul, morality, and the like. The result is that the truly human questions are relegated to the subjective.

This narrowing of reason necessarily entails the loss of the coherence and intelligibility of the natural order, since the ability to see the natural order as the embodiment of divine wisdom manifestly requires a philosophical insight which transcends the empirical and quantifiable. Accordingly, the problem for the Church, according to Long, is that the *natural* basis for many of its teaching—whether moral, or simply the preambles of the faith such as God's existence, the soul, and the like—

---

10. Ibid., 45.

11. See Pope Benedict, *Regensburg Address*, "Faith, Reason, and the University" September, 2006 cited in Schall, *The Regensburg Lecture*, emphases added.

has been forfeited, with the result that one is left with "faith alone," so to speak, a kind of fideism that can appeal only to authority or emotion.

With Long's concern in mind, let us turn to consider the following statement from Conor Cunningham, who represents just this very juxtaposition of Christian faith along with this Enlightenment reduction of reason. This results for Cunningham in an extreme form of intrinsicism, one which illustrates precisely Long's concern. Cunningham states:

> Quite simply, the idea of nature, the idea of the purely natural is a fiction, and this is revealed, for example, in the default position of our intellectual culture, namely, ontological naturalism, which is itself a true progeny of *natura pura*. . . . *In short, in the absence of theology there is no such thing as language. . . . There is no such thing as a person, thus there is no such thing as belief, any belief; and lastly, there is no such thing as life. . . . In light of such naturalism the Twin Towers never fell, and people never died, for the simple reason that there are no such entities as towers or people—especially the latter.* This is pure nature—a nature purified of anything at all—this is not just ethnic cleansing, but ontological cleansing . . .[12]

12. Cunningham, "*Natura Pura*, the Invention of the Anti-Christ," 243–54, here 245–246, emphasis added. One wonders whether this assessment is the result of an eclectic mix of Willard van Orman Quine (1908–2000), A. J. Ayer (1910–1989), and Richard McKay Rorty (1931–2007), doused with a little Christianity on top. I do not think de Lubac would ever put matters so intemperately, but Cunningham does represent at least one development in the *Communio* school of theology. In the face of such "theological nihilism" is it any wonder that the resurgence of a robust realism seems to have taken the form that it has in the so-called "New Atheists"? For this reason, Long writes: "Consequent upon the eclipse of *natura*, what would one expect to occur in the ensuing apologetic void? As a metaphysical realist, one might anticipate a resurgence of doctrinaire atheism and agnosticism—clothed in ideology masquerading as science. . . . Precisely, this is what has happened" (Long, *Natura Pura*, 106). On the other hand, we should note that some Christian thinkers have allied themselves successfully with postmodern sentiments in order to marshal a critique against modernity. Much of Alasdair MacIntyre's work is a good example of this hermeneutic. See *After Virtue* and *Three Rival Versions of Moral Enquiry*. For example: "The encyclopaedist's [i.e., Enlightenment] conception is of a single framework within which knowledge is discriminated from mere belief, progress towards knowledge is mapped, and truth is understood as the relationship of *our* knowledge to *the* world, through the application of those methods whose rules are the rules of rationality as such. Nietzsche, as a genealogist [representing postmodernity], takes there to be a multiplicity of perspectives within each of which truth-from-a-point-of-view may be asserted, but no truth-as-such. . . . There are no rules of rationality as such to be appealed to; there are rather strategies of insight and strategies of subversion" (MacIntyre, *Three Rival Versions*, 42, emphasis original). See also Vanhoozer, *Is There a Meaning in this Text?*: "Reality is a text to be

For Long, such a view of nature and the natural order (or lack thereof) forfeits the *"natural presuppositions* of Christian moral life."[13] For this reason, Long suggests that the inevitable outcome will look something like this: "It is not hard to see with what ease culture will then incline to the supine supposition that religious conviction is largely an emotive affair."[14]

Further, the loss of the integral coherence of the natural order has Christological implications as well: for if we cannot know *what* human nature is apart from Christ, then how can we even begin to understand *what* the Son became when He became *"man"*? And so Long writes:

> *The mode* [or condition] *of being of human nature is distinct in Christ, and in St. Peter, but the definition of human nature as such is not.* That is what is required for the intelligibility of the doctrine of Nicea, and anything that impedes or contradicts this by so doing [also implicitly] impedes and contradicts the most foundational truth of Christianity.[15]

---

interpreted, mediated by language, history, culture, and tradition. . . . Nietzsche held that, in the absence of a Creator, it was up to human beings to impose meaning and order on the world" (20–21). Vanhoozer expresses his *modus operandi* this way: "The present work takes an unabashedly Augustinian approach to these queries: '*credo ut intelligam*' ('I believe in order to understand')" (ibid., 30). And finally: "If postmodernity stands for anything, it is for the demise of a universal standpoint and the subsequent celebration of the diverse particular perspectives from which we view the world, each other, and our texts" (168). One can see how such an approach relativizes the Enlightenment rationalistic perspective and thereby offers Christian intellectuals a place at the academic table. However, as Long implicitly warns throughout, such an approach equally relativizes Christianity's truth claims as well, and may on that account, prove more deleterious in the long run for the promulgation of the faith.

13. Long, *Natura Pura*, 97, italics are Long's.

14. Ibid., 103. Accordingly, Long assesses the contemporary pastoral situation this way: "Which is the proper framework to instruct people that something is wrong: 'because the Church and Scripture say so', with no further consideration; or to show the way that vice is disruptive, and virtue perfective, with respect both to the natural end and the life of grace? The teleology that specifies human virtue and perfection is critical for moral theology, and it is of special importance in the apologetic engagement of the Church with a culture that assumes that moral limitations are mere dictatorial means for controlling and suppressing normal human spontaneity . . ." (ibid., 99).

15. Long, *Natura Pura*, 87, Long's italics. Here, Long anticipates our next section where he will set forth the distinction between *nature*, taken abstractly, and its existential *conditions* in which it exists.

In fact, Cunningham registers this very Christological dilemma as well,[16] but actually dismisses it flippantly, stating that "this is a case of the ontic tail wagging the ontological dog."[17] Cunningham unapologetically holds that we simply cannot know what it means to be human apart from Christ: "we *only* are as *humans* in being sons in the Son. . . . [D]eification is hominization."[18] Now no Christian theologian true to the name would ever assert that man can be *fully* comprehended in his totality apart from Christ; but conceding this much—not only can we understand something of man's nature apart from Christ—but it is imperative that we do so for the very integrity of the faith.

This point can be seen in St. Thomas as well when he states: "Christ is called a man *univocally* with other men, as being of the same species."[19] The meaning of "univocally" here is that "human nature" is predicated of Christ *in the exact same way* as it is predicated of any other human being (despite the vast difference in the condition between His human nature and ours). Hence, we must be able to appre-

16. Cunningham describes the problem as: "the fear that if there is not some sort of autonomous human nature then how can Christ become human?" (Cunningham, "*Natura Pura*, the Invention of the Anti-Christ," 252).

17. Ibid.

18. Ibid., 244, 249, emphasis added.

19. *ST* III, q. 2, a. 5, emphasis added. In this passage, Aquinas cites Phil 2:7: "[Christ] emptied himself, taking the form of a servant, being born in the likeness of men." The passage in the Vulgate reads: "sed semet ipsum exinanivit formam servi accipiens in similitudinem hominum factus et habitu inventus ut homo" (emphasis added). And similarly, Aquinas states: "For nature . . . designates the specific essence which is signified by definition" (*ST* III, q. 2, a. 2). St. Thomas makes the importance of the philosophical notion of nature explicit when treating the Incarnation in the following: "To make this question clear we must consider what is nature. Now it is to be observed that the word nature comes from nativity. Hence this word was used first of all to signify the begetting of living beings, which is called birth or sprouting forth, the word *natura* meaning, as it were, *nascitura* ['about to be born']. Afterwards this word nature was taken to signify the principle of this begetting; and because in living things the principle of generation is an intrinsic principle, this word nature was further employed to signify any intrinsic principle of motion: thus the Philosopher says (*Phys. ii*) that *nature is the principle of motion in that in which it is essentially and not accidentally*. Hence sometimes form is called nature, and sometimes matter. And because the end of natural generation, in that which is generated, is the essence of the species, which the definition signifies, this essence of the species is called the nature. And thus Boethius defines nature (*De Duab. Nat.*): *Nature is what informs a thing with its specific difference*—i.e., which perfects the specific definition. But we are now speaking of nature as it signifies the essence, or the *what-it-is*, or the quiddity of the species" (*ST* III, q. 2, a. 1).

hend something of *what* human nature is before we can even begin to profess faith in the Incarnation. If Christ is said to be "consubstantial" with both God and man, we must have some prior understanding of what these terms refer to.

For this reason, Long contends that the surest way to preserve the integrity of the faith and of supernatural grace is *not* to follow Cunningham's denigration of the natural order and its integral coherence, but as we have seen—just the opposite. For Long, the only answer to de Lubac's deepest fears regarding secularism is not to dilute the claims of nature—in order to exalt grace—but rather to restore the full theonomic character of the natural order, as such.

With this in mind, let us now turn to the distinction between man's nature and the conditions of his nature. To some extent, de Lubac's rejection of this distinction (or at the very least, his rejection of its implications) constitutes his rejection of the pure-nature tradition as a whole; and conversely, the acceptance of this distinction leads directly to the very logic of the pure-nature tradition.

Nature and the Conditions of Nature

Long helpfully distinguishes two issues in the debate over the legitimacy of the pure-nature tradition: namely, (1) "pure nature" taken as a state or condition *of* human nature, independent of grace in a hypothetical economy; and (2) the definition of human nature, as such, which excludes grace as part of its essence.[20] The latter exists in *any* condition in which human beings exist (e.g., pre-lapsarian, post-lapsarian, etc.); but the former, on the other hand, is only a hypothetical *state* or condition—which is to say that it is logically dependent upon the latter. In this light, Long writes: "The *condition* of pure nature is only a hypothesis; but human nature *simpliciter—pure nature* in the sense of *all that defines human nature as such*—is found in all who have the nature, irrespective of *the condition* in which they have it . . ."[21]

As we have seen, grace for St. Thomas must be extrinsic or "accidental" with respect to human nature, as such, precisely because grace is not included in the definition of man. Aquinas writes: "Because grace is

20. Long, *Natura Pura*, 81, 142.
21. Ibid., 81, emphasis original.

above human nature, it cannot be a substance or a substantial form, but is an *accidental* form of the soul . . ."[22]

Importantly, the fact that grace is said here to be "accidental" or extrinsic to human nature does not mean that grace fails to touch the individual deeply; it only means that grace is not contained within the definition of man, as such, and is therefore "above" his nature, strictly speaking. The abstract distinction of nature and grace in this sense, as we have said, need not be taken to negate the pervasiveness of their existential interplay in the life of the individual person. Accordingly, Long states: "It is not grace as *extrinsic* principle—for that is what grace *is*, since grace *is not* nature—but grace as *transmutative* principle that constitutes a deformation of Christian teaching."[23] By "transmutative" Long means here some kind of ontological distancing or separation between nature and grace. In other words, the intelligible distinction between nature and grace does not require that grace is "extrinsic" to the individual human person (which would be "transmutative" in the less-than-felicitous language used here by Long). For this reason, speaking of Balthasar (though the same applies in his assessment to de Lubac), Long states:

> If [one means] there is no pure nature in the sense of a nature *existentially unaffected* by sin and grace, that is true, and it is completely consistent with the *abstract intelligibility* of nature and of its being *distinct* from that which affects it (nature is not sin; nature is not grace). The reason? Being and essential nature are really distinct.[24]

In order to attain greater clarity on this point, let us consider the generically similar example of sin, the existential power of which provides an excellent illustration of that which is "accidental" with respect

22. *ST* I-IIae, q. 110, a. 2, ad 2, emphasis added. Similarly: "man partakes of the life of grace accidentally" (*ST* I-IIae, q. 112, a. 4, ad 3). And: "Although grace is more efficacious than nature, yet nature is more essential to man, and therefore more enduring" (*ST* I-IIae, q. 94, a. 6, ad 2). And further: "Grace is reduced to the first species of quality" (*ST* I-IIae, q. 110, a. 3, ad 3), which is one of the ten predicamentals (i.e., categories of Aristotle): substance, quantity, quality, relation, action, passion, when, where, position, possession. The latter nine are all "accidents" with respect to the essence of a particular thing. Long makes the important point that "accidental" in Thomistic-Aristotelian parlance certainly does not mean "unimportant" (Long, *Natura Pura*, 148 n. 44). "Accident" here just means that a certain feature, property, or attribute is not contained within the definition of the *essence* of a particular thing.

23. Long, *Natura Pura*, 36, emphasis added.

24. Ibid., 80, emphasis added.

to human nature, but simultaneously all-pervasive in its personal and existential influence. Indeed, this antinomy of "sin," so powerful and yet so *contrary* to nature—so *normal* and yet so *unnatural*—seems to have caught the attention of the likes of both the pagan Aristotle, as well as St. Paul. In fact, Aristotle almost seems to anticipate the disciple of Gamaliel in the following:

> Just as paralyzed parts of a body, when we decide to move them to the right, do the contrary and move off to the left, *the same is true of the soul*; for incontinent people have impulses in contrary directions. . . . We should [therefore] suppose that the soul also has something apart from reason, countering and opposing reason.[25]

Indeed, here Athens almost prefigures Jerusalem, as St. Paul writes:

> I do not do what I want, but I do the very thing I hate. Now if I do what I do not want, I agree that the law is good. So then it is no longer I that do it, but *sin* which dwells within me. . . . I can will what is right, but I cannot do it. For I do not do the good I want, but the evil I do not want is what I do. Now if I do what I do not want, it is no longer I that do it, but sin which dwells within me. So I find it to be a law of God, in my inmost self, but I see in my members another law at war with the law of my mind and making me captive to the law of sin which dwells in my members. (Rom 7:15b–23)

St. Thomas likewise recognizes the power of sin, but with the additional emphasis that the pull of sin is *contrary* to man's nature, absolutely speaking, in which case—despite the presence of this "law" of sin, sin is not *natural*, strictly speaking:

> The *law of man* [i.e., natural law], which by the Divine ordinance is allotted to him according to his proper natural condition, *is that he should act in accordance with reason*. . . . So, then, this very inclination [to sin] of sensuality which is called the "fomes" ["instigator"] in other animals has simply the nature of a law by

---

25. Aristotle, *Nicomachean Ethics*, Bk. I, ch. 13 (1102b 20–25), emphasis and brackets added: "ἀτεχνῶς γὰρ καθάπερ τὰ παραλελυμένα τοῦ σώματος μόρια εἰς τὰ δεξιὰ προαιρουμένων κινῆσαι τοὐναντίον εἰς τὰ ἀριστερὰ παραφέρεται, καὶ ἐπὶ τῆς ψυχῆς οὕτως· ἐπὶ τἀναντία γὰρ αἱ ὁρμαὶ τῶν ἀκρατῶν. ἀλλ᾽ ἐν τοῖς σώμασι μὲν ὁρῶμεν τὸ παραφερόμενον, ἐπὶ δὲ τῆς ψυχῆς οὐχ ὁρῶμεν· ἴσως δ᾽ οὐδὲν ἧττον καὶ ἐν τῇ ψυχῆς νομιστέον εἶναί τι παρὰ τὸν λόγον ἐναντιούμενον τούτῳ καὶ ἀντιβαῖον."

reason of a direct inclination. *But in man, it has not the nature of law in this, rather it is a deviation from the law of reason.*[26]

Hence, for St. Thomas, despite its pervasive power, sin is nonetheless contrary to man's nature, as he states again here: "By human nature [if we] mean . . . that which is proper to man . . . [then] all sins, as being against reason, are also against nature."[27] Referring to the sinless human nature of Christ, Aquinas likewise states: "The truth of His human nature is not proved by sin, since sin does not belong to human nature . . ."[28]

Therefore, strictly speaking, sin (and the same goes for grace) is *not* part of man's nature, and is therefore "extrinsic" or "accidental with respect to human nature, as such—despite its obvious existential influence over man in his current state. Accordingly, the important point is that the pervasive existential influence of either sin or grace does not thereby undermine the intelligibility of human nature, *qua* nature, and it is this very point which is captured by the distinction between nature and the conditions of nature.

For this reason, according to Long, the hypothetical state of pure nature must be possible for two reasons: (1) God's freedom and (2) the independent intelligibility of nature, *vis-à-vis* its conditions. He states:

> The *state* of pure nature is simply a state or condition of nature in which God would not have called man to the beatific vision and would have provided only natural aids to man. Its *possibility*

---

26. *ST* I-IIae, q. 91, a. 6, emphasis added. "If the inclination of sensuality be considered as it is in other animals, thus it is ordained to the common good, namely, to the preservation of nature in the species or in the individual. And this is in man also, in so far as sensuality is subject to reason. *But it is called the 'fomes' in so far as it strays from the order of reason*" (*ST* I-IIae, q. 91, a. 6, ad 3, emphasis added). Also: "The 'fomes' has the nature of law in man, in so far as it is a punishment resulting from Divine justice; and in this respect it is evident that it is derived from the eternal law. *But in so far as it denotes a proneness to sin, it is contrary to the Divine law, and has not the nature of law* . . ." (*ST* I-IIae, q. 93, a. 3, ad 1, emphasis addded). By *nature*, Aquinas writes: "Each rational creature . . . has a natural inclination to that which is in harmony with the eternal law" (*ST* I-IIae, q. 93, a. 6). And likewise: "To the natural law belongs everything to which a man is inclined according to his nature. . . . Since the rational soul is the proper form of man, *there is in man a natural inclination to act according to reason*; and this is to act according to virtue. Consequently, considered thus all acts of virtue are prescribed by the natural law, since each one's reason naturally dictates to him to act virtuously" (*ST* I-IIae, q. 94, a. 3, emphasis added).

27. *ST* I-IIae, q. 94, a. 3, ad 2, emphasis added.

28. *ST* III, q. 15, a. 1.

seems to follow simply from the divine omnipotence and from the definition of human nature.[29]

However, contrary to Feingold, Long rejects the possibility of a purely natural end in *this* economy for two reasons: (1) in this economy, God has further ordered nature to grace, ordering man to the beatific vision; and (2) the present condition of sin inhibits nature's ability to attain even *natural* good, with the result that nature is in need of healing grace (as well as elevating grace).

Let us take the second reason in St. Thomas first since it is easier to see. Distinguishing between the conditions of "integrity" and "corrupted" human nature, Aquinas clearly holds that man is now in need of healing grace, simply for the restoration of nature, *as* nature:

> Man's nature may be looked at in two ways: first in its *integrity*, as it was in our first parent before sin; secondly as it was *corrupted* in us after the sin of our first parent. Now in both states human nature needs the help of God as First Mover, to do or wish any good whatsoever. But *in the state of integrity . . . man by his natural endowments could wish and do the good proportionate to his nature*, such as the good of acquired virtue; but not surpassing good, as the good of infused virtue. But *in the state of corrupt nature, man falls short of what he could do by his nature*, so that he is unable to fulfill it by his own natural powers. . . . And thus in the *state of perfect nature* [i.e., integrity] man needs gratuitous strength superadded to natural strength [not just] for *one* reason . . . in order to do and wish supernatural good, but for *two* reasons in the *state of corrupted nature . . .* in order to be healed, and furthermore in order to carry out works of supernatural virtue.[30]

29. Long, *Natura Pura*, 61, emphasis original.

30. *ST* I-IIae, q. 109, a. 2, emphases added. See also: "In the state of perfect nature man referred the love of himself and of all other things to the love of God as to its end; and thus he loved God more than himself and above all things. But in the state of corrupt nature man falls short of this in the appetite of his rational will, which, unless it is cured by God's grace, follows its private good, on account of the corruption of nature. *And hence we must say that in the state of perfect nature man did not need the gift of grace added to his natural endowments, in order to love God above all things naturally,* although he needed God's help to move him to it; *but in the state of corrupt nature man needs even for this, the help of grace to heal his nature*" (*ST* I-IIae, q. 109, a. 3, emphasis added). Further: "Man without grace may be looked at in two states . . . the first, a state of *perfect nature*, in which Adam was before his sin; the second, a state of *corrupt nature*, in which we are before being restored by grace. Therefore, if we speak of man in the first state, there is only one reason why man cannot merit eternal life without grace, by his purely natural endowments . . . [namely] because man's merit depends

In other words, given the context of sin, man cannot attain the good of nature on his own, and so the concrete possibility of realizing man's purely natural end must be modified accordingly. St. Thomas writes:

> We may speak of man in two ways: first, in the *state of perfect nature*; secondly, in the state of *corrupted nature*. Now in the state of perfect nature, man, without habitual grace, could avoid sinning either mortally or venially. . . . But in the state of corrupt nature, man needs grace to heal his nature in order that he may entirely abstain from sin.[31]

It is this perspective regarding the need for healing grace which explains the necessity, for example, of the infused moral virtues. St. Thomas clearly distinguishes between infused theological virtues and a separate kind of infused "habit" or virtue, which in context refers to infused *moral* virtue:

> God bestows on us the theological virtues whereby we are directed to a supernatural end. . . . Wherefore we need to receive from God *other habits* corresponding, in due proportion, to the theological virtues, which habits are to the theological virtues what the moral and intellectual virtues are to the natural principles of virtue.[32]

Thus, the condition of sin necessarily modifies the prospect of realizing man's purely natural end, making it no longer possible in the concrete economy. Let us now turn to the first reason given above by Long:

---

on the Divine pre-ordination. . . . But if we speak of *man as existing in sin*, a second reason is added to this . . . the impediment of sin. For since sin is an offense against God, excluding us from eternal life . . . no one existing in a state of mortal sin can merit eternal life unless first he be reconciled to God, through his sin being forgiven, which is brought about by grace" (*ST* I-IIae, q. 114, a. 2, emphasis added).

31. *ST* I-IIae, q. 109, a. 8, emphasis added. Similarly: "In the state of corrupted nature, man cannot fulfill all the Divine commandments without healing grace" (*ST* I-IIae, q. 109, a. 4).

32. *ST* I-IIae, q. 63, a. 3. "The theological virtues direct us sufficiently to our supernatural end. . . . But the soul needs further to be perfected by *infused virtues* in regard to other things . . ." (*ST* I-IIae, q. 63, a. 3, ad 2, emphasis added). And: "All moral virtues are infused together with charity" (*ST* I-IIae, q. 65, a. 3). See Cessario, *Christian Faith and the Theological Life*, 3–5: "The infused moral virtues . . . develop within the theological life of the believer, that is, a life suffused with faith, hope, and charity." Again, St. Thomas states: "Those infused moral virtues, whereby men behave well in respect of their being *fellow-citizens with the saints* . . . differ from the acquired virtues, whereby man behaves well in respect to human affairs" (*ST* I-IIae, q. 63, a. 4).

namely, that since God has actually ordered man to the beatific vision, this ordination of divine providence is itself enough to preclude the possibility of a purely natural end—even apart from sin. Long writes: "Paradoxically, the attainment of the natural end will require *medicinal grace*, but not because it is itself supernatural, *but because nature is itself further ordered in grace from its creation and is thus harmed by the loss of grace*."[33]

It is here that Long most decidedly differs from Feingold: while both fully accept the intelligible integrity of the natural order, and the resultant hypothetical possibility of man's purely natural end, Long goes on to reject the notion that this intelligible integrity of the natural order can be simply transposed onto the actual divine economy—as if the actual governance of the eternal law did not modify the concrete possibilities of pure nature. In other words, the intelligible possibilities of pure nature, abstractly considered, are necessarily modified by the concrete ordination of divine providence, a point which Matthias Scheeben will especially bring home in the following chapter by recourse to the Incarnation.

At this point, let us now turn to Long's appropriation of Aquinas' teaching on eternal and natural law and its implications for the nature-grace debate.

Eternal and Natural Law: Distinction in Unity

The first thing to note here is that both the natural law and the new law of grace derive from the *one* eternal law of God; yet the intelligibility of the natural law abides *along with* and *after* the gift of grace, as Aquinas implies here: "For just as grace presupposes nature, so must the Divine law presuppose the natural law."[34] Accordingly, the intelligibility of the natural law does not vanish upon the onset of grace. For Long, to say otherwise: "is to imply that no definitive distinction can be made between our *natural rational participation* of the eternal law that is known as the *natural law* and that *essentially higher participation of the eternal law* which is that of the *lex nova* and *gratiae*."[35]

---

33. Long, *Natura Pura*, 200–201. Cf. *ST* I-IIae, q. 99, a. 2, ad 1.

34. *ST* I-IIae, q. 99, a. 2, ad 1.

35. Long, *Natura Pura*, 72–74, emphasis added.

The eternal law is nothing other than God's providence, as is evident by the similar language used by Aquinas in both settings.[36] All creatures, in virtue of their natures participate in the eternal law, and this very participation—in accordance with their natures—is itself the natural law. Aquinas writes:

> It is evident that all things partake somewhat of the eternal law, in so far as, namely, from its being imprinted on them, they derive their respective *inclinations* to their *proper acts* and *ends*. Now among all others, the rational creature is subject to Divine providence in the most excellent way, in so far as it partakes of a share of providence, by being provident both for itself and for others. Wherefore it has a share of the Eternal Reason whereby it has a natural inclination to its proper act and end: *and this participation of the eternal law in the rational creature is called the natural law.*[37]

For St. Thomas, it is precisely on account of man's divine call to a disproportionate end that brings about the necessity of an *additional* law, over and above the natural law, just as we saw earlier with predestination. Accordingly, Aquinas writes:

36. "It is necessary that the *type* of the order of things towards their end should pre-exist in the divine mind: and the *type* of things ordered towards an end is, properly speaking, *providence*" (*ST* I, q. 22, a. 1, emphasis added). And consider: "The *type* of Divine Wisdom, as moving all things to their due end, bears the character of law. . . . The *eternal law* is nothing else than the *type* of Divine Wisdom . . ." (*ST* I-IIae, q. 93, a. 1, emphasis added). Further: "The eternal law is nothing else than the type of Divine Wisdom, as directing all actions and movements" (*ST* I-IIae, q. 93, a. 1). Also: "The eternal law is the plan of government in the Chief Governor . . ." (*ST* I-IIae, 1. 93, a. 3). Finally: "The eternal law is the type of Divine government" (*ST* I-IIae, q. 93, a. 4). And: "thus all actions and movements of the whole of nature are subject to the eternal law" (*ST* I-IIae, q. 93, a. 5). And: "Now it is manifest that things made by nature receive determinate forms. This determination of forms must be reduced to the divine wisdom as its first principle, for divine wisdom devised the order of the universe, which order consists in the variety of things. And therefore we must say that in the divine wisdom are the types of all things, which types we have called ideas—i.e., exemplar forms existing in the divine mind" (*ST* I, q. 44, a. 3). Similarly: "It is necessary to suppose ideas in the divine mind. . . . By ideas are understood the forms of things, existing apart from the things themselves" (*ST* I, q. 15, a. 1). And finally: "In the divine mind there are the proper ideas of all things" (*ST* I, q. 15, a. 2).

37. *ST* I-IIae, q. 91, a. 2, emphasis added. "God imprints on the whole of nature the principles of its proper actions. . . . And thus all actions and movements of the whole of nature are subject to the eternal law" (*ST* I-IIae, q. 93, a. 5). Further: "The impression of an inward active principle is to natural things, what the promulgation of law is to men" (*ST* I-IIae, q. 93, a. 5, ad 1).

If man were ordained to no other end than that which is proportionate to his natural faculty, there would be no need for man to have any further direction on the part of his reason, beside the natural law and human law which is derived from it. But since man is ordained to an end of eternal happiness which is disproportionate to man's natural faculty . . . it was necessary . . . that man should be directed to his end by a law given by God.[38]

Long rightly points out that these diverse participations in the eternal law—by way of grace and by way of the natural law—do not lose their distinctiveness simply because they both have their common source in the eternal law. For this reason, St. Thomas writes the following: "By the natural law the eternal law is participated in *proportionately* [according] to the capacity of human nature. But to his supernatural end, man needs to be directed in a yet *higher* way."[39] As we mentioned, Aquinas' language is here reminiscent of his teaching on predestination, which arises for the very same reason. And so St. Thomas states:

The end towards which created things are directed by God is twofold, one which exceeds all proportion and faculty of created nature; and this end is life eternal, that consists in seeing God which is above every creature. . . . The other end, however, is proportionate to created nature, to which end created being can attain according to the power of its nature. . . . Hence the type of the aforesaid direction of a rational creature towards the end of life eternal is called predestination.[40]

38. *ST* I-Iae, q. 91, a. 4. Similarly: "There are two ways in which a thing may be instilled into man. *First*, through being *part of his nature*, and thus the natural law is instilled into man. *Secondly*, a thing is instilled into man by being, as it were, *added* on to his nature by a gift of *grace*. In this way the New Law is instilled into man . . ." (*ST* I-IIae, q. 106, a. 1, ad 2, emphasis added).

39. *ST* I-IIae, q. 91, a. 4, ad 1, emphasis added. Aquinas writes: "If anything needs to be done that is above nature, it is done by God immediately. . . . Happiness is a good surpassing created nature . . . by God alone is man made happy—if we speak of perfect Happiness" (*ST* I-IIae, q. 5, a. 6).

40. *ST* I, q. 23, a. 1, emphasis added. Also: "Man's happiness is twofold . . . one proportionate. . . . The other . . . surpassing man's nature, and which man can obtain by the power of God alone, by a kind of participation of the Godhead, about which it is written (2 Pet 1:4) that by Christ we are made partakers of the Divine nature. And because such happiness surpasses the capacity of human nature, man's natural principles . . . do not suffice to direct man to this . . . happiness. Hence it is necessary for man to receive from God some additional principles, whereby he may be directed to supernatural happiness. . . . Such principles are called theological virtues . . ." (*ST* I-IIae, q. 62, a. 1). See also: "Acts conducing to an end must be proportioned to the end. But

For the Thomist tradition, man's natural proportionate end is indeed God—but God as First Cause of all things, which is the object of man's *natural* love of God and is thereby ordained by the natural law. This proportionate natural end stands in contrast to man's disproportionate supernatural end by way of grace and supernatural charity. St. Thomas writes:

> Man by his nature is proportioned to a certain end for which he has a natural appetite, and which he can work to achieve by his natural powers. This end is a certain contemplation of the divine attributes, *in the measure in which this is possible for man through his natural powers*; and in this end even the philosophers placed the final happiness of man. But God has prepared man *for another end*, one that exceeds the proportionality of human nature. This end is eternal life, which consists in the vision of God in his essence, an end which exceeds the proportionality of any created nature, being connatural to God alone.[41]

This distinct intelligibility of the orders of nature and grace in no way takes away from their ceaseless interaction in the concrete life of the individual person. For this reason, Long writes: "The order of natural ends does not disappear with revelation. And to say that there *is* no nature

---

no act exceeds the proportion of its active principle; and hence we see in natural things, that nothing can by its operation bring about an effect which exceeds its active force, but only such as is proportionate to its power. *Now everlasting life is an end exceeding the proportion of human nature.* . . . Hence man, by his natural endowments, cannot produce meritorious works proportionate to everlasting life; *and for this a higher force is needed . . . the force of grace*" (*ST* I-IIae, q. 109, a. 5, emphasis added). And: "Now it is established throughout all natural things, that every action is commensurate with the power of the agent, *nor does any natural agent strive to do what exceeds its ability*" (*ST* II-IIae, q. 130, a. 1, emphasis added). And finally: "Now everything has a natural inclination to accomplish an action that is *commensurate* with its power" (*ST* II-IIae, q. 133, a. 1, emphasis added).

41. *De Veritate*, q. 27, a. 2, emphasis added. See also: "Now no act of anything whatsoever is divinely ordained to anything exceeding the proportion of the powers which are the principles of its act; for it is the law of Divine providence that nothing shall act beyond its powers. Now everlasting life is a good exceeding the proportion of created nature. . . . And hence it is that no created nature is a sufficient principle of an act meritorious of eternal life, unless there is added a supernatural gift which we call grace" (*ST* I-IIae, q. 114, a. 2). Also: "When nature is perfect, it can be restored by itself to its befitting and proportionate condition; but without exterior help it cannot be restored to what surpasses its measure . . . but [once] corrupted . . . [it] can [no longer] be restored, by itself, to its connatural good, much less to the supernatural good of justice" (*ST* I-IIae, q. 109, a. 6, ad 3).

as such—because it always exists concretely in some relation to grace and supernatural beatitude—is to say that nature is itself intrinsically unintelligible."[42] Hence, as we saw in the last section, the abiding intelligibility of the natural order is implied in the distinction between nature and its conditions; and likewise, the intelligibility of the natural law does not disappear because man is gifted with an essentially higher participation in the eternal law through grace.

In the present economy, the condition of human nature includes the *lex nova* of grace, which is not included in the definition of human nature, as such; but this concrete and existential state of affairs does not nullify the integrity of the natural order—and in accepting this claim, we are implicitly accepting the legitimacy of the distinction between the nature of a thing and its particular condition.

In order to deny the legitimacy of this distinction, we would have to state that the natural order is no longer intelligible, on account of its existential interaction with grace—in which case, we can no longer apprehend the natural order, as natural; in other words, we could no longer speak of an abiding "natural law," precisely because it is too intertwined with supernatural grace. This is precisely the import of de Lubac's claim that the specifying or "constitutive" feature of human nature is its ordination to the beatific vision; for in this claim, he refuses to allow for the abstraction of human nature apart from its concrete existential condition of being called by God to the beatific vision.

For this reason, the issue here really comes down to metaphysical realism, as we suggested in the previous chapter; Long appears to concur with this assessment in the following: "The radical and permeating reordering of human nature in and by grace does not annul that of nature, nor does it deny it its specific intelligibility . . ."[43]

We will now turn to anticipate our overall conclusion, suggesting how this pure-nature analysis can be reconciled with the Christocentrism mentioned at the outset. Here we are beginning to bring together the two all-important aspects of the nature-grace mystery—captured by both de Lubac and the pure-nature tradition respectively, a project which will come to fruition more fully in the subsequent chapter. Here we wish to point the way forward to our proposed solution.

42. Long, *Natura Pura*, 81.
43. Ibid., 89.

Christocentrism and the Intelligibility of Nature

As we saw briefly in the introduction, for Aquinas, the eternal law is expressed in the very Person of the Word—as the Divine Intellect's conception of all things: "Among other things expressed by this Word, the eternal law itself is expressed thereby."[44] And as we have also seen, Aquinas likewise insists upon the abiding reality of the natural order, alongside the gift of grace. Thus, while the natural order is *ontologically* dependent upon the Word in an ultimate sense, the natural order retains its own distinctive perfection and intelligibility nonetheless. The finite natural perfections of creatures constitute the independent intelligibility of the natural order; "independent" here refers to each creature's own way of being, in accordance with its nature—it does not mean any kind of autonomous natural existence, as Long so painstakingly made clear. Understood in this light, the notion of the "independent" intelligibility of the natural order is perfectly compatible with the Christocentric foundation of all reality, as taught by St. Paul and the early Fathers of the Church.

While all creatures were made through the Word,[45] the Word has bequeathed a share of His own Logos to the world, as it were. This "bequeathed logos" constitutes the "natural order," which is both independently intelligible on the one hand, and simultaneously dependent

44. *ST* I-IIae, q. 93, a. 1, ad 2. See also: "God the Son . . . is Himself the eternal law by a kind of appropriation" (*ST* I-IIae, 1. 93, a. 4, ad 2). See also: "*Word*, said of God in its proper sense, is used personally, and is the proper name of the person of the Son. For it signifies an emanation of the intellect: and the person Who proceeds in God, by way of emanation of the intellect, is called the Son" (*ST* I, q. 34, a. 2). At the very beginning of the *Summa theologiae*, Aquinas writes: "The Word is an exemplar form" (*ST* I, q. 3, a. 8, ad 2). And: "Word implies relation to creatures. For God by knowing Himself, knows every creature. . . . Because God by one act understands Himself and all things, *His one only Word is expressive not only of the Father, but of all creatures. . . .* The Word of God is [not] only expressive of what is in God the Father, but is both expressive and operative of creatures; and therefore it is said (Ps. xxxii. 9): *He spake, and they were made; because in the Word is implied the operative idea of what God makes*" (*ST* I, q. 34, a. 3, emphasis added). Finally, in a Trinitarian and creational context, St. Thomas states: "God the Father made creatures through His Word, which is His Son; and through His Love, which is the Holy Ghost. And so the processions of the Persons are the types of the productions of creatures inasmuch as they include the essential attributes, knowledge and will" (*ST* I, q. 45, a. 6).

45. See John 1:1–3; Col 1:16b; and Ps 33:6 which states: "By the word of the Lord the heavens were made and all their host by the breath of his mouth"; MT: בִּדְבַר יְהוָה שָׁמַיִם נַעֲשׂוּ וּבְרוּחַ פִּיו כָּל־צְבָאָ

ontologically upon the Logos, on the other hand. Christoph Schönborn makes this very point as follows:

> In the beginning was the Logos and the Logos was with God, and the Logos was God" (John 1:1). What does "*Logos*" mean? It does mean "word," certainly—but also "meaning," "reason," and "essential determining factor." "All things were made through the Logos and without the Logos was not anything made that was made" (John 1:3).[46] The great tradition of Christian thought has understood that there exists an inner connection between the *Logos* and the *logoi* of things. The "logos" of a thing is what makes it what it is, what determines it in its inmost being, what decides its nature. If each creature thus has its own "logos," then the trace of the Creator-Logos is found in each one. . . . God's traces in creation are the signs of the Logos, of Christ, in whom and through whom and toward whom everything was created. . . . But this means that the *Logos* is the Word of creation that re-echoes in the inmost part of every creature; it is the creative rationality that gives meaning to all things and that grants them their nature and their effective action. And the *Logos* is the light that is active in our reason, illuminating it and making it clear, so that it can penetrate the realm of creatures and is able to recognize in things the signs of the Creator. The Logos of God is at work both as the trace of the Creator in the creatures and as light in human reason, so that this reason may become aware of the signs of the Creator and may recognize them.[47]

In this light, the unity in *origin* of both the natural law and the new law of grace—as grounded in the eternal law—does not nullify the *intelligible distinction* between the two orders. In other words, the unity of all created things in the Logos does not preclude the distinctiveness of each creature's natural intelligibility, that is, its specific embodiment as a participation in God's Creative Reason.

Conclusion

As we have seen, Long is sympathetic to de Lubac's efforts in context, noting that de Lubac accurately diagnosed much of the problem on nature and grace at mid-century. However, as we have seen, a weakened

---

46. πάντα δι᾽ αὐτοῦ ἐγένετο, καὶ χωρὶς αὐτοῦ ἐγένετο οὐδὲ ἕν. ὃ γέγονεν (John 1:3).

47. Schönborn, *Chance or Purpose*, 138–39.

notion of "nature" ultimately undermined his proposed solution. Thus, for Long, in order to get to the root of the problem, we must recover a theonomic conception of the natural order, a notion which calls for a return to St. Thomas' teaching on the metaphysics of creation, providence, and law—as can be apprehended by natural reason.

In the second section, we saw that the distinction between a thing's *nature* and its existential *conditions* enables one to preserve the independent intelligibility of nature and the natural order on the one hand, while still fully acknowledging the radical existential effects of sin and grace upon the life of the concrete individual, on the other. The intelligible distinction of nature and grace need not be taken to imply that "nature" exists in a vacuum, devoid of the influence of sin and grace; conversely, this existential influence of sin and grace in no way nullifies the intelligibility of man's "nature," as an independently abiding metaphysical principle, intelligible in its own right.

The same point was equally driven home in the third section on eternal and natural law: the fact that the *lex nova* of grace and the natural law both derive from the eternal law in no way vitiates the meaningful and intelligible distinction between the the two, as diverse participations in the one eternal law. In this sense, the integrity of the natural law abides along with the gift of grace.

In conclusion, then, let us note that both distinctions (nature and condition, natural and eternal law) clarify the solution toward which this work has been tending: namely, (1) the paramount need to *distinguish* nature and grace intelligibly, so as to preserve the *supernatural* character of the Christian faith; and (2) the paramount need to embrace the Christocentric unity of all reality, so as to preserve the primacy of the concrete and actual ordination of divine providence which includes nature's ordination to grace.

In order to bring this project to completion, let us now turn to the nineteenth-century German theologian from Cologne, Matthias J. Scheeben.

PART THREE

The Reconciliation of Extrinsicism and Intrinsicism in Matthias Joseph Scheeben

6

Matthias J. Scheeben on the Relationship of Nature and Grace

Let us take a moment here to recapitulate the course we have taken thus far. In Part One, we traced the thought of Henri de Lubac on nature and grace, noting especially the evangelical élan of his work, as he tried to correlate nature and grace more closely in the face of modern secularism. Here he shows us just how much is at stake, for the issue of nature and grace touches upon the very problems of secularism, pluralism, relativism and the like—a point on which Henri de Lubac, Lawrence Feingold, and Steven A. Long all agree.

Part Two treated the contemporary resurgence of the pure-nature tradition by recourse to Lawrence Feingold and Steven Long, whose work was at pains to point out that—despite the merits of de Lubac—difficulties still remain in his overall account. We also saw that many of de Lubac's allegations against the pure-nature tradition were unfounded, as for example was the case with regard to his critique of obediential potency.

In Part Three, we will now introduce Matthias Joseph Scheeben (1835–1888) with the aim of demonstrating his ability to reconcile the insights of intrinsicism and extrinsicism. It is our contention that his synthesis most satisfactorily captures the contributions of both sides of this debate, and so we will proceed as follows: (1) we will present Scheeben's *prima facie* credentials for accomplishing this reconciling task; (2) we will demonstrate his congruity with the pure-nature tradition; then (3) we will treat Scheeben's teaching on the grace of divine sonship; and finally, (4) we will demonstrate his appropriation of Christocentrism which he captures by way of the Incarnation. With Scheeben, let us now begin.

Introduction

After studying in Rome at the Gregorianum under Jesuits of the "Roman School,"[1] Scheeben became a professor at the seminary in Cologne at the age of twenty-five in 1860.[2] By 1865, he had already written three of his most important works: *Natur und Gnade* ("Nature and Grace," 1861); *Die Mysterien des Christentums* ("The Mysteries of Christianity," 1865); and *Die Herrlichkeiten der göttlichen Gnade* ("The Glories of Divine Grace," 1862).[3] Toward the end of his life, he began a truly massive and integrative work entitled the *Handbuch der katholischen Dogmatik* ("Handbook of Catholic Dogmatics"), published between the years of 1874 and 1887.[4]

As we will see, Scheeben is exceptional in that his writings are unmarked by polemic, political or theological, a somewhat surprising feature given that he lived under the rule of Protestant Chancellor, Otto von Bismarck (1815–1898), notorious for his *Kulturkampf* ("culture war" 1871–1887) against Catholics at the time.[5] Nonetheless, Scheeben absorbs much of the Romantic spirit of the age, witnessed especially in his penchant for biological metaphors, most notably his frequent usage of the term *Leben* ("life").[6] Yet at the same time, it must be said that he is

---

1. Nichols, *Romance and System*, 6.

2. Ibid., 9.

3. Ibid., 12–13. Scheeben, *Die Mysterien des Christentums*; Scheeben, *Natur und Gnade*; Scheeben, *Die Herrlichkeiten der Göttlichen Gnade*. In English translation: Scheeben, *The Mysteries of Christianity*; Scheeben, *Nature and Grace*; Scheeben, *The Glories of Divine Grace*.

4. Scheeben, *Handbuch der katholischen Dogmatik*.

5. See Nichols, *Romance and System*, 9–10.

6. See ibid., 345. Nichols discusses the centrality of the Incarnation in Scheeben's thought along these very lines: "It fits with Scheeben's generous use of the language of life (*Leben*), indebted as this was . . . to the Romantic background of nineteenth-century German thought, that everything he has . . . said about the new dignity which accrues to humanity from its divine-human head he reiterates in terms of a new resource of super-abundant, overflowing life drawn from the Son through the Spirit" (ibid., see also 271, 381).

uncompromising in distilling the genuinely supernatural and "mysteric" character of Christianity.[7]

His serene intellectual termperament can also be witnessed by the way in which he appropriates a wide array of Christian sources. Though he is clearly at root a Thomist, he reads St. Thomas in light of the Church Fathers, especially the Greek Fathers. This Greek patristic influence can be seen readily in his unabashed embrace of the Christocentrism found in the Letters to the Colossians (1:16–17) and Ephesians (1:10), a point which will be very important for us later on when we seek to demonstrate Scheeben's ability to accommodate the intrinsicist contribution of de Lubac.[8]

In order to further illustrate Scheeben's uniqueness, let us take note of the fact that in agreement with Bl. John Duns Scotus (1265–1308) Scheeben holds that the ultimate basis for the Incarnation is man's deification or divinization, not sin—as was taught by St. Thomas. [9] For Scheeben, there is nothing untoward about supposing that the Incarnation would have occurred *regardless* of sin,[10] a view certainly

---

7. Ibid., 1–2, 101.

8. See ibid., 19. Nichols writes: "His . . . habitual references to the Greek patristic sources, Cyril of Alexandria above all, in far more than a merely illustrative sense, and his reliance on the power of images, both biblical and more generally cosmic, differentiated him from many modern Schoolmen" (ibid.). Nichols comments further on Scheeben's preference for Cyril this way: "Cyril's thought is key to Scheeben's doctrine of the Incarnation and of the Eucharist, but more widely, he admired Cyril as a defender of Christianity's supernatural character against a version of theological rationalism."

9. This is not to say that Aquinas is unaware of other reasons for the Incarnation besides sin, such as man's "full participation in Divinity" which is made possible through "Christ's humanity" (*ST* III, q. 1, a. 2), as well as the fact that it belongs "to the essence of goodness to communicate itself to another" (*ST* III, q. 1, a. 1), which makes the Incarnation incredibly *conveniens*, to use Aquinas' customary Latin expression: "hence, it is manifest that it was fitting [*conveniens*] that God should become incarnate" (*ST* III, q. a. 1). Nonetheless, it is still true that *the* reason for the Incarnation given by Aquinas is due to man's sin: "Hence, since everywhere in the Sacred Scripture the sin of the first man is assigned as the reason of the Incarnation, it is more in accordance with this to say that the work of the Incarnation was ordained by God as a remedy for sin; so that, had sin not existed, the Incarnation would not have been" (*ST* III, q. 1, a. 3).

10. Nichols, *Romance and System*, 366–68. See also ibid., 337–38. Scheeben writes: "And so the Incarnation could have taken place without man's sin; there is no reason why it could not have occurred on this supposition, since its very highest goal, *the infinite glory of God*, could have been attained" (Scheeben, *The Mysteries of Christianity*, 423, emphasis added). "Und so hätte die Inkarnation auch stattfinden können ohne Sünde der Menschen; sie hätte um so mehr stattfinden können, da in diesem Falle gerade ihr

at home in the Greek Fathers.[11] Similarly, on the issue of predestination, Scheeben very clearly stands in the Jesuit tradition, not the strict Thomist.[12] These examples show forth Scheeben's uniqueness and constitute the reason why his thought can often build bridges between various theological traditions.

Aidan Nichols describes the fruit of this hermeneutic as it is borne out in Scheeben's masterpiece, *The Mysteries of Christianity*, this way: "The outcome in *Die Mysterien* [is] . . . a patristically inspired mystery theology of the Trinitarian enfolding of human life."[13] For this reason, Scheeben is esteemed not only by Neoscholastic representatives of the

---

höchster Zweck, die unendliche Verherrlichung Gottes, hätte erreicht werden können" (Scheeben, *Die Mysterien des Christentums*, 350).

11. See Athanasius, *On the Incarnation*, ch. 8 where he states: "He, indeed, assumed humanity that we might become God" (93).

12. Nichols, *Romance and System*, 420–21. For example, Scheeben sees the "infallibility" of predestination as flowing from God's *foreknowledge*—not His Will—as St. Thomas teaches. Scheeben writes: "The infallibility of particular predestination [as opposed to God's universal salvific Will] consists in the fact that God infallibly foresees the result of the efficacy of universal salvation, which in itself is unfailing. The infallibility that corresponds to God's love and faithfulness is not necessarily rooted in a special preference of God for the effectively predestined; rather it flows *ipso facto* from His universal salvific will under the prevision of human cooperation" (Scheeben, *The Mysteries of Christianity*, 709): "Die Unfehlbarkeit der besondern Prädestination als solcher liegt nur darin, daß Gott die Wirkung der an sich unfehlbaren Kraft der allgemeinen unfehlbar voraussieht. Die der Liebe und Treue Gottes entsprechende Unfehlbarkeit derselben wurzelt nicht notwendig in einer speziellen Zuneigung Gottes zu den effectiv Prädestinierten; sie fließt vielmehr 'ipso facto' unter Voraussicht der menschlichen Mitwirkung aus dem allgemeinen Heils willen" (Scheeben, *Die Mysterien des Christentums*, 595). A few pages later, Scheeben tells us that "effective predestination involves God's prevision [foreknowledge] of man's free cooperation" (Scheeben, *The Mysteries of Christianity*, 711): "effektive Prädestation die Präszienz der freien Mitwirkung des Menschen involviert" (ibid., 596). Aquinas, on the contrary, holds that God's Will must contain the ultimate reason for the predestination of one man over another, as the Angelic Doctor writes here: "The number of the predestined is certain . . . not only by reason of His knowledge . . . but by reason of His deliberate choice and determination" (*ST* I, q. 23, a. 7). Further, what is known as the "principle of predilection" in Aquinas is the principle that states that one man is better than another—*not* because of one man's consent and cooperation with grace—but because God *loved* the one more than the other; that is, God's love is the *cause* of goodness in things, including individual persons. Aquinas writes: "For since God's love is the cause of goodness in things . . . no one thing would be better than another, if God did not will greater good for one than for another" (*ST* I, q. 20, a. 3).

13. Nichols, *Romance and System*, 78.

pure-nature tradition, but also by prominent *Ressourcement* thinkers of the twentieth century:

> The sympathetic citation of his work by twentieth century theologians as different as Hans Urs von Balthasar, a child of the so-called "new theology" of the 1940s and 50s, and Réginald Garrigou-Lagrange, champion, in the years immediately preceding the Second Vatican Council, of "strict observance" Thomism, attests to his *mediating* role.[14]

Making much the same point, Herman-Emiel Mertens seeks to set Scheeben apart, as unique against the general backdrop of Neoscholasticism:

> Semi-rationalism was quite out of keeping with the doctrine of grace proposed by Matthias Scheeben (1835–1888), perhaps the greatest Scholastic theologian of the nineteenth century and a thinker whose influence lasted into the twentieth. Though he had been formed by the Roman school . . . he went his own way particularly in the stress he laid on the supernatural character of the mysteries of faith which are to be clarified from within.[15]

Though having much in common with Neoscholasticism on the surface, the following passage is indicative of Scheeben's surprising kinship with de Lubac:

> Who can fail to perceive . . . that the doctrine of supernature, which is an elevation of human nature above its own level, clarifies and specifies the transcendence of Christian morality over all philosophical, rational, and rationalistic morality. . . .

---

14. Ibid., 19, emphasis added. Let us note that Feingold also cites Scheeben approvingly (Feingold, *Natural Desire to See God*, 118–19).

15. Mertens, "Nature and Grace," 249. Nichols writes: "Despite the idiom of the two worlds, one superimposed on the other, Scheeben's *principal* organizing metaphor for the nature/grace relation is very different. It is drawn not from architecture but from marriage. It is nuptiality. Yes, he makes a sharp ontological distinction between nature and grace. But he treats nature and grace as intimately conjoined in a matrimonial bond, co-inhabiting, according to the divine covenant, in a connubial relationship, inter-penetrating in life and love. Scheeben is not only a theologian of the difference between the natural and the supernatural, he is *the* theologian of their *connubium* as well" (Nichols, *Romance and System*, 289, Nichols' italics). Elsewhere Nichols, writes: "Scheeben's conviction . . . [is that] the sharp distinction of nature and supernature . . . [enables one] to reunify them in the spiritual marriage God has arranged for them" (ibid., 63). Also: "The absolute distinction between the orders [of nature and grace] serves to underscore the marvel of their intimate inter-connection" (ibid., 74).

Philosophical ethics, in the sense of a system set up in opposition
and defiance against theological morality, is unquestionably not a
true and genuine morality. *For in the present order purely natural
relationships do not exist alone and apart, and therefore cannot be
made to prevail in isolated self-sufficiency.*[16]

It is no doubt on account of such sentiments that Scheeben receives
approbation from prominent twentieth-century *Ressourcement* thinkers; and let us note that these sentiments occur with great frequency in
his thought, as seen again here:

How poverty-stricken and mean Christian morality appears
when it is regarded merely as the morality of man (that is, the
ethics based on man's natural moral dignity as found in his reason and free will) *rather than as the morality of the sons of God!.*
. . . To grasp the truth that we are really Christ's brothers, we
must go into the question of our conformity with Him in His
divine no less than in His human nature. And grace may not be
regarded merely as a corroborating factor in moral life; it must
be apprehended and presented as the new foundation of that life,
pertaining to a higher order. *Then we shall develop a true moral
theology, as distinct from a moral philosophy.* Then we shall be

16. Scheeben, *Nature and Grace*, 275, emphasis added; "Wer erkennt nicht. . .daß
gerade durch die Lehre von der Übernatur, einer Erhebung der menschlichen Natur
über sich selbst, die eigentümliche Erhabenheit der christlichen Moral über alle auch
sonst noch so durchgebildete philosophische, rationelle . . . und rationalistische Moral.
. . . Freilich ist die philosophische Moral, wie sie sich im Gegensatze und zum Trotze
gegen die theologische geltend machen will, keine wahre und echte Moral. Aber sie
ist dies nur deshalb nicht, weil gegenwärtig die rein natürlichen Verhältnisse nicht
allein und getrennt bestehen, folglich auch nicht als einzig und absolut bestehend
geltend gemacht werden können; nicht aber deshalb, weil diese Verhältnisse in sich
falsch oder fingiert wären" (Scheeben, *Natur und Gnade*, 164–65). Consider also
this statement: "To buttress belief in Christian truth and to defend it, they [Christian
apologists] desired to resolve it into a rational science, to demonstrate articles of faith
by arguments drawn from reason, and so to reshape them that nothing would remain
of the obscure, the incomprehensible, the impenetrable. They did not realize that by
such a procedure they were betraying Christianity into the hands of her enemies and
wresting the fairest jewel from her crown" (Scheeben, *The Mysteries of Christianity*,
4); "Um den Glauben an die christlichen Wahrheiten zu stützen und zu verteidigen,
wollten sie ihn in Vernunftwissenschaft auflösen, die Glaubenslehren durch Vernunft-
gründe beweisen und sie so zustutzen, daß des Dunkeln, Unbegreiflichen und durch
ein solches Verfahren das Christentum an seine Feinde verrieten und den schönsten
Edelstein aus seiner Krone herausrissen" (Scheeben, *Die Mysterien des Christentums*, 1).
Scheeben's comments here could have been made by de Lubac in regards to his teaching
on fundamental theology, over against the customary procedure of Neoscholastic
apologetics.

able to preach from the pulpit a morality that shares in the excellence of dogmatic theology, a morality *rooted in faith, grace, and the mysteries of Christianity.*[17]

On the other hand, Scheeben and de Lubac diverge most profoundly when it comes to their respective emphasis (or lack thereof) upon the distinction of nature and grace. As Long pointed out previously, de Lubac's context in the 1940s led him to oppose what he saw as an exaggerated distinction between nature and grace; yet Scheeben, on the other hand, insists that *only* in light of this very distinction can the splendor of the nature-grace union truly shine through. Accordingly, he writes:

> In this relationship the sharp distinction between the two factors is preserved in unity, and the necessary independence is maintained in subordination. Indeed, *union* of both is based upon their very *difference*, and the subordination of the lower to the higher is shown to be the supreme elevation of the former.[18]

For Scheeben, as was the case for Long, it is the *loss* of this very distinction that has brought about the spiritual malaise of modernity, as

---

17. Scheeben, *Nature and Grace*, 343, emphasis added; "O wie arm, wie niedrig erscheint uns die christliche Moral, wenn man sie nur als die Moral des Menschen (auf seine natürliche moralische Würde, die in Vernunft und freiem Willen besteht, gegründete), nicht als die der Kinder Gottes betrachtet! . . . .Um zu begreifen, wie wir wahrhaft Brüder Christi seien, muß man auf die Gleichförmigkeit mit ihm in der göttlichen nicht weniger als in der menschlichen Natur eingehen. Und die Gnade darf nicht nur als ein unterstützendes Moment im moralischen Leben, sie muß als seine neue höhere Grundlage aufgefaßt und dargestellt werden. Dann gewinnen wir eine wahre Moraltheologie im Gegensatz zur Moralphilosophie. Dann können wir auf der Kanzel eine *dogmatische*, eine auf dem Glauben, der Gnade und den Geheimnissen des Christentums gegründete Moral predigen" (Scheeben, *Natur und Gnade*, 204, emphasis original).

18. Scheeben, *The Mysteries of Christianity*, 788, emphasis added; "In der Einheit den strengsten Unterschied, in der Unterordnung die notwendige Selbständigkeit beider Faktoren wahrt, ja die Vereinigung beider auf ihren Unterschied gründet und in der Unterordnung des Niederen unter das Höhere die höchste Erhebung des ersteren darstellt" (Scheeben, *Die Mysterien des Christentums*, 665). Similarly, he writes: "When grace is transformed into the light of glory, the union [between nature and grace] will become an indissoluble spiritual marriage, a *matrimonium spirituale ratum et consummatum.* The freedom of nature at the side of grace will cease, because it will be thoroughly pervaded by grace and taken up into grace" (Scheeben, *Nature and Grace*, 337); "Wenn die Gnade in das Licht der Herrlichkeit übergegangen ist, wird die Verbindung eine unauflösliche, ein, matrimonium spirituale ratum et consummatum. Die Freiheit der Natur neben der Gnade hört auf, weil sie ganz von ihr durch-drungen und eingenommen wird" Scheeben, *Natur und Gnade*, 200–201).

Scheeben states emphatically here: "The crisis [of rationalism and indif-
ferentism] . . . will not be settled until the supernatural order is frankly,
adequately, and radically distinguished from the natural order."[19] The
distinction between nature and grace is therefore absolutely essential, in
Scheeben's mind, for the purpose of preserving the supernatural character of the Christian faith—a point which of course brings him squarely
into accord with Feingold, Long, and the pure-nature tradition. And for
Scheeben, the supernatural character of Christianity especially stands in
need of vindication:

> My cherished aim is to bring out the supernatural character of
> the Christian economy of salvation in its full sublimity, beauty,
> and riches. The main task of our time, it seems to me, consists
> in propounding and emphasizing the supernatural quality of
> Christianity, for the benefit of both science and life. Theoretical
> as well as practical naturalism and rationalism, which seek to
> throttle and destroy all that is specifically Christian, must be
> resolutely and energetically repudiated.[20]

19. Scheeben, *Nature and Grace*, 13; "Die Krisis . . . wird man nie kommen, solange
man nicht unumwunden und konsequent allseitig und gründlich die übernatürliche
Ordnung von der natürlichen unterscheidet" (Scheeben, *Natur und Gnade*, 12).

20. Scheeben, *Nature and Grace*, xvii; "Vorzüglich soll dadurch erreicht werden, daß
die Übernatürlichkeit der christlichen Heilsordnung in ihrer ganzen Erhabenheit und
ihrem vollen Glanze und Reichtum hervortrete. Diese Hervorhebung und Entwicklung
des übernatürlichen Charakters des Christentums scheint uns eine Hauptaufgabe der
Zeit für Wissenschaft und Leben zu sein, um dem theoretischen und praktischen
Naturalismus und Rationalismus, der alles spezifisch Christliche zurückzudrängen und
aufzuheben sucht, entschieden und kräftig entgegenzutreten" (*Natur und Gnade*, 1).
Since the preservation of this supernatural character of grace, for Scheeben, requires a
sharp distinction of nature and grace—and thereby a strong sense of the coherence of
the natural order—one can find readily enough in Scheeben passages which illustrate
the very same extrinsicism which de Lubac so deplored in Neoscholastic thinkers,
as for example here: "On the created plane the natural is really distinct from the
supernatural, and is not necessarily connected with it. The supernatural is added to
nature as a new, higher reality, a reality that is neither included in nature, nor developed
from it, nor in any way postulated by it. . . . God exhibits two kingdoms . . . two worlds,
which are erected one on top of the other . . . one natural and the other supernatural"
(Scheeben, *The Mysteries of Christianity*, 202); "Der Kreatur hingegen ist das Natürliche
vom Übernatürlichen reell verschieden und auch nicht notwendig mit ihm verbunden;
das Übernatürliche tritt hier als eine neue, höhere Realität zur Natur hinzu, als eine
Realität, die weder in ihr eingeschlossen, noch aus ihr entwickelt, noch überhaupt
durch sie postuliert wird. Wie also Gott nur für unser Auge zwei Reiche darstellt,
ein sichtbares und ein geheimnisvolles: so finden wir in der Kreatur zwei wirklich
verschiedene Reiche, gleichsam zwei Welten, die übereinander aufgebaut sind, eine
sichtbare und eine unsichtbare, eine natürliche und eine übernatürliche, von denen

It is not hard to see here the general affinity between Scheeben and the pure-nature tradition; but no less important is his clear affinity at points with de Lubac and other *Ressourcement* thinkers. For now, we will turn to his teaching on nature and grace, drawing out his congruity with the pure-nature tradition. This will be the first phase in demonstrating Scheeben's ability to reconcile the contributions of both extrinsicism and intrinsicism.

Scheeben on Nature and Grace

For Scheeben, it is the *origin* of an action that indicates whether or not it is properly of the natural or supernatural order: if man is the sole cause of an action, then it is of the natural order; if the act requires the direct elevation by God, then it is of the supernatural order. Accordingly, he describes the coherence of the natural order this way:

> Although nature can pursue and attain its natural end only in consequence of divine destination and activity, God has placed the seed of its growth in nature itself; as long as it unfolds in its own sphere, the entire movement can be regarded as proceeding from nature.[21]

---

zwar auch die erste für die bloß natürliche Vernunft in ihren Tiefen unerschöpflich, die zweite aber geradezu in jeder Beziehung unerreichbar, unerforschlich und darum im absoluten Sinne geheimnisvoll ist" (Scheeben, *Die Mysterien des Christentums*, 168). One can readily find this sentiment in his work, *Nature and Grace*, 19–31. For this reason, Nichols is correct when he writes: "Right from his earliest work, *Natur und Gnade* of 1861, Scheeben has insisted on an extremely sharp distinction between . . . nature and grace. Indeed, were one looking for texts to illustrate what early twentieth-century critics of neo-Scholasticism called 'extrinsicism' and [what] mid-twentieth-century theologians of the *nouvelle théologie* movement [called] 'a two-story model' of the nature/grace relationship, one could do a lot worse than quarry some texts from Scheeben's writings" (Nichols, *Romance and System*, 288).

21. Scheeben, *The Mysteries of Christianity*, 700; "Obgleich die Natur nur durch göttliche Bestimmung und Bewegung ihr natürliches Ziel erstreben und erreichen kann, so hat doch Gott den Keim ihrer Entwicklung in sie selbst hineingelegt, und solange sie sich auf ihrem Gebiet entwickelt, kann man die ganze Bewegung als von ihr ausgehend betrachten; sie braucht nicht von einer neuen, zu ihr hinzutretenden Kraft gehoben und getragen zu werden" (Scheeben, *Die Mysterien des Christentums*, 587). Let us note that this does not mean that man acquires natural goods *without* God's help, simply speaking. Scheeben is just as insistent as Long that it is a metaphysical mistake of the first order to suggest that the natural order is self-sufficient and autonomous. Rather, the natural order is at every moment dependent upon God's providence *in the natural order*. On the Thomistic account, God is the source of the teleological ordination

Analogously, he describes the supernatural order as follows:

> The specific character of supernatural activity is therefore best defined by the fact that it does not, like natural activity, proceed from nature. . . . Rather, supernatural activity proceeds from God immediately, not through a created medium, and therefore leads back to God immediately, not through a created medium; it unites us with God in His very divinity.[22]

As we have noted, the very notion of the word "supernatural" is itself a relative term: for Scheeben, it ultimately refers to an act which is *natural* to God alone, but in which man can share by way of graced participation and divine elevation. Such an act on the part of the creature constitutes a supernatural act because it transcends the powers of its nature, simply speaking. For this reason, Scheeben states:

> The supernatural, as understood in Christianity, does not mean precisely the superiority of one created nature as compared with another; rather it means the elevation of a nature above the natural limits of created existence to participation in the divine nature.[23]

---

and existence of the natural order. Accordingly, while on the one hand, Scheeben does write that: "[The] help needed by pure nature is neither supernatural revelation nor supernatural grace," this does not imply that the natural order has *no* need of divine providence (*Nature and Grace*, 91); "Diese Aushilfe, welche die reine Natur notwendig hat, ist näher weder übernatürliche Offenbarung noch übernatürliche Gnade" (Scheeben, *Natur und Gnade*, 56).

22. Scheeben, *Nature and Grace*, 230; "Der spezifische Charakter der übernatürlichen Tätigkeit wird also vorzüglich dadurch bestimmt, daß sie nicht wie die natürliche von der Natur ausgeht, darum auch wieder zunächst auf dieselbe zurückgeht, und nur durch sie sich zu dem Wesen erhebt, von dem die Natur selbst abhängt; sondern daß sie vielmehr unmittelbar, nicht durch das geschaffene Wesen, von Gott ausgeht, darum auch unmittelbar, nicht durch ein geschaffenes Wesen, auf ihn zurückgeht und so unmittelbar und nach der Eigentümlichkeit seiner Gottheit sich mit ihm vereinigt" (Scheeben, *Natur und Gnade*, 138).

23. Scheeben, *The Mysteries of Christianity*, 238; "Das Übernatürliche im Christentum ist nicht so sehr die Erhabenheit einer geschaffenen Natur über die andere, als die Erhebung derselben über die natürlichen Schranken des geschöpflichen Daseins zur Teilnahme an der göttlichen Natur" (Scheeben, *Die Mysterien des Christentums*, 198). Similarly: "[The supernatural] is, in a word, an activity by which God elevates the creature above its own nature and makes it participate in His nature" (Scheeben, *The Mysteries of Christianity*, 205); "wodurch er mit einem Worte die Kreatur über ihre eigene Natur erhebt und der seinigen teilhaft macht" (Scheeben, *Die Mysterien des Christentums*, 172). Hence, the supernatural life of faith, hope, and charity is supernatural for the following reason: "the special way and manner in which they

[these three theological virtues] grasp their supernatural object and rest in it [thus] making it clear [that] they are essentially raised above nature and natural acts and entail a participation in divine life" (Scheeben, *Handbuch der Katholischen Dogmatik*, 339); "Und in der Tat läßt sich bei ihnen nicht bloß aus dem übernatürlichen Werte, den sie haben sollen, auf ihren übernatürlichen Gehalt schließen, sondern auch unmittelbar aus der besonderen Art und Weise, wie sie ihr übernatürliches Objekt erfassen und in ihm ruhen, klarmachen, daß sie über die Natur und die natürlichen Akte wesentlich erhaben sind und eine Teilnahme am göttlichen Leben enthalten." I would like to thank my colleague in philosophy, Dr. Jamie Spiering, for her help in translating passages from Scheeben's *Dogmatik*. Let us note here that Scheeben describes the mystery of predestination along similar lines: "In Christian predestination . . . man is destined by God for an end which lies beyond the range of natural powers, which nature of itself can neither attain nor merit, and to which of itself it stands in no vital relationship. The divine love manifested in ordaining man to this end is truly lavish and gracious. No less imposing is the divine power that comes into play in communicating to nature an activity it could never attain by itself. That man may receive the power to strive after the supernatural end, he must mount above his nature. He must let himself be elevated, raised by God. Here the full force of the *transmissio in finem* is revealed; for man progresses toward his goal not by any power lying in his own nature, but is raised up and carried by a higher power that speeds him toward it. *Hence Christian predestination is essentially supernatural*"(Scheeben, *The Mysteries of Christianity*, 701, emphasis added); "Bei der christlichen Prädestination . . . der Menschen von Gott zu einem Ziel bestimmt, welches schlechtweg über die Trageweite der natürlichen Kräfte hinausliegt, welches die Natur aus sich weder erschweigen noch verdienen kann, zu dem sie aus sich in keinem lebendigen Verhältnis steht. Ebenso freigebig und gnädig, als sich bei dieser Bestimmung die göttliche Liebe offenbart, ebenso großartig muß sich hier die göttliche Macht geltend machen, indem sie der Natur eine Bewegung mitteilt, welche dieselbe aus sich in keiner Weise gewinnen könnte. Damit der Mensch nach jenem übernatürlichen Ziele zu streben vermöge, muß er über seine Natur emporsteigen; er muß sich von Gott erheben, emporziehen, gleichsam auf den Flügeln seiner Gnade sich seinem Ziel entgegentragen lassen. Hier tritt folglich die 'transmissio in finem' im vollsten Sinne ein, weil der Mensch nicht durch eine in seiner Natur liegende Kraft demselben entgegengeführt wird. Die christliche Prädestination ist also wesentlich übernatürlich . . ." (Scheeben, *Die Mysterien des Christentums*, 588). Scheeben understands the beatific vision in just this very light, as a beatitude which is *natural* to God alone: "This happiness is the same as that which God Himself enjoys, which belongs to Him alone by nature. . . . The immediate intuition of God in His very essence is in itself natural and proper only to the three persons who possess the divine nature" (Scheeben, *The Mysteries of Christianity*, 662, 659, respectively): "Es ist dieselbe Seligkeit, die Gott selbst genießt, die von Natur ihm allein zukommt, und die deshalb nur denjenigen zum Mitbesitze zufallen kann, welche Gott seiner eignenen Würde und Natur teilhaft gemacht und aus dem Zustand der Knechtschaft heraus in seine Familie hineingezogen hat. . . . Die unmittelbare Anschauung Gottes in seinem eigenen Wesen ist an sich bloß den Inhabern der göttlichen Lichtes, in dem allein das göttlichen Natur natürlich und eigentümlich" (Scheeben, *Die Mysteriern des Christentums*, 551, 549, respectively). And similarly: "This is the love which truly loves God above all things in the Christian sense, that is, which not only esteems God as superior to all creation,

Since the supernatural is relative to the natural, the preservation of the supernatural character of grace requires a conceptual grasp of the integral coherence of the natural order, as distinct from grace. As we have seen, this point is crucial for the pure-nature tradition, and Scheeben likewise echoes this emphasis in the following:

> The treatment of those doctrines of Christianity which are really mysteries in the sense explained cannot be fruitful and successful *unless we clearly determine and keep before our eyes the position of reason and its natural objects* with respect to these suprarational and supernatural objects. If this is not done, there is a proximate danger of confusing the higher objects with the lower, of drawing the higher down within the orbit of reason, and of treating them in the same manner as the lower.[24]

---

with whom no other good can be compared, in the way that even nature can love Him, *but which rises to His level*, embraces Him ardently with a divine strength surpassing all created force, and clasps Him so closely that no creature can separate it from Him (Rom., ch. 8)" (Scheeben, *Nature and Grace*, 267, emphasis added): "Darum ist sie auch die Liebe, welche wahrhaft Gott über alles liebt in christlichem Sinne, d. h. die Gott nicht nur hochachtet als den über alles Geschaffene Erhabenen, dem kein anderes Gut gleichzustellen ist, wie auch die Natur es vermag, sondern die sich auch zu seiner Höhe erhebt, ihn auch auf das innigste mit einer alles Geschaffene übersteigenden göttlichen Kraft umfängt und ihn so fest umschlossen hält, daß keine Kreatur sie davon trennen kann (Rom 8)" (Scheeben, *Natur und Gnade*, 160).

24. Scheeben, *The Mysteries of Christianity*, 18, emphasis added; "Die Behandlung derjenigen Lehren des Christentums, die wirklich Geheimnisse in dem erklärten Sinne sind, kann nicht fruchtbar und gedeihlich werden, wenn man nicht genau die Stellung fixiert und im Auge behält, in der die Vernunft und die natürlichen Objekte zu diesen übervernünftigen und übernatürlichen Objekten stehen. Wo das nicht geschieht, liegt die Gefahr nahe, die höheren Objekte mit den niederen zu vermengen, sie ganz in den Gesichtskreis der Vernunft herabzuziehen und auf gleiche Weise mit den übrigen zu behandeln" (Scheeben, *Die Mysterien des Christentums*, 17–18). Scheeben gives a summary definition of "Christian mystery" as follows: "a truth communicated to us by Christian revelation, a truth to which we cannot attain by our unaided reason, and which, even after we have attained to it by faith, we cannot adequately represent with our rational concepts" (ibid., 13): "Das christliche Mysterrium ist eine durch die christliche Offenbarung uns kundgewordene Wahrheit, die wir mit der bloßen Vernunft nicht erreichen und, nachdem wir sie durch den Glauben erreicht, mit den Begrifffen unserer Vernunft nicht ausmessen können" (Scheeben, *Die Mysterien des Christentums*, 11). The natural order, then, is integral in its own right: "Without doubt Christianity comprises many truths knowable by reason. To such belongs all that concerns the nature of man, man's utter dependence on God, and the existence of this personal God Himself (apart from the precision of His personality in the Trinity). These truths constitute a *definite system in themselves*" (Scheeben, *The Mysteries of Christianity*, 14–15, emphasis added): "Ohne Zweifel enthält das Christentum viele Wahrheiten, die auch durch die Vernunft erkennbar sind; dahin gehört alles, was sich auf die Natur des Menschen, seine absolute

In Scheeben's mind, neglecting the coherence of the natural order risks distorting the mysteries of faith, and so reminiscent of Long's treatment earlier, Scheeben likewise states:

> Thus, for instance, the mystery of the Trinity can neither be revealed nor be grasped without a further elucidation of God's nature; nor can we form an idea of the compass and meaning of the supernatural elevation of human nature, as effected by grace and glory, or by the hypostatic union, *unless we take into account human nature itself and its natural condition.*[25]

For Scheeben's part, any attempt to extol the supernatural order of grace at the *expense* of the natural order only serves to undermine the supernatural transcendence of grace:

> Our intention is not to extol grace at the expense of nature. Rather, we shall do justice to nature and give it its due; thereby we shall also do justice to grace and more easily and surely vindicate for it its rightful position of preeminence. *Both endeavors require of us a clear, definite, and sharply delineated philosophical notion of nature.*[26]

Without a doubt, this sentiment aligns him well with the pure-nature tradition. At this point, we will now turn to demonstrate his agreement with the pure-nature tradition more specifically, in terms of the basic issues treated earlier; we will begin with obediential potency.

Abhängigkeit von Gott und das Dasein dieses perönlichen Gottes selbst (abgesehen von der Spezifikation seiner Persönlichkeit in der Trinität) bezieht. Diese Wahrheiten bilden ein gewisses System für sich" (Scheeben, *Die Mysterien des Christentums*, 13).

25. Scheeben, *The Mysteries of Christianity*, 741, emphasis added: "So z. B. läßt sich das Mysterium der Trinität ohne eine nähere Beleuchtung der Natur Gottes weder offenbaren noch auffassen; ebensowenig kann man sich einen Begriff von dem Umfange und der Bedeutung der übernatürlichen Erhebung der menschlichen Natur, wie sie durch die Gnade und Glorie sowie durch die hypostatische Union geschieht, bilden, wenn d as Wesen und die natürliche Beschaffenheit der menschlichen Natur nicht mit in Betracht gezogen wird" (Scheeben, *Die Mysterien des Christentums*, 624).

26. Scheeben, *Nature and Grace*, 50 emphasis added: "Unsere Absicht ist es nun, nicht auf Kosten der Natur die Gnade zu erheben, sondern eben dadurch, daß wir der Natur gerecht werden und ihr das zugestehen, was ihr gebührt, gegen die Gnade erst wahrhaft gerecht zu werden und derselben ihren eigentümlichen und erhabenen Vorrang desto leichter und sicherer zu vindizieren. Beides hängt einfach davon ab, daß wir uns einen klaren, bestimmten und scharf abgegrenzten philosophischen Begriff von der Natur bilden" (Scheeben, *Natur und Gnade*, 31).

Obediential Potency

Similar to Feingold and Long (who of course were following the likes of Cajetan), Scheeben, too, describes man's capacity for the beatific vision in terms of a specific obediential potency, as can be seen here:

> Since not all created natures are capable of receiving the same effect of God, it remains true that the particular *potentia oboedientialis* with which we are concerned here, is a *specific privilege of spiritual nature as such*, and coincides with the capacity for a supernatural similitude of God to be brought forth out of the simple image of God.[27]

As we have seen, while grace is supernatural and brings about a supernatural perfection in man, this perfection nonetheless remains a *human* perfection insofar as the supernatural elevation is still positively founded upon man's integral nature and is perfective of his nature. The following statement from Scheeben bears this out and implicitly assumes the framework of *specific* obediential potency:

> Grace alone, coming as it does to man from outside, cannot give him the first capacity for the spiritual life or for union with God. It necessarily presupposes that such a capacity is already found in man's nature. *It is a higher, more perfect form that is not acquired by an internal development but comes to the natural power and disposition from outside.* The subject must be essentially spiritual, intellectual, and capable of love, before it can receive a higher spirituality, intelligence, and love.[28]

27. Scheeben, *Handbuch der Katholischen Dogmatik*, III/IV, 441, emphasis added: "Aber nicht alle geschaffene Naturen auch derselben Einwirkung Gottes fähig sind, so ist und bleibt diejenige potentia oboedientialis, von welcher hier die Rede, ein spezifischer Vorzug der geistigen Naturen als solchen und deckt sich hier mit der Fähigkeit, aus einem einfachen Bilde Gottes zum übernatürlichen Gleichnis Gottes zu werden."

28. Scheeben, *Nature and Grace*, 322, emphasis added: "Die Gnade allein, als von außen zum Wesen hinzutretend, kann ihm nicht die erste Anlage zum geistigen Leben, noch auch zur Verbindung mit Gott geben; sie setzt notwendig schon eine solche Anlage als im Wesen des Menschen begründet voraus; sie ist eine höhere, vollkommenere, nicht durch innere Entwicklung gewonnene, sondern von außen hinzugetretene Bestimmung (forma) der natürlichen Kraft und Anlage. Das Subjekt muß seinem Wesen nach schon geistig, intellektuell und der Liebe fähig sein, um eine höhere Geistigkeit, Intellektualität und Liebe empfangen zu können" (Scheeben, *Natur und Gnade*, 191). Regarding natural love of God, Scheeben writes: "The creature as such can love God only with the love of a stranger or of a handmaid [i.e., natural love]. But when the creature loves God with the love of a bride or of a son [i.e., charity], its act is

We turn next to Scheeben's teaching on man's natural desire, where we will witness his further agreement with the pure-nature tradition.

Natural Desire

Let us recall that the "problem," so to speak, with regard to man's natural desire stems from the fact that man seems to have an inexorable desire for his final end of supernatural happiness in the beatific vision. The problem, then, is whether or not this desire for the beatific vision can be described as a "natural" desire—since if such is the case, it would seem that the gratuity of grace would thereby be forfeited.

With this in mind, Scheeben takes up the following passages from St. Augustine and St. Thomas, the first of which is taken from the *Confessions*: "The thought of you stirs him [man] so deeply that he cannot be content unless he praises you, because you made us for yourself and our heart finds no peace until it rests in you."[29] Such a statement from St. Augustine seems to imply that beatitude, simply speaking, can only be found in a supernatural union with God—necessarily precluding the possibility of a purely natural beatitude (this, of course, would be de Lubac's position). The following from St. Thomas (which Scheeben also takes up) seems to echo this same sentiment: "Final and perfect happiness can consist in nothing else than the vision of the Divine Essence."[30]

However, Scheeben's interpretation of these and like texts is exactly the same as that of the pure-nature tradition: namely, St. Augustine and St. Thomas here aim to assert only the *possibility* and fittingness of man's elevation to the beatific vision; that is, they do not intend to suggest that

---

supremely supernatural, and its love is closely linked and exalted to the supernatural love which God has for the creature, and by which He unites Himself to the creature in grace" (Scheeben, *The Mysteries of Christianity*, 639); "Denn die bräutliche resp. kindliche Liebe der Kreatur zu Gott, welchen dieselbe aus sich nur als eine Fremde oder als eine Magd zu lieben vermag, erscheint einesteils schon in sich selbst als ein höchst übernatürlicher Akt und steht anderseits in der innigsten Beziehung und Verwandtschaft mit der übernatürlichen Liebe Gottes zur Kreatur, durch welche er sich mit derselben in der Gnade vereinigt" (Scheeben, *Die Mysterien des Christentums*, 529). Similarly: "Natural love unites one with God only in the measure of the creature's proximity to the Creator" (Scheeben, *Nature and Grace*, 265); "Darum vereinigt die Liebe der Natur mit Gott nur nach dem Maße, in dem das Geschöpf seinem Schöpfer nahesteht" (Scheeben, *Natur und Gnade*, 159).

29. Augustine, *Confessions*, Bk. I, ch. 1.

30. *ST* I-IIae, q. 3, a. 8.

the beatific vision is man's *only* possible end. Accordingly, Scheeben writes:

> This point has to be considered in the inquiry whether the be-atific vision of God, which is proper for His children, must be the unique end and natural consummation of the created spirit. The occasion of this question confronts the history of dogma with the difficulty that the holy Fathers, especially St. Augustine, and even St. Thomas, who is noted for his accuracy, seem to con-nect the destiny for the beatific vision directly with the rational, intellectual nature of the soul. *However, they do not intend to as-sign reasons why the soul must have received such a destiny;* their purpose is to show why spiritual creatures *could* receive it. And if they say that that end is the unique last end of man, the reason is that it alone actually is the highest and last end which man can attain, [whereas] the *natural end* is much lower and, in a certain sense, is but a first step toward it.[31]

Thus, in agreement with the pure-nature tradition, Scheeben ex-plains that a "natural" desire for the beatific vision must be viewed as a mere "wish" (cf. *velleitas*)—the non-fulfillment of which does *not* entail suffering (as opposed to what would be the case regarding the non-fulfillment of a *natural* or *innate* desire).[32] Accordingly, drawing from Aristotle, a "wish" here refers to something which one may desire—but

31. Scheeben, *Nature and Grace*, 57 emphasis added; "Dieser Punkt ist namentlich in Betracht zu ziehen bei der Untersuchung, ob die 'visio beatifica', die beseligende Anschauung Gottes, die seinen Kindern eigentümlich ist, des geschaffenen Geistes einziges Ziel und natürliche Vollendung sein müsse oder nicht. Die Veranlassung dazu bietet die dogmenhistorische Schwierigkeit, daß die heiligen Väter, vorzüglich der heilige Augustinus, und selbst der doch so genaue heilige Thomas die Bestimmung zu jener Anschauung unmittelbar zu verbinden scheinen mit der vernünftigen, intellektuellen Natur des Geistes. Sie wollen aber nicht den Grund angeben, warum der Geist jene Bestimmung habe erhalten *müssen*, sondern warum er sie habe erhalten *können*. Und wenn sie jenes Ziel das einzige *letzte* Ziel des Menschen nennen, geschieht es nur darum, weil es wirklich allein das höchste und letzte ist, zu dem der Mensch gelangen kann, während das natürliche Ziel viel tiefer liegt und gewissermaßen nur eine Vorstufe zu jenem bildet" (Scheeben, *Natur und Gnade*, 36, emphases original).

32. Likewise, Feingold writes: "A conditional natural desire may be frustrated. . . . A conditional [natural desire]—a wish (*velleitas*)—nothing prohibits a natural desire of this kind from being 'in vain' in all men" (Feingold, *Natural Desire to See God*, 272). "Conditional" desires and "wish" also correspond to "elicited" desires in the following passage from Feingold: "Innate appetite is limited to what is proportionate to the nature of the faculty, and is incapable of growth or self-transcendence, whereas elicited natural desire, based on knowledge, can aspire to disproportionate objects, transcending the limits of human nature" (ibid., 26).

which is beyond the powers of one's own agency—with the result that its non-fulfillment does not necessitate suffering. Aristotle writes: "[We] wish for impossible things—for immortality, for instance. . . . We wish [not only for results we can achieve], but also for results that are [possible, but] not achievable through our own agency."[33] In this light, the non-fulfillment of a wish *can* be in vain, without entailing any frustration or suffering on the part of the creature—and by implication, therefore, there is no injustice on the part of God if He leaves a mere "wish" unfulfilled.[34]

33. Aristotle, *Nicomachean Ethics*, Bk. III, ch. 2 (1111b 22–24), brackets original; "καὶ ἡ βούλησίς ἐστι καὶ περὶ τὰ μηδαμῶς δι' αὐτοῦ πραχθέντα ἄν." One can see here how in the pure-nature framework, the category of "wish" would be seen to indicate a desire which is beyond the order of man's nature, and which therefore does not result in suffereing, if left unfulfilled. Commenting on the above passage from Aristotle, Aquinas states: "Wishing designates an act of this power [rational appetite] related to good *absolutely*. But choice designates an act of the same power related to good according as it belongs to an act by which we are ordered to some good" (Aquinas, *Commentary on Aristotle's Nicomachean Ethics*, bk. III, Lect. V, emphasis added).

34. Similarly and certainly related to the issue at hand, when Aristotle discusses the interplay of chance and purpose in the second book of his *Physics*, he understands chance as referring to that which comes about accidentally when something *else* is intended; in his discussion here, he is arguing that chance presupposes teleology. For our purposes, however, he refers to a chance happening as one which is "in vain," since the intended teleology of the natural order did not come about. The import for our discussion is this: nature is *not* ordered to what is "in vain," which means that man's natural desire cannot be inherently ordered to what might be in vain—as would be the case in de Lubac's analysis. Aristotle writes: "Hence it is clear that events which belong to the general class of things that may come to pass for the sake of something, when they come to pass not for the sake of what actually results . . . may be described by the phrase 'from spontaneity' [i.e., chance]. These spontaneous events are said to be from [luck] if they have the further characteristics of being the objects of choice and happening to agents capable of choice. This is indicated by the phrase 'in vain', which is used when one thing which is for the sake of another, does not result in it. . . . *This implies that what is naturally for the sake of an end is in vain, when it does not effect the end for the sake of which it was the natural means.* . . . Thus the spontaneous is even according to its derivation the case in which the thing itself happens in vain" (Aristotle, *Physics* bk. II, ch. 6, (197b 18–30), cited in *The Complete Works of Aristotle*, 337, emphasis added). In Greek: "ὥστε φανερὸν ὅτι ἐν τοῖς ἁπλῶς ἕνεκά του γιγνομένοις ὅταν μὴ τοῦ συμβάντος ἕνεκα γένηται ὧν ἔξω τὸ αἴτιον, τότε ἀπὸ τοῦ αὐτομάτου λέγομεν· ἀπὸ τύχης δέ, τούτων ὅσα ἀπὸ τοῦ αὐτομάτου γίγνεται τῶν προαιρετῶν τοῖς ἔχουσι προαίρεσιν. σημεῖον δὲ τὸ μάτην, ὅτι λέγεται ὅταν μὴ γένηται τὸ ἕνεκά ἄλλου ἐκείου ἕνεκα, οἷον εἰ τὸ βαδίσαι λαπάξεως ἕνεκά ἐστιν, εἰ δὲ μὴ ἐγένετο βαδίσαντι, μάτην, τὸ πεφυκὸς ἄλλου ἕνεκα, ὅταν μὴ περαίνῃ ἐκεῖνο οὗ ἕνεκα ἦν καὶ ἐπεφύκει, ἐπεὶ εἴ τις λούσασθαι φαίη μάτην ὅτι οὐκ ἐξέλιπεν ὁ ἥλιος, γελοῖος ἄν εἴη· οὐ γὰρ ἦν τοῦτο ἐκείου ἕνεκα. οὕτω δὴ τὸ αὐτοματον καὶ τὸ ὄνομα ὅταν αὐτὸ μάτην γένηται."

The non-fulfillment of a wish forms the backdrop of Feingold's critique of de Lubac, since as we have seen de Lubac argued that "essential
suffering" was the inevitable result if man failed to reach the beatific
vision as his final end. And so Feingold responds this way:

> Ultimately, de Lubac's thesis that the natural desire to see God is
> an absolute or unconditional desire has the effect of assimilating
> or identifying it with the natural desire for happiness in general.
> It is clear for St. Thomas that the natural desire for happiness in
> general is an absolute and innate desire, to which our will itself
> is determined by nature, and whose lack of realization obviously
> causes an essential suffering. *De Lubac's fundamental thesis con-
> sists in transferring these four qualities also to the natural desire to
> see God.*[35]

In agreement with the pure-nature tradition, Scheeben, too, describes man's desire for the beatific vision along these very lines:

> The desire [for the beatific vision] is not of such a nature that it
> necessarily requires satisfaction, or postulates the real existence
> of its object, thus presupposing the possibility of the object; this
> is against Catholic doctrine. If such a desire is assumed, it can be
> nothing else than the general *wish* of nature to be united with
> God as perfectly and intimately as possible. This longing exists.
> . . . Nothing is more agreeable to the natural bent and wishes of
> the rational creature than perfect knowledge and intuition of its
> Creator. But nothing more transcends the creature's natural pow-
> ers and destiny, and therefore nothing more surpasses all natural
> concepts than this very intuition, by which the creature is raised
> above itself. . . . Accordingly, if we choose to admit a natural long-
> ing for the beatific vision—*but only in the sense mentioned* [i.e.,
> as "wish"]—we must add that the object of the desire is an abso-
> lutely supernatural mystery, which natural reason, left to itself, is
> unable to conjecture.[36]

35. Feingold, *Natural Desire to See God*, 353, emphasis added.

36. Scheeben, *The Mysteries of Christianity*, 661–62, emphasis added; "Denn erstens
ist das Verlangen auf keinen Fall derart, daß es notwendig Befriedigung forderte, die
Verwirklichung seines Gegenstandes erheischte und darin die Möglichkeit desselben
voraussetzte: das widerspricht der katholischen Lehre. Wenn man ein solches
Verlangen annimmt, so kann es nichts anderes sein, als der allgemeine Wunsch der
Natur, so vollkommen als nur immer möglich und so innig als nur immer möglich
mit Gott verbunden zu werden. . . . Will man daher auch ein natürliches Verlangen
nach der 'visio beatifica'—aber auch nur in dem erwähnten Sinne—zugeben, so muß
man hinzufügen, daß hier der Gegenstand des Verlangens ein absolut übernatürliches

Let us now turn to what we have suggested all along is likely the most central concept in this debate, namely, the *debitum naturae*. As we will see, Scheeben once again expresses his agreement with the pure-nature tradition.

Debitum Naturae

Scheeben's acceptance of the *debitum naturae* is already implicit above, but we will make it explicit here. In the following, we have placed brackets throughout the passage in order to draw out the elements of his teaching witnessed so far, as well as to show how they lead to and imply the *debitum naturae*. Scheeben writes:

> [The] *elevation* of a faculty [cf., *obediential* potency] is not necessary to its perfection and does not pertain to its *due* development [cf. *debitum naturae*], which takes place within its own sphere. . . . They [e.g., Baius and Jansensius] confounded the *active* striving [natural potency or natural inclination] for a good that is involved in the power to procure it, with a sort of passive aspiration [i.e., a "wish"] that is nothing but a *receptivity* [cf., the obediential potency] for the good if it should be given. Only the former [active striving] can imply a *necessity* for reaching the good [cf., *debitum naturae*]; the latter [passive striving] implies only an indifferent capacity [cf., "wish"] which awaits the *free* decision of the giver and *is not the basis for any claim to the good that may be desired* [cf., *debitum naturae*].[37]

As we can see, for Scheeben, man's natural desire *does* constitute an "active striving," and this active striving, flowing from the ordination of the natural order, does indeed provide a basis for the creature's "claim" to a certain good (i.e., the *debitum naturae*). Accordingly, this "claim" ne-

---

Mysterium ist, von dem die Natur und die Vernunft aus sich nichts ahnen können" (Scheeben, *Die Mysterien des Christentums*, 550–51).

37. Scheeben, *Nature and Grace*, 58, emphases added; "Eine Erhebung der Kraft ist aber nicht eine *notwendige* Vervollkommnung derselben und gehört nicht zu der ihr eigentümlichen Entwicklung; diese findet nur in der ihr eigenen Sphäre statt. . . . Sie verwechselten das aktive *Streben* nach einem Gute, das mit der Kraft, dasselbe zu *bewirken*, verbunden ist, mit jenem, sozusagen passiven Streben, welches nichts ist als die Empfänglichkeit für das Gute, *wenn* es gegeben wird. Nur jenes kann offenbar eine *Notwendigkeit* in sich schließen, das Gute zu erreichen; dieses schließt nur eine indifferente Möglichkeit in sich, welche die freiwillige Entscheidung des Gebers erwartet und keinen Anspruch auf das etwa Gewünschte begründet" (Scheeben, *Natur und Gnade*, 36, emphasis original).

cessitates at least the possibility of its realization, a point which Scheeben makes even more explicitly here: "Man's *claim* to all the goods necessary for his natural happiness is sufficiently cared for by his nature and the natural providence of God."[38]

The notion of God's "natural providence" in this passage is simply another way of referring to the *debitum naturae*. Despite the utter gratuity of creation—once God has willed to create—He has simultaneously willed into existence an intelligible natural order, which can then be distinguished from the order of grace. It is this perspective which lies behind Scheeben's comments here:

> Nature is a principle of activity necessarily proceeding from the substance and essence of a being; it has a definite power and tendency by which it strives for a *definite end* and a definite development and perfection. . . . Each nature has assigned to it a development and perfection *proportionate* and *corresponding to its* [innate natural] *powers*.[39]

---

38. Scheeben, *The Mysteries of Christianity*, 340, emphasis added; "Der Anspruch des Menschen auf alle zu seiner natürlichen Seligkeit notwendigen Güter ist hinreichend durch seine Natur und die natürliche Vorsehung Gottes begründet" (Scheeben, *Die Mysterien des Christentums*, 282).

39. Scheeben, *Nature and Grace*, 50, emphasis added; "*Natur* ist der aus der Substanz und Wesenheit eines Wesens *an sich notwendig hervorgehende Lebensgrund, mit einer bestimmten Kraft und Tendenz, welche aus sich nach einem bestimmten Ziele und nach einer bestimmten Entwicklung und Vollendung strebt*. . . . Ferner, für jede Natur gibt es eine *bestimmte*, ihren Kräften angemessene und entsprechende *Entwicklung und Vollendung*" (Scheeben, *Natur und Gnade*, 32 emphasis original). Similarly, in summary fashion, he concludes: "In assigning a certain rank and destiny to His creature, God endows him with the power to live up to his position and to attain his destiny; and together with this power He infuses a tendency, a desire for their realization. . . . *All of this, of course, happens in the natural order quite otherwise than in the supernatural order*, because goodness and justice themselves are entirely different in the two cases. *The necessary power and inclination for the realization of the creature's natural position and destiny are contained in nature itself*" (Scheeben, *The Mysteries of Christianity*, 247, emphasis added): "Indem Gott seiner Kreatur eine gewisse Stellung und Bestimmung gibt, verleiht er derselben auch die Kraft, ihrer Stellung zu genügen, ihre Bestimmung zu erreichen, und mit der Kraft die Tendenz, das Streben, dieselbe zu betätigen; er bringt sie von seiner Seite in Einklang mit ihrere Stellung und Bestimmung. . . . Alles das geschieht aber natürlich in ganz anderer Weise in der natürlichen und der übernatürlichen Ordnung, weil die Güte und Gerechtigkeit selbst in den beiden Fällen von ganz anderer Art ist. Für die natürliche Stellung und Bestimmung der Kreatur liegt die notwendige Kraft und Tendenz in der Natur derselben" (Scheeben, *Die Mysterien des Christentums*, 206–7).

Although our next concept is again already implicit in the above, we will now turn directly to Scheeben's teaching on man's natural end. Here we will find some ambiguity in his thought, as he oscillates back and forth between the positions represented earlier by both Feingold and Long. The key question here, again, is whether or not—in addition to the hypothetical possibilty of a purely natural end—Scheeben also accepts the possibility of its concrete realization in the present divine economy. Though there is textual evidence supporting both views in Scheeben's writings, by the end of the chapter we will argue that the passages which share Long's view of the matter (hypothetical possibility, but no concrete possibility) better align with the internal logic of Scheeben's thought, and will therefore be privileged in our overall presentation and appropriation of his thought.

The Possibility of a Purely Natural End

First, let us observe that there is no question as to whether or not Scheeben affirms the hypothetical possibility and coherence of man's purely natural end; he assumes this possibility quite readily, as he states very clearly here:

> Rational creatures, with the nature they have, cannot improve indefinitely. Their progress lasts just so long as the development of their natural faculties will last. But since their natural faculties are finite, *the development of rational creatures must also have a determined and limited end.*[40]

Moreover, the following could be read as a summary charter for the logic of the pure-nature tradition:

40. Scheeben, *Glories of Divine Grace*, 46, emphasis added; "Selbst die vernünftigen Kreaturen können ihrer Natur nach sich nicht ins Unendliche vervolllkommnen; ihr Fortschritt dauert nur so lange als die Entwicklung ihrer natürlichen Kräfte, und da diese endlich sind, so muß auch ihre Entwicklung ein bestimmtes und begrenztes Ziel und Ende erreichen" (Scheeben, *Die Herrlichkeiten der Göttlichen Gnade*, 42). For him, this seems to be a settled question: "The Church necessarily supposes that there is a natural goal and end; for it teaches that the end now appointed for nature, consisting as it does in the beatific vision of God, is absolutely supernatural, and is to be communicated to us by a special grace. *And yet there must be a necessary end for nature*" (Scheeben, *Nature and Grace*, 93, emphasis added); "Daß es ein natürliches Ziel und Ende gebe, muß die Kirche notwendig voraussetzen, wenn sie lehrt, das der Natur jetzt in der seligen Anschauung Gottes bestimmte Ziel sei ein absolute übernatürliches, nur durch eine besondere Gnade uns zuteil" (Scheeben, *Natur und Gnade*, 58).

In addition to the supernatural order of human development established, revealed, and inaugurated by Christ, man has a natural
order, based on his nature. This would be the permanent order
destined for man if God had not decreed something better. . . .
*This means that a purely natural state would be possible, that is, a
state without any genuine supernatural elements.*[41]

41. Scheeben, *Nature and Grace*, 86–88, emphasis added; "Kurz, es gibt für den
Menschen eine von der übernatürlichen, durch Christus hergestellten, offenbarten und
eingeleiteten Ordnung seiner Entwicklung auch eine natürliche, die sich auf seine Natur
gründet. Diese Ordnung würde für den Menschen ohne weiteres an sich bestehen, wenn
Gott nicht etwas Höheres bestimmt hätte. . . . Damit ist es ausgesprochen, daß es *einen
reinen Naturzustand* geben könne, einen Zustand ohne alle eigentlich übernatürlichen
Elemente . . ." (Scheeben, *Natur und Gnade*, 53, emphasis original). Scheeben seeks
to distinguish *natural* post-mortem life from supernatural eternal life envisioned by
the Gospel in the following: "If we should entertain the idea that the mystery of faith
consists only in the fact that man's destiny in the future world is beyond the reach
of present experience, and that only the darkness of the grave veils it from our sight,
we would completely mistake its true nature. To the extent that man's state beyond
the grave is his *natural end* and pertains to his natural destiny, it cannot be entirely
impervious to reason. . . . That the soul is immortal, that it will continue its spiritual
life on the other side of death, and will enjoy a *happy*, peaceful repose in the *knowledge*
and *love* of God . . . these are simple philosophical truths which . . . pertain properly to
the sphere of sound reason" (*The Mysteries of Christianity*, 651–52, emphasis added):
"Wenn man das eigentliche Mysterium des Glaubens nur darin finden wollte, daß
das jenseitige Ziel des Menschen unserer diesseitigen Erfahrung entrückt ist, daß
die Finsternis des Grabes uns davon scheidet, würde man sein eigentliches Wesen
gänzlich verkennen. Sofern der Zustand des Menschen jenseits des Grabes dessen
natürliches Ziel ist, zu seiner natürlichen Bestimmung gehört, kann er der Vernunft
nicht gänzlich verborgen sein; der richtig geleiteten und ausgebildeten Vernunft muß
er mit hinreichender Sicherheit in ziemlich deutlichen Umrissen vor Augen treten. Daß
die Seele unsterblich ist, daß sie jenseits des Grabes ihr geistiges Leben fortsetzen und
in der Erkenntnis und Liebe Gottes eine selige, friedliche Ruhe genießen wird, oder,
falls sie in der Feindschaft Gottes aus dieser Welt geschieden, auch ewig im Unfrieden
mit Gott und sich selbst ihre Sünde büßen wird: das sind eigentlich keine Mysterien,
das sind einfache philosophische Wahrheiten, die zwar vielfach durch die Zerrüttung
der Vernunft verdunkelt warden können, aber doch recht eigentlich zur Sphäre der
gesunden Vernunft gehören" (Scheeben, *Die Mysterien des Christentums*, 541). Thus,
Scheeben distinguishes between two senses of "eternal life," one which corresponds
to (*natural*) everlasting life, and the other (*supernatural*) which corresponds to the
Christian participation in God's own eternal beatitude: "The eternal life we await is
not thus called in the Christian sense simply because it never comes to an end. That
would be the case even in natural beatitude. Rather it is called eternal life because it
is a participation in the absolutely eternal life of the eternal Godhead in which the
soul is immersed. Through the gift of supernature, the soul achieves supreme unity in
its supernatural life; it does not, like nature, merely direct its various activities to its
one end; when it is united with God in the state of perfection and sensible happiness,
it extends its activity to other objects through its immediate vision and love of God.

The more difficult question of course is whether or not this coherent possibility of a purely natural end can be realized in the present economy, especially given the reality of sin and man's ordination by divine providence to the beatific vision.

The Possibility of a Purely Natural End in this Economy

At places Scheeben seems to accept the possibility of a purely natural end in this economy; but in other places he seems to deny this very proposition. Indeed, as we mentioned above, there is a clear tension and ambivalence in Scheeben's thought on this matter, and it appears that he never fully made up his mind. Let us begin by considering the following passage where at first glance Scheeben seems as if he were going to *deny* the possibility of man's realization of a purely natural end in the present economy, but then he turns surprisingly to the contrary by the end of the passage. He writes:

> In consequence of the privation of sanctity which was rejected by the racial guilt [i.e., original sin], he [man] finds himself in a relationship to God and His providence other than that of the purely natural man, who would have been originally created without a supernatural destiny. He [post-lapsarian man] has forfeited the true destiny actually assigned to him by God. [However] *we are not obliged to assume—and I even believe that we may not assume it—that God would entirely deny him the assistance absolutely necessary for the attainment of his natural end . . .*[42]

The blessed in heaven know all things in and through God; even on earth the saints love things in and through God, rather than because of the natural goodness in them" (Scheeben, *Nature and Grace*, 195–96 n. 7): "Das ewige Leben, das wir erwarten, heißt im christlichen Sinne nicht eben deshalb ewiges Leben, weil es überhaupt nicht aufhört. Dies würde auch in der natürlichen Seligkeit der Fall sein. Es heißt so vielmehr, weil es eine Teilnahme ist an dem absolut ewigen Leben der ewigen Gottheit, in die sich der Geist ganz versenkt. So erlangt die Seele durch die Übernatur auch die höchste Einheit in ihrem übernatürlichen Leben, da sie nicht nur alle verschiedenen Tätigkeiten auf ihr eines Ziel zurückführt wie die Natur, sondern im Zustande der Vollkommenheit und sinnlichen Seligkeit nur aus und in der Verbindung mit der göttlichen Einheit durch deren unmittelbare Anschauung und Liebe ihre Tätigkeit auf andere Gegenstände erstreckt. Denn die Seligen erkennen alles in und aus und durch Gott, wie die Heiligen die Dinge nicht so sehr wegen ihrer eigenen natürlichen Güte, als nur in und durch Gott lieben" (Scheeben, *Natur und Gnade*, 117 n. 6).

42. Scheeben, *The Mysteries of Christianity*, 306, emphasis added; "Wohl befindet er sich infolge der durch die Geschlechtsschuld verscherzten Heiligkeit in einem andern Verhältnis zu Gott und seiner Vorsehung als der bloße Naturmensch, der ursprünglich

For Scheeben here, despite the Fall and the reality of sin, he still maintains that God would not withhold from man His natural providence (i.e., the *debitum naturae*), implying the possibility of man's purely natural end, as potentially realizable in this concrete economy. Elsewhere, he writes likewise:

> It is, on the contrary, highly probable, that the final state of [one who dies in original sin, but not personal sin] is overall not painful; and since he is not at all closed off from God by hatred, there is a certain *inner peace* and *satisfaction*. The [one who dies in original sin, but not personal sin] reaches at least such a state which, outside of the supernatural order, would be his natural end.[43]

In this passage, he seems to be at ease with the notion of limbo as a final state, which—as was the case with Feingold—he takes to be the equivalent of man's purely natural end, as concretely realized in this economy. As it appears here, Scheeben's teaching is in agreement with the position of Feingold. Again, Scheeben writes:

> Those who are lost without any personal fault of their own [i.e., unbaptized infants] can have no complaints concerning the gratuitous providence which effectively extends grace to others, because they neither had any right to such grace, nor are held personally responsible for the non-possession of grace, and *hence do not suffer the loss of their natural goods and rights*.[44]

---

ohne übernaturliche Bestimmung erschaffen worden wäre. Er ist der wahren, ihm faktisch von Gott gegebenen Bestimmung verlustig, und wenn man auch nicht annehmen muß—ich glaube, nicht einmal annehmen darf—, daß Gott ihm die zur Erreichung seines natürlichen Zieles . . ." (Scheeben, *Die Mysterien des Christentums*, 255).

43. Scheeben, *Handbuch der Katholischen Dogmatik*, III/IV, 733, emphasis added: "Es ist im Gegenteil sogar höchst wahrscheinlich, daß der definitive Zustand des Erbsünders überhaupt gar kein schmerzlicher ist und leidvoller ist und, wie er gar keine Gott widerstrebende Gesinnung einschließt, so auch eine gewisse innere Ruhe und Befriedigung läßt, daß der Erbsünder wenigstens einigermaßen denjenigen Zustand erreicht, welcher außer der übernatürlichen Ordnung sein natürliches Endziel gewesen ware."

44. Scheeben, *The Mysteries of Christianity*, 727, emphasis added; "Diejenigen, welche ohne ihre persönliche Schuld verloren gehen, können sich nicht über die gnädige Vorsehung, welche andern die Gnade effektiv zukommen läßt, beklagen, weil sie weder ein Recht auf dieselbe hatten, noch für den Nichtbesitz derselben persönlich verantwortlich gemacht werden, darum aber auch ihre natürlichen Güter und Anrechte nicht verlieren" (Scheeben, *Die Myseterien des Christentums*, 610–11). He explains that

However, in what follows Scheeben states the opposite, *denying* the very possibility of man's realization of a purely natural end in the present economy—and his reasons are more or less the same as Long's given previously. Scheeben states:

> The existence of the divine [eternal] law, which gives the creature's supernatural ordination, includes much more than that of natural beatitude, to which the creature would have been otherwise determined by nature. *And therefore a final natural end is in fact no longer possible as an ultimate end.* In other words, if the creature is determined by divine law to a supernatural beatitude . . . a purely natural beatitude does not remain possible. . . . *Thus there is in fact no double final end, one for the natural order and one for the supernatural.*[45]

Similarly, despite the obvious correlation between man's purely natural end and the final state of limbo, Scheeben seeks to distinguish between the two states. Implicitly, his reasoning here follows the pattern set by Long—in that man's purely natural end pertains to the hypothetical possibilty of pure nature, whereas limbo purports to be a purely natural end for man in *this* concrete economy. Hence, the very attempt to distinguish

---

God's providence "appoints one end for those who are in the state of grace [i.e., the beatific vision] . . . [and another end] for those who lack grace through their own fault [i.e., damnation]; (and [*an additional end*] for those who are without fault, *in the case of unbaptized children*)" (*The Mysteries of Christianity*, 728, emphasis added, brackets are mine, parentheses are original). Here is the whole sentence as it occurs in the German original: "Wie Gott sich durch die Verweigerung der Kooperation vonseiten des Menschen nicht immer sogleich aufhalten läßt und oft durch neue Mittel den Menschen anzuziehen sucht, so spendet er auch vor der eintretenden Kooperation und abgesehen von derselben dem einen größere, dem andern geringere Gnaden, dem einen solche, die er als 'effectrices' voraussieht, dem andern solche, deren Erfolglosigkeit ihm nicht unbekannt ist, und steckt dem einen das Ziel der Bewegung da, wo derselbe durch oder ohne seine Schuld (oder ohne dieselbe bei den ungetauften Kindern) sich im Stande der Ungade befindet" (Scheeben, *Die Mysterien des Christentums*, 611).

45. Scheeben, *Handbuch der Katholischen Dogmatik*, III/IV, 467, emphasis added: "Die Existenz des allgemeinen göttlichen Gesetzes, welches der Kreatur eine übernatürliche Bestimmung gibt, schließt wesentlich ein, daß diejenige endliche Vollendung oder Seligkeit, zu welcher die Kreatur sonst von Natur bestimmt gewesen wäre und die darum das natürliche Endziel wird, tatsächlich nicht mehr das letzte Endziel ist und überhaupt nicht und erreichbaren Endzieles hat. Mit andern Worten: Wenn die Kreatur durch göttliches Gesetz zu einer übernatürlichen Seligkeit bestimmt ist . . . Gott nicht gestatten, daß eine bloß natürliche Seligkeit. . . . Es gibt also in Wirklichkeit für der Kreatur kein doppeltes Endziel, eins für die natürliche, eins für die übernatürliche Ordnung."

between the final state of limbo and man's purely natural end implicitly affirms the way in which the eternal law (i.e., man's concrete ordination to the beatific vision)—as well as the concrete conditions of the present economy (i.e., sin)—necessarily modify the prospects of man's realization of his purely natural end in this economy. Accordingly, Scheeben states:

> The children dying without baptism, *whose state . . . is not simply identical with the purely natural end*, which they would have received without such an appointment; because in the latter case their state would have been the normal situation [i.e., pure nature] . . . now they are, as a result of [original sin], *against God himself, in a state contrary to one of his laws* [i.e., contrary to the ordination of the eternal law].[46]

He is even more explicit on this point in the following when he refers to the lack of the beatific vision in post-lapsarian man as a *"privation,"* in contradistinction to the lack of the beatific vision in purely natural man, which he describes here as a mere *"absence."* This language is very significant, since in the Thomistic-Aristotelian tradition, the term "privation" signifies not just an absence, but an absence in a thing which *should ordinarily possess that particular quality*, as St. Thomas writes here: "A privation is said only of a certain subject, in which it is natural for the positive state to come to be, just as blindness is only said of things which can see by nature."[47] While we might refer to a rock as "non-sighted" or "non-literate," we would never describe a rock as "blind" or "illiterate"— since the latter terms only apply to things which ordinarily can see or read, respectively. In other words, terms such as "blind" and "illiterate" signify not just an absence, but a privation—since the kinds of things they describe are things which ordinarily can see or read; whereas, terms such as "non-sighted" or "non-literate" signify merely an absence of these qualities, strictly speaking.

---

46. Scheeben, *Handbuch der Katholischen Dogmatik*, III/IV, 468, emphasis added: "Die ohne Taufe sterbenden Kinder . . . der Zustand, in welchen sie eingehen, nicht schlechthin identisch mit dem rein natürlichen Endziele, welches ihnen ohne eine solche Berufung vorgesteckt gewesen wäre; denn im letzteren Falle wäre der Zustand ihre normale Lage gewesen, während sie jetzt infolge der Geschlechtsschuld Gott gegenüber sich in einer seinem Gesetze zuwiderlaufenden Lage befinden."

47. St. Thomas Aquinas, *On the Principles of Nature*, cited in Rioux, *Nature, The Soul, and God*, 114. Also see St. Thomas Aquinas, *On the Principles of Nature* in Aquinas, *Thomas Aquinas*, 18–29.

Therefore, Scheeben's use of privation here is certainly not without significance. Since he undoubtedly has this Thomistic-Aristotelian backdrop in mind, his use of "privation" is tantamount to the very logic employed above by Long: in other words, the divine ordination of the eternal law in *this* economy makes all the difference, since the failure to actualize God's concrete ordination necessarily results in some kind of frustration and suffering. For this reason, Scheeben's own logic here militates against the very possibility of a purely natural end being realized in the present economy—despite its otherwise hypothetical coherence. Scheeben implies as much in the following when he uses the term "privation" in the very sense described above with reference to post-lapsarian man's relation to grace and the beatific vision:

> What distinguishes the man born in original sin [Erbsünder] from the natural man [Naturmenschen] is not properly a positive or a negative quality [i.e., they do not differ in nature]. *It is the relationship to the sinful act*. . . . Without this relationship the withdrawal of supernatural justice [after sin for post-lapsarian man] would merely be an *absence*, not a *privation* of a perfection which *ought* to be present, nor [would it be] a subversion of an order established by God.[48]

The key to the inner logic animating Scheeben's teaching here is that reality is ultimately one. There are not "two" economies—one natural and another supernatural—but one concrete economy which is rooted in the unity of God's providence. For this reason, Scheeben's insistence upon the distinction between nature and grace is ultimately ordered toward preserving the splendor of the concrete *union* between nature and grace in the actual order of divine providence. It is for this reason that Scheeben shares an unexpected kinship with de Lubac, one which runs much deeper than might appear at first glance. For example, Scheeben again writes:

48. Scheeben, *The Mysteries of Christianity*, 301–12, emphasis added; "Was an dem Erbsünder mehr haftet als an dem Naturmenschen, ist keine ihm eigene positive oder negative Beschaffenheit; es ist die Beziehung auf den sündhaften Akt. . . . Ohne diese Beziehung ware der Abgang der übernatürlichen Gerechtigkeit ein bloßer Mangel, keine Privation dessen, was da sein sollte, keine Verkehrung einer von Gott gesetzten Ordnung" (Scheeben, *Die Mysterien des Christentums*, 251). Given the fact that the German word used here for original sin, "Erbsünder," is built upon the root for "inheritance" (Erbe), Scheeben seems to have in mind the fact that original sin forfeits the original inheritance of grace—the absence of which in post-lapsarian man now constitutes a privation.

> Philosophical ethics, in the sense of a system set up in opposition
> and defiance against theological morality, is unquestionably not a
> true and genuine morality. *For in the present order purely natural
> relationships do not exist alone and apart, and therefore cannot be
> made to prevail in isolated self-sufficiency.*[49]

Accordingly, despite Scheeben's ardent insistence upon the intelligible
distinction between nature and grace—and his insistence upon the abiding coherence of the former—the ultimate result is certainly no material
or existential separation between nature and grace. Rather, in his mind,
as we have stated, the rigor of this distinction is precisely what preserves
the supernatural splendor of their union. And this feature in Scheeben
is perhaps witnessed in no greater fashion than in his teaching on the
grace of divine sonship, to which we will now turn.

Scheeben on the Grace of Divine Sonship

For Scheeben, the grace of divine adoption unquestionably surpasses
the natural order, since supernatural grace engages man from without,
inviting him to share in a sublime and supernatural participation in the
very life and beatitude of God. And so Scheeben writes:

> We could never, in all eternity, attain to such an intimate, spiritu-
> al union with God even by the most perfect development of our
> natural spiritual powers, and by the conformity of our natural life
> with the divine will. This union is contained only in the super-
> natural grace of divine sonship, which makes us, as children of
> God, partakers of His nature and His life.[50]

49. Scheeben, *Nature and Grace*, 275, emphasis added; "Freilich ist die philosophische
Moral, wie sie sich im Gegensatze und zum Trotze gegen die theologische geltend
machen will, keine wahre und echte Moral. Aber sie ist dies nur deshalb nicht, weil
gegenwärtig die rein natürlichen Verhältnisse nicht allein und getrennt bestehen,
folglich auch nicht als einzig und absolut bestehend geltend gemacht werden können;
nicht aber deshalb, weil diese Verhältnisse in sich falsch oder fingiert wären" (Matthias
Scheeben, *Natur und Gnade*, 164–65).

50. Scheeben, *The Mysteries of Christianity*, 489; "Eine so innige, geistige Einheit
mit Gott Erlangen wir aber nie und nimmer auch durch die volkommenste, reinste
Entwicklung unserer natürlichen Geistes-kräfte und durch die Übereinstimmung
unseres natürlichen Lebens mit dem göttlichen Willen: sie ist nur in der übernatürlichen
Gnade der Kindschaft enthalten, die uns als Kinder Gottes seiner Natur und seines
Lebens teilhaftig macht" (Scheeben, *Die Mysterien des Christentums*, 402). Regarding
the absolute gratuity of grace with respect to merit, he writes: "If you suffer all that
Christ suffered, you could not merit even the least degree of grace" (Scheeben, *The

He points to the Incarnation as the ultimate foundation of the supernatural order of grace. For the entering into time and space of the Eternal Son, and the gifts flowing to man thereof, imply a divine condescension which inaugurates something fundamentally *new* into human existence, over and above that allotted to man by his nature, simply speaking. Indeed, in Scheeben's words, the Incarnation constitutes a veritable "hypostatic" order of reality:

> We must mount above the natural order of things, and even above the order of grace as considered in itself, and think of the Incarnation not as a factor in another order, conceivable apart from it, *but as the basis of its own proper order, of a special and altogether sublime order of things*, in which the orders of nature and of grace are absorbed.[51]

Glories of Divine Grace, 65); "Hättest du alles das zu dulden, was der Heiland gelitten hat, hättest du selbst alle Peinen der Hölle zu tragen, du könntest damit nicht den geringsten Grad der Gnade verdienen" (Scheeben, *Die Herrlichkeiten der Göttlichen Gnade*, 56). And similarly: "Indeed, we can by no means acquire grace for ourselves through our own efforts. No more than we can call ourselves out of nothingness and give to ourselves natural being or existence could we bring forth in ourselves supernatural life. For grace does not grow out of our natural powers as plants from their roots, *but it comes to our nature from without*" (Scheeben, *The Glories of Divine Grace*, 315, emphasis added; "Noch viel weniger können wir durch unsere eigene Kraft die Gnade in uns *hervorbringen*. Ebensowenig als wir uns selbst aus dem Nichts hervorbringen und uns das natürliche Dasein zu geben vermochten, vermögen wir auch uns selbst das übernatürliche Dasein zu geben. Denn die Gnade wächst nicht, wie die Pflanze aus ihrer Wurzel, aus unserer natürlichen Kraft hervor, sondren tritt zu unserer Natur von außen hinzu" (Scheeben, *Die Herrlichkeiten der Göttlichen Gnade*, 228, emphasis original).

51. Scheeben, *The Mysteries of Christianity*, 356, emphasis added; "Muß man sich nicht nur über die natürliche Ordnung der Dinge, sondern auch über die Gnadenordnung an sich betrachtet hinausschwingen, und sie nicht als Moment einer andern, schon außer ihr denkbaren, sondern als Basis einer eigenen, ganz besonders erhabenen Ordnung der Dinge denken, in welche die Ordnung der Natur und der Gnade aufgenommen ist" (Scheeben, *Die Mysterien des Christentums*, 295). According to Scheeben, the communication of divine life proceeds as follows: "First, by the substantial and total communication of the divine essence in the Trinity; secondly, by hypostatic union in the Incarnation of the Son; and thirdly, by participation in grace and glory on the part of men" (Scheeben, *The Mysteries of Christianity*, 738); "Erstens durch substantielle und totale Wesensmitteilung in der Trinität, zweitens durch hypostatische Union in der Meschwerdung des Sohnes, durch Partizipation in der Gnade und Glorie der Menschen" (Scheeben, *Die Mysterien des Christentums*, 621). For Scheeben, "[the] order of grace . . . proceeds from the Trinity" (*The Mysteries of Christianity*, 146): "Dem Gesagten gemäß haben wir die Dreifaltigkeit der Personen insofern als die Wurzel einer übernatürlichen Ordnung der Dinge in den Geschöpfen der Gnaden-ordnung

For Scheeben, the grace of sonship offered to man by way of supernatural grace derives from Christ and constitutes a real participation in His filial relation to the Father. For this reason, Scheeben seeks to distinguish between God's presence as Creator on the one hand, and His supernatural presence through grace, on the other hand. For him, the grace of divine sonship brings man into a relation with the Father analogous to that of the Eternal Son:

> In the ordinary created thing, God is present only as its maker and conserver. Without His presence in this way, things could not exist. But in the soul having grace He is present as sanctifier, giving Himself to the creature and sharing with him the holiness of His own being. *That recalls the way in which God the Father is in His only-begotten Son.* The Holy Ghost is in us by reason of the gracious sharing of the holiness which is proper to the Divine Nature. *Thus, as the presence of the Father in His Son is different from His presence in creatures, similarly the presence of the Holy Ghost in the souls of the just is different from His ordinary manner of dwelling in creatures.*[52]

zu betrachten, als die letztere auf ihr und aus ihr als ihrem Grunde sich entwickelt und aufbaut und somit als Nachbildung ihrer innerer Verhältnisse und Produktionen auch eine reale Offenbarung derselben ist" (Scheeben, *Die Mysterien des Christentums*, 125). Again, for Scheeben, the Incarnation is the exemplar and cause of the man's graced elevation: "The hypostatic union is the ideal, as well as the principle and end of the union by grace. It is the principle, because by it the Godhead is brought close to all mankind in inseparable union; the fullness of divinity was united with one individual of human nature, to be communicated to all others by participation" (*Nature and Grace*, 328): "Jene hypotatische Union ist wie das Ideal, so auch das Prinzip und Ziel dieses letzteren durch die Gnade. Sie ist Prinzip, weil durch sie die Gottheit der ganzen Menschheit in untrennbarer Verbindung nahegebracht wurde und in dem einen Individuum der menschlichen Natur die Fülle der Gottheit niedergelegt war, um von da aus durch Partizipation allen andern mitgeteilt zu wereden" (Scheeben, *Natur und Gnade*, 195). Similarly, he writes: "The God-man . . . is the principle of the supernatural order in virtue of His personal and natural dignity. Grace belongs to Him essentially as His own, and through Him it belongs to the race as its own" (Scheeben, *The Mysteries of Christianity*, 386); "Der Gottmensch hingegen ist kraft seiner persönlichen, natürlichen Würde Prinzip der übernatürlichen Ordnung, dem die Gnade wesentlich eigen ist, und durch den sie auch dem Geschlecht wahrhaft eigen wird" (Scheeben, *Die Mysterien des Christentums*, 320). See also: "The Incarnation places man, in Christ, upon God's throne, inaugurates his fellowship of dignity with the divine persons, and ushers him into relations with the Trinity" (Scheeben, *The Mysteries of Christianity*, 395–96): "Wie sie den Menschen in Christus auf den Thron Gottes, in die Gemeinschaft der Würde mit den göttlichen Personen setzt, ihn in die trinitarischen Verhältnisse einführt" (Scheeben, *Die Mysterien des Christentums*, 327).

52. Scheeben, *The Glories of Divine Grace*, 74 emphasis added; "In den bloßen

He makes this same point by distinguishing between God's "creative" power and His "generative" power, the latter referring to the eternal generation of the Son—a filiation in which man shares by virtue of the supernatural grace of divine adoption. Accordingly, for Scheeben, God the Father *begets* children by grace after the model of His begetting of the Eternal Son. As startling as this may sound, he does not back away from it in the least. Indeed, this familial begetting and generation within the Godhead provides, according to Scheeben, the archetype for understanding the full grandeur of man's salvation in Christ. He writes:

> God can give existence to finite beings because He is infinite being itself; in the contemplation of His perfection He finds the exemplar and ideal of their essence . . . but the case is otherwise with the grace of divine filiation . . . the gratuitous communication of the divine nature to creatures. God's power to communicate His nature externally and to beget children of grace is conceived by us not on the ground of His *creative* power, but as correlative to the infinite *generative* power by which He communicates his nature substantially and begets a Son equal to Himself. Not God's creative power, but His generative power enables us to apprehend that the generation of adoptive children is possible. . . . *The doctrine of the generation of the Son of God from the Father provides us with the key to understanding our elevation to the status of children of God.* Nothing is truer than this; and we need feel no misgiving in maintaining that God has revealed the inner life of the Trinity for the very purpose of enlightening us concerning our supernatural relationship to Him.[53]

Kreaturen ist er nur als ihr Schöpfer, ohne welchen sie nicht sein können; in den begnadeten aber als Heiligmacher, der sich ihnen zu eigen gibt und ihnen die Tiefen seines eigenen Wesens erschließt; er ist in ihnen auf ähnliche Weise, wie Gott der Vater in seinem eingeborenen Sohne ist. Der Vater ist im Sohne durch die substantielle und wesentliche Mitteilung seiner Natur, und so ist der Heilige Geist in uns kraft der gnadenvollen Mitteilung der Teilnahme an der göttlichen Natur. Sosehr also die Gegenwart des ewigen Vaters in seinem Sohne verschieden ist von seiner Gegenwart in seinen Geschöpfen, so sehr ist auch die Gegenwart des Heiligen Geistes in der begnadeten Seele von derjenigen verschieden, durch die er in den bloßen Geschöpfen wohnt" (Scheeben, *Die Herrlichkeiten der Göttlichen Gnade*, 62).

53. Scheeben, *Mysteries of Christianity*, 141–44, emphasis added; "Weil Gott das Sein selbst ist, deshalb kann er endlichen Wesen das Dasein geben. . . . Nicht so mit der Gnade der Kindschaft . . . der gnädigen Mitteilung der göttlichen Natur an die Geschöpfe. Die *Macht*, seine Natur nach außen mitzuteilen, Kinder aus Gnade zu zeugen, begreifen wir in Gott nicht auf Grund seiner Schöpfermacht, sondern als Korrelativ der unendlichen Zeugungskraft, durch die er seine Natur wesenhaft mitteilt und einen natürlichen, ihm gleichen Sohn zeugt. Nicht die Schöpfermacht, sondern nur die

For Scheeben, the Incarnation prolongs the very procession of the Eternal Son, and the same is true of the descent of the Holy Spirit, which prolongs the spiration of the Holy Spirit from the Father and the Son. The supernatural order of grace, therefore, brings man into this Trinitarian heart of God, as Scheeben writes here:

> The divine Trinity, consisting in the substantial communication of the divine nature to several persons, is the beginning, the middle, and the end of the supernatural economy of salvation. For this economy is based on the communication of the divine nature to man through the gift of grace. It consists in a union of man with God as his Father; and this is analogous with the union which the only-begotten Son of God has with the Father in the Holy Spirit. And it leads us back to the Trinity; for, as St. John tells us, it introduces us into a fellowship, a companionship with the Father and with the Son in the Holy Spirit (cf. I John 1:3), in which we love and glorify the divine Persons and share in their happiness.[54]

Zeugungskraft in Gott läßt uns die Zeugung von Adoptivkindern als möglich denken. ... Nichts ist also so wahr, als daß die Lehre von der Zeugung des Sohnes Gottes aus dem Vater allein uns den Schlüssel gibt zum Verständnisse unserer Erhebung zu Kindern Gottes, und wir brauchen daher keinen Anstand zu nehmen, zu behaupten, daß Gott eben deshalb, um uns über unser übernatürliches Verhältnis zu ihm aufzuklären, das Innere der Dreifaltigkeit offenbart habe" (Scheeben, *Mysterien des Christentums*, 120–21). Similarly, in *Nature and Grace*, he writes: "It [grace] requires a communication which, much more than creation, resembles that inconceivable, heavenly production and generation by which God the Father communicates His entire nature and essence to His only-begotten Son. ... By the grace flooding his soul he becomes a son of the heavenly Father and a brother of the only-begotten Son, that, like the latter, he may embrace the Father with filial love, reposing with the Son on the heart of the Father ..." (Scheeben, *Nature and Grace*, 102–3); "Es erfordert eine Mitteilung, die weit mehr als die Schöpfung, jener unbegreiflichen, himmlischen Hervorbringung und *Zeugung* ähnlich ist, durch welche Gott der Vater seinem eingeborenen Sohne seine ganze Natur und Wesenheit in ihrer Fülle mitteilt. ... Damit er dem Geiste nach *durch Gnade werde ein Sohn des himmlischen Vaters und Mitbruder des eingeborenen Sohnes*; damit auch er, wie dieser, in wahrhaft kindlicher Liebe dem Vater anhange, mit ihm *im Schoße des Vaters ruhend, ihn von Angesicht schaue*, in alle seine Geheimnisse eingeweiht werde; damit er so in der innigsten Gemeinschaft mit jenen Personen, welche die göttliche Natur *wesentlich* besitzen, als Sohn des Vaters, Mitbruder des Sohnes, Tempel des Heiligen Geistes." (Scheeben, *Natur und Gnade*, 61–62, emphases original).

54. Scheeben, *Nature and Grace*, 339–40; "Die Dreifaltigkeit in Gott, als in der wesenhaften Mitteilung der göttlichen Natur an mehrere Personen bestehen, ist der Ausgangs-, Mittel- und Zielpunkt der übernatürlichen Heilsordnung. Denn diese wird begründet durch eine gnadenvolle Mitteilung der göttlichen Natur an den Menschen; sie besteht in einer Verbindung des Menschen mit Gott als seinem Vater, die derjenigen

Elsewhere, he makes the same point, again, without qualification:

> The mystery of the Godhead, the inner communication of the
> divine nature, prolongs and reproduces itself exteriorly. . . . Thus
> by a prolongation of His eternal procession from the Father, the
> Son of God goes forth from the Father and enters into the hu-
> man race as a real member thereof. . . . Thus our participation in
> the divine nature and divine life becomes a reproduction of the
> fellowship in nature and life which the Son of God has with His
> Father . . .[55]

analog ist, welche der eingeborene Sohn Gottes mit dem Vater im Heiligen Geiste
besitzt; und sie führt uns zur Dreifaltigkeit zurück, indem sie, wie der heilige Johannes
sagt, uns 'eine Gemeinschaft, Gesellschaft mit dem Vater und dem Sohne' (I Jo I, 3)
im Heiligen Geiste eingehen läßt, in der wir sie lieben un verherrlichen und an ihrer
Seligkeit teilnehmen" (Scheeben, *Natur und Gnade*, 202). In a different work, he
likewise states: "If the internal divine relations and processes are externally imitated
and reproduced by the communication of the divine nature to rational creatures . . .
the Trinity is clearly the basis for the possibility, as well as the exemplar and goal of the
supernatural order of grace as we actually find it among creatures. The very essence
of the Trinity consists in the substantial communication of the divine nature from
the Father to the other two divine persons. Hence the true meaning of the Trinity for
creatures raised to the supernatural order must be apprehended in the fact that on
its basis, according to its model, and for its glorification, a participation in the divine
nature is gratuitously communicated to them. Consequently, the Trinity is the root
from which arises the order of things called forth by this communication" (Scheeben,
The Mysteries of Christianity, 141): "Wenn durch Mitteilung der göttlichen Natur an
die vernünftigen Geschöpfe in der erklärten Weise die innergöttlichen Verhältnisse
und Vorgänge nach außen nach gebildet und reproduziert werden, dann erscheint
die Trinität als der Möglichkeitsgrund, als das Ideal und das Ziel der übernatürlichen
Gnadenordnung in den Geschöpfen. Das innerste Wesen der Trinität liegt in der
wesenhaften Mitteilung der göttlichen Natur andere Personen; und so muß auch
ihre eigentümliche Bedeutung darin bestehen, daß auf ihrem Grunde, nach ihrem
Vorbilde und zu ihrer Verherrlichung eine gnadenreiche Mitteilung der Teilnahme an
der göttlichen Natur nach außen stattfindet, und daß sie folglich für die durch diese
Mitteilung hervorgerufene Ordnung der Dinge die Wurzel bildet, woraus dieselbe
entspringt" (Scheeben, *Die Mysterien des Christentums*, 119).

   55. Scheeben, *The Mysteries of Christianity*, 481; "Das Mysterium der Gottheit, die
innere Mitteilung der göttlichen Natur, nach außen hin sich fortsetzt und nachbildet.
. . . So tritt der Sohn Gottes, von seinem Vater ausgehend, in das menschliche Geschlecht
in der realsten, innigsten Weise hinein, durch eine Fortsetzung seines ewigen Ausganges
vom Vater. . . . und unsere dadurch vermittelte Teilnahme an der göttlichen Natur und
am göttlichen Leben erscheint als Nachbild der durch die höchste substantielle Einheit
bedingten Gemeinschaft der Natur und des Lebens, die der Sohn Gottes mit seinem
Vater besitzt" (Scheeben, *Mysterien des Christentums*, 395–96). The result is that the
gift of divine sonship actually approximates a state of "natural" sonship: "Our adoption
is rooted in this procession for the very reason that it is rooted in the procession of
the Son from the Father and in the Son's relationship to the Father" (ibid., 143); "Sie

Hence, for Scheeben, the gift of divine sonship entails a real ontic share in the filiation of the Eternal Son. Indeed, for him, the grace of divine sonship is no mere metaphor; like the order of nature, the order of grace constitutes its own a metaphysical order of reality:

> Thus the incarnation of the Son of God is the real basis for the divine adoption of the human race, and likewise conducts that adoption to a consummation that is unique in its sublimity. It is the bridge leading to the extension of the divine Trinitarian

---

wurzelt schon deshalb in dieser, weil sie in dem Ausgang des Sohnes vom Vater und in dessen Verhältnis zum Vater wurzelt" (Scheeben, *Die Mysterien des Christentums*, 122). Moreover, for Scheeben, the gift of the Holy Spirit is a "real prolongation of His eternal procession" (Scheeben, *The Mysteries of Christianity*, 386; "wahre Fortsetzung seines ewigen Ausganges" (Scheeben, *Die Mysterien des Christentums*, 320). Nichols comments on some of the sources of Scheeben's thinking here: "In the Alexandrian theology, the descent of the Son of God through the acceptance of human nature has its counterpart in the exaltation of that humanity through sharing in the divine nature, such that the Incarnation brings about a supernatural *Gottesgemeinschaft* ('community with God') for humankind at large. Scheeben, who has in mind in particular Cyril's great commentary on the Gospel according to St. John, is insistent that in no way can this doctrine be considered a local peculiarity of Lower Egypt. His favored Latin Father, Peter Chrysologus, teaches no differently in the Ravenna sermons which celebrate, in addresses to neophytes, the 'lifting up of man to adoptive sonship in a wonderful sublimity which emulates the hypostatic union in Christ'" (Nichols, *Romance and System*, 82–83). Nichols' quotation is from Scheeben, *Handbuch der Katholischen Dogmatik*, III/IV, 314: "die Erhebung der Menschen zur Adoptivkindschaft Gottes an wunderbarer Erhabenheit wetteifere mit der hypostatischen Union in Christus." Similarly, Scheeben writes: "The communication of divine life to the creature and to mankind is to be regarded as an extension and continuation of that communication of life which is transmitted from the Father to the Son in God" (Scheeben, *The Mysteries of Christianity*, 391–92); "Die Mitteilung des göttlichen Lebens an die Kreatur und die Menschheit ist ferner als seine *Ausbreitung und Fortsetzung jener Lebensmitteilung zu betrachten, die in Gott vom Vater auf den Sohn übergeht*" (Scheeben, *Die Mysterien des Christentums*, 324, emphasis original). See also Scheeben, *The Mysteries of Christianity*, 138–46 and Scheeben, *Nature and Grace*, 339–40). With remarkable daring, he writes further: "Every child that is born receives its nature from its father. Therefore, the Second Person of the Holy Trinity is called Son and the First is called Father, because the Latter has shared His own Divine Nature with the Former. . . . When through grace we receive a sharing of the Divine Nature and of the divine life, it is then true in a strict sense that we are born of God" (Scheeben, *The Glories of Divine Grace*, 100); "Die Zeugung ist der Akt, wodurch der Vater dem Kinde seine eigene Natur mitteilt. So zeugt Gott seinen eingeborenen Sohn, indem er seine eigene göttliche Natur und Wesenheit auf ihn übergehen laßt. . . . Wenn auch wir durch die Gnade wahrhaft der göttlichen Natur und des göttlichen Lebens teilhaftig warden, dann ist es im eigentlichen Sinne wahr, daß wir, ähnlich wie der natürliche Sohn Gottes, aus dessen Schoß gezeugt und geboren warden" (Scheeben, *Die Herrlichkeiten Der Göttlichen Gnade*, 83).

fatherhood to the race. This fatherhood is not merely imitated in God's relationship to man, out of sheer grace, but is joined to man substantially. . . . The Incarnation sets up a real *continuity* between the Trinitarian process and the human race, in order that this process may be prolonged in the race. *The Incarnation raises the human race to the bosom of the eternal Father* that it may receive the grace of sonship *with all its implied dignities and rights* by a real contact with the source, rather than by a purely gratuitous influx from without.[56]

For this reason, Scheeben is fond of pointing out that man's natural state before God is more properly designated by the terms "creature" and "servant,"[57] in contrast to "sonship" which is made possible only through

56. Scheeben, *The Mysteries of Christianity*, 384–85; "So legt die Inkarnation des Sohnes Gottes in dem Menschen-geschlechte den eigentlichen Grund zur Adoption desselben und führt sie zugleich zu einer ganz besonders hohen Vollendung. Sie bilden den Übergang für die *Ausbreitung der göttlichen trinitarischen Vaterschaft über das Geschlecht.* Diese Vaterschaft wird hier nicht schlechtweg aus reiner Gnade in dem Verhältnisse Gottes zum Menschen nachgebildet, sondern substantiell mit demselben in Verbindung gebracht. . . . Die Inkarnation setzt den trinitarischen Prozeß in reale Kontinuität mit dem Menschengesschlechte, damit er in demselben weitergeführt werde; sie erhebt das Menschengeschlecht wirklich in den Schoß des ewigen Vaters, damit dasselbe nicht bloß durch eine gnadenvolle Zuströmung von außen her, sondern durch realen Kontakt mit der Quelle die Gnade der Kindschaft mit allen in ihr engeschlossenen Würden und Rechten erhalte" (Scheeben, *Die Mysterien des Christentums*, 319, emphasis original). In context, "substantial" union, in contrast to "sheer grace," Scheeben is referring to the implications of the Incarnation, in contrast to the hypothetical gift of grace *apart from* Incarnation. See Scheeben, *The Mysteries of Christianity*, 382.

57. "The creature stands to God in the position of a servant" (Scheeben, *The Mysteries of Christianity*, 245); "Seiner Natur nach steht das Geschöpf zu Gott in der Stellung eines Knechtes" (Scheeben, *Die Mysterien des Christentums*, 205). Scheeben cites St. Irenaeus who states: "The Word became man for this reason, that man, by accepting the Word and receiving the grace of sonship, might become the son of God" (*Against heresies*, Bk. III, ch. 2, cited in Scheeben, *The Mysteries of Christianity*, 380): "Deshalb ist das Wort Mensch geworden, damit der Mensch, das Wort aufnehmend und die Gnade er Kindshaft emfangend, Kind Gottes würde" (Scheeben, *Die Mysterien des Christentums*, 315). He also cites St. Cyril of Alexandria who writes: "Through the Word, who joined human nature to Himself by means of the flesh united to Him, but who is by nature joined to the Father . . . *servitude is raised to sonship*, being summoned and elevated by its participation in the true Son to the dignity which pertains to Him by nature" (*Commentary on Gospel of John*, Bk. I, ch. 9, cited in ibid., emphasis added: "Vermittelst des Wortes, welches die Menschheit (das Geschlecht) durch das mit ihm vereinigte Fleisch mit sich verbindet, aber von Natur mit dem Vater verbunden ist . . . steigt das Knechtliche zur Kindschaft auf, indem es durch die Mitgenossenschaft des wahren Sohnes zu der diesem von Natur eigentümlichen Würde berufen und erhoben

the gift of divine grace. Hence, as Scheeben writes, it is only "through the grace of sanctity and deification [that] the creature becomes a child of God."[58]

For Scheeben, this order of supernatural grace has such an ontological density that he goes on to speak of a certain "equality" between man and God: "Grace gives us, not only the freedom necessary for true friendship with God, but also the other condition of friendship, *equality*."[59] For him, mystical and mysterious as this may sound, it is no mere figure of speech or exaggerated hyperbole. Rather, this supernatural elevation and transformation is simply the outworking of the ontological grace of the Incarnation and its effects. Scheeben writes:

wird" (Scheeben, *Die Mysterien des Christentums*, 315).

58. Scheeben, *The Mysteries of Christianity*, 245–46; "Durch die Gnade der Heiligkeit und Vergöttlichung wird das Geschöpf ein Kind Gottes" (Scheeben, *Die Mysterien des Christentums*, 206). Through grace man stands before God: "in the manner of son [Sohn], brother [Bruder], and bride [Braut] *in equal rank*" (Scheeben, *Handbuch der Katholischen Dogmatik*, VIII, 29, emphasis added). Here is the fuller passage from which this passage has been taken: "Bei der Mitteilung der Übernatur wirkt Gott als causa efficiens, strenggenommen auch nur durch die den Personen gemeinschaftliche Natur, aber da er hier einigermaßen secundum participationem similitudinis specificae vel quasi specificae seiner eigenen Natur in ihren eigentümlichen Vorzügen nach außen sich mitteilt, wird hier die innere substantiaelle Mitteilung der göttlichen Natur das Ideal, nach dem sie nach außen wirkt, und ein Zentrum, mit dem das Geschöpf durch seine Übernatur in Verbindung tritt, so daß es in Gemeinschaft des Heiligen Geistes Gesellschaft habe mit dem Vater und dem Sohn, mit dem Vater als dessen Kind nach Art seines Sohnes, mit dem Sohn als dessen Bruder und Braut im ebenbürtigen Rang, mit beiden durch jene höchste Liebe, als deren Blüte aus beiden Heilige Geist hervorgeht." Likewise, he writes: "Through grace an entirely new world is opened to it [the soul], and an entirely different activity is made possible. Through it the spirit is made capable of knowing God Himself, not only in His external works, but in His infinite holiness . . . *in His own inner life*. By grace the soul is put in position to love God and to deal with Him, not only as the creature with the Creator . . . *but as the child with its father*" (Scheeben, *The Glories of Divine Grace*, 86 emphasis added); "Durch die Gnade aber wird dieser Kreis unendlich erweitert und erhoben; durch sie wird die Seele befähigt, Gott selbst unmittelbar in seiner Herrlichkeit zu erkennen und sich liebend in die Tiefe seiner unendlichen Güte zu versenken, um das höchste Gut in sich aufzunehmen und es so zu genießen, wie Gott selbst es genießt. Und so gibt die Gnade der Seele ein Leben, unendlich reicher und erhabener als alles natürliche Leben nicht zu vergleichen ist" (Scheeben, *Die Herrlichkeiten der Göttlichen Gnade*, 73).

59. Scheeben, *The Glories of Divine Grace*, 116, emphasis original; "Doch die Gnade gibt uns nicht nur die *Freiheit*, die zur wahren Freundschaft mit Gott notwendig ist; auch die andere Bedingung der Freundschaft, die *Gleichheit* mit dem Freunde, ist in ihr eingeschlossen" (Scheeben, *Die Herrlichkeiten der Göttlichen Gnade*, 96, emphasis original).

By reason of nature, God loves us as His creatures and servants. But the distance between Him and us is infinite and is therefore too great to allow us to be called His true friends. Consequently, it is understandable that the pagan philosophers said that a true friendship between God and man is impossible. Only grace raises man to such a high degree of similarity—*even to a certain equality with God*—that the distance between God and man is spanned, and friendship between them no longer appears unbecoming.[60]

We will turn next to develop this familial analogy further, where we will see a point of contact between Scheeben and de Lubac in terms of what I will refer to below as a certain "familial" logic.

"Familial" Logic: a Convergence between Scheeben and de Lubac

Scheeben's comments regarding man's "rights" before God in a graced state, even to the point of suggesting a certain "equality" between man and God, bear a striking similarity to the way in which de Lubac juxtaposed his teaching on man's natural desire, alongside his insistence that he could still retain the gratuity of grace. For de Lubac, man's natural

60. Scheeben, *The Glories of Divine Grace*, emphasis added; "Gott liebt uns auch schon unserer Natur nach als seine Geschöpfe und seine Diener. Aber der Abstand zwischen uns und ihm ist unendlich und mithin zu groß, als daß wir so seine wahren Freunde genannt werden könnten. Selbst jene heidnischen Weltweisen, welche von der menschlichen Seele sagten, sie sei ein Ausfluß und ein Teilchen der göttlichen Substanz, wagten darum doch noch nicht zu behaupten, daß zwischen Gott und den Menschen eine wahre Freundschaft möglich sei. Nur die Gnade erhebt den Menschen zu einer so hohen Stufe der Ähnlichkeit mit Gott und einer gewissen Gleichheit mit Gott, daß der Abstand zwischen ihm und Gott nicht mehr zu groß ist und die Freundschaft mit ihm Gottes nicht mehr ganz unwürdig erscheint" (Scheeben, *Die Herrlichkeiten Der Göttlichen Gnade*, 96). Similarly, "Thus we belong to God's kind [by grace] in the same manner as the palm tree belongs to the class of plants, and the lion to that of animals" (Scheeben, *The Glories of Divine Grace*, 21); "und so gehören wir in ähnlicher Weise zum Geschlechte Gottes wie die Palme zum Geschlechte der Pflanzen und der Löwe zum Geschlechte der Tiere" (Scheeben, *Die Herrlichkeiten der Göttlichen Gnade*, 24). He also writes: "Insofar as grace implies divine sonship, it raises us high above the state of servitude. It removes the condition of estrangement, the relation of slavery and the immeasurable inequality that exists between God and us by nature, and places us in a condition of freedom as members of God's family, *and thus gives us a certain equality with God*" (Scheeben, *The Glories of Divine Grace*, 114, emphasis added); "Schon die Kindschaft Gottes erhebt uns unendlich hoch über den Stand der Knechtschaft; sie hebt den Zustand der Entfremdung, das Verhältnis der Dienstbarkeit und allzu großer Ungleichheit, worin wir von Natur zu Gott stehen, auf und versetzt uns in den Zustand der Freiheit und einer gewissen Gleichheit mit Gott" (Scheeben, *Die Herrlichkeiten der Göttlichen Gnade*, 95).

desire for the beatific vision constitutes no less than a *call* from God, an invitation, as it were, and one which should be embraced with trust and confidence. However, the presence of this desire for de Lubac though indicative of a call, is not itself grounds for a strict *demand*, and here de Lubac contends that such "juridical" logic necessarily falls short of the reality at hand. Yet he insists that the absence of juridical necessity should in no way undermine man's confident expectation that this inexorable and innate desire is itself a sign pointing to his ultimate end in the beatific vision. Accordingly, de Lubac writes: "Once such a desire exists in the creature *it becomes the sign not merely of a possible gift from God, but of a certain gift.*"[61]

In a similar vein, Scheeben so exalts man's graced status before God that man can now lay claim to certain "rights" before God. Though this language sounds provocative, his purpose is simply to accentuate the full reality of man's graced sonship. As is the case with de Lubac, this juxtaposition of *radical gratuity* and *confident expectation* can be seen in the human analogy of the father-son relation. For example, let us observe that a child does not bring himself into existence, since his natural begetting is pure gift. But once in existence certain proprieties do indeed follow, and to a large extent as a matter of justice. Accordingly, for Scheeben, if the reality of grace is as real as he describes, then the same must be true of man's supernatural begetting before God: while utterly gratuitous, his graced sonship nonetheless brings about a new filial relationship with God, one which brings with it certain "rights" or proprieties, and which therefore should be acknowledged unreservedly; for such acknowledgement is indicative of man's trust and confidence in Almighty God. In this light, Scheeben states:

> The divine dignity which falls to man's portion by his incorporation in Christ, gives him a *right* to deification, that is, to divine transfiguration of his nature that corresponds to this dignity. . . . The natural consequence of the Incarnation is to confer on men the *right* and power to become children of God.[62]

61. De Lubac, *The Mystery of the Supernatural*, 207, emphasis added; "Toute question d'exigence de la part de la créature est bannie. Mais il n'en reste pas moins, dira-t-on peut-être, qu'un tel désir existant dans la créature devient alors le signe, non seulement d'un don possible de la part de Dieu, mais d'un don certain" (De Lubac, *Le Mystère du Surnaturel*, 257).

62. Scheeben, *Mysteries of Christianity*, 378 emphasis added; "Die göttliche Würde, die dem Menschen durch seine Eingliederung in Christus zuteil wird, gibt ihm ein Recht

Accordingly, the language of "inheritance," "rights," and even "equality" in Scheeben's thought is best understood as his attempt to stress this fundamental posture of trust—the trust proper to a child. Both de Lubac and Scheeben make use of this "familial" logic, which enables them to navigate a "third path," so to speak, between juridical necessity and gratuity—between confident trust and improper demand. With this in mind, let us conclude here with the following from Scheeben:

> Because of Christ this sonship is no longer a mere adoptive sonship, since we receive it not as strangers, but as kinsfolk, as members of the only-begotten Son, and can lay claim to it as a *right*. The grace of sonship in us has something of the natural sonship of Christ Himself, from which it is derived. Because we are not mere adoptive children, because we are members of the natural Son, we truly enter into the personal relationship in which the Son of God stands to His Father. *In literal truth, and not by simple analogy or resemblance*, we call the Father of the Word our Father, and in actual fact He is such not by purely analogous relationship, but by the very same relationship which makes Him the Father of Christ. He is our Father in somewhat the way He is

---

auf die Vergöttlichung, d. h. auf die dieser Würde entsprechende göttliche Verklärung seiner Natur. . . . Die natürliche Folge der Inkarnation sei die, daß die Menschen dadurch das Recht und die Macht erhielten, Kinder Gottes zu werden" (Scheeben, *Die Mysterien des Christentums*, 314, 315, respectively). Similarly: "If, then, the human race . . . becomes the body of Christ, and its members become the members of God's Son, if the divine person of the Son of God bears them in Himself as His own, then, with due proportion, *must not the divine dignity of the Son of God flow over to men, since they are His members? Must not God the Father extend to these members the same love as that which He bears for His natural Son, must He not embrace them in His Son with one and the same love, inasmuch as they belong to Him?*" (Scheeben, *The Mysteries of Christianity*, 377–78, emphasis added); "Wenn nun das Menschengeschlecht . . . Weise der Leib Christi und seine Glieder Glieder des Sohnes Gottes werden, wenn die göttliche Person desselben sie als zu sich selbst gehörig in sich trägt: muß dann nicht verhältnismäßig die göttliche Würde des Sohnes Gottes den Menschen als seinen Gliedern zuströmen? Muß nicht Gott der Vater dieselbe Liebe, die er zu seinem natürlichen Sohne trägt, auch auf seine Glieder ausdehnen, muß er sie nicht in seinem Sohne, als zu ihm gehörig, mit einer und derselben Liebe umfangen?" (Scheeben, *Die Mysterien des Christentums*, 313). See also: "*Since grace makes us partakers of the Divine Nature, we are taken into the very family of God. God becomes our Father, His only-begotten Son our brother, and we ourselves children of God*" (Scheeben, *Glories of Divine Grace*, 91); "Indem die Gnade uns der göttlichen Natur teilhaftig macht, den Geist Gottes in uns wohnen läßt und uns ein göttliches Leben einpflanzt, macht sie uns zu wahren Kindern Gottes, und Gott wird unser wahrer Vater" (Scheeben, *Die Herrlichkeiten der Göttlichen Gnade*, 76).

Father to the God-man in His humanity by the same relationship whereby He is Father of the eternal Word.[63]

63. Scheeben, *Mysteries of Christianity*, 383, emphasis added; "Die Kindschaft selbst ist daher auch durch Christus keine *bloße* Adoptivkindschaft mehr, da wir nicht als Fremde, sondern als Verwandte, als Glieder des eingeborenen Sohnes dieselbe erhalten und sie als ein Recht beanspruchen können. Die Gnade der Kindschaft in uns hat etwas von der natürlichen Sohnschaft Christi selbst, von der sie getragen wird. Weil wir nicht bloße Adoptivkinder, weil wir Glieder des natürlichen Sohnes sind, deshalb treten wir als solche auch wirklich mit in das persönliche Verhältnis ein, in welchem der Sohn Gottes zu seinem Vater steht. Wir nennen in Wahrheit, nicht nur der Analogie oder der Ähnlichkeit nach, den Vater des Wortes unseren Vater, und er ist es in der Tat nicht durch ein bloßes analoges Verhältnis, sondern durch ein und dasselbe Verhältnis, durch das er der Vater Christi ist. Er ist das auf ähnliche Weise, wie er auch durch dasselbe Verhältnis dem Gottmenschen in seiner Menschheit Vater ist, durch welches er Vater des ewigen Wortes ist" (Scheeben, *Die Mysterien des Christentums*, 317–18, emphasis original). He writes further: "As children of God, we have a far more intimate relation with God than adopted children have to their father. We are children of God, not only because we have been accepted and considered as children, but also because He shares His Divine Nature and life with us and because He fills and enlivens us with His own Spirit. We are His *heirs* and we have a *right* to the inheritance. This *right* is based on our [re-] birth" (Scheeben, *The Glories of Divine Grace*, 100–101, emphases added); "Wir demnach als Kinder Gottes zu unserem himmlischen Vater in einem ungleich innigeren Verhältnisse als unter uns Menschen die angenommenen Kinder zu ihrem Adoptivvater. Wir sind Kinder Gottes, weil wir nicht nur von ihm als Kinder angenommen und betrachtet, sondern auch, wie sein natürlicher Sohn, aus seinem Schoße gezeugt und geboren worden, indem er uns seine göttliche Natur und sein göttliches Leben mitteilt und uns mit seinem eigenen Geiste erfüllt und belebt. Wir sind nicht nur seine *Erben*, sondern das Recht auf die Erbschaft stützt sich auf unsere *Wiedergeburt*, wie der heilige" (Scheeben, *Die Herrlichkeiten der Göttlichen Gnade*, 83, emphasis original). Similarly, Scheeben writes: "The grace of divine sonship [makes us] children of God . . . brothers of Christ" (*Handbuch der Katholischen Dogmatik*, VIII, 39, 33 respectively): "die Gnade der Kindschaft" and "Kindes Gottes und Mitbruders Christi." Supernatural grace transforms the creature into child, bride, and friend of God: "kindliche, bräutliche oder freundschaftliche" (ibid., III/IV, 376). Also: "For by reason of Sanctifying Grace, which makes us partakers of the Divine Nature, we are true sons of God, and the works that we perform in virtue of this grace are divine, heavenly works. Thus, we stand in a relation of equality to heavenly glory, and when God actually promises this to us, He promises it as an *inheritance* and as a reward that is not above the dignity of our person and the value of our works" (Scheeben, *The Glories of Divine Grace*, 236–37, emphasis added); "Wir sind nämlich durch die heiligmachende Gnade, die uns der göttlichen Natur teilhaftig macht, wahre Kinder Gottes, und die Werke, die wir in ihrer Kraft verrichten, sind göttliche, himmlische Werke. Wir stehen also dadurch in einem ebenbürtigen Verhältnisse zu der himmlischen Herrlichkeit, und wenn Gott uns diese nun wirklich verspricht, dann verspricht er sie uns als ein Erbteil und einen Lohn, der nicht über den Bereich der Würde unserer Person und des Wertes unserer Werke hinaus liegt" (Scheeben, *Die Herrlichkeiten der Göttlichen Gnade*, 179).

In order to further explore the implications of Scheeben's teaching here, let us observe that he goes so far as to say that man's graced sonship actually lies somewhere between "natural" and "adopted" sonship. Ultimately, it is the indwelling of the Holy Spirit that makes this possible and completes the gift of man's graced adoption—and so to the Holy Spirit's role in the grace of this divine sonship, we now turn.

The Holy Spirit: Seal of a Sonship "between" Natural and Adoptive

In Sacred Scripture, the grace of divine sonship is often connected with the gift of the Spirit, as for example here in St. Paul's Letter to the Romans:

> For all who are led by the Spirit of God are sons of God. For you did not receive the spirit of slavery to fall back into fear, but you have received the spirit of *sonship*. When we cry, "Abba! Father!" it is the Spirit himself bearing witness with our spirit that we are children of God, *and if children, then heirs*, heirs of God and fellow heirs with Christ, provided we suffer with him in order that we may also be glorified with him. (Rom 8:14–17)[64]

The New Testament speaks of the Holy Spirit as the seal of man's divine sonship: "In him . . . [we] were sealed [ἐσφραγίσθητε] with the promise of the Holy Spirit (Eph 1:13)," which is the "guarantee of our inheritance" (Eph 1:14). For this reason, Scheeben sees the indwelling of the Spirit as the "constitutive" element of man's graced sonship:

> The indwelling of the Holy Spirit is absolutely the most important constitutive moment of [man's divine] sonship with God in this sense: that therein is contained a partaking in the substance of the divine nature, a substantial fellowship and unity in connection with God. In this indwelling, the Spirit of God, appears in a certain sense as a "form informing the soul" and a "form

---

64. Emphases added. Scheeben himself makes this connection by alluding to this very passage: "We are through grace children of God, consequently His heirs and co-heirs with Christ" (*The Glories of Divine Grace*, 148); "Ferner sind wir durch die Gnade wahre Kinder Gottes, folglich seine Erben und Miterben Christi" (Scheeben, *Die Herrlichkeiten der Göttlichen Gnade*, 118). At the conclusion of *Gaudium et Spes* 22, we likewise have an allusion to this passage in Rom 8:15, drawing this same connection between the gift of the Spirit and the gift of divine sonship: "Christ has risen again, destroying death by his death, and has given life abundantly to us so that, *becoming sons in the Son, we may cry out in the Spirit: Abba, Father!*" (*Gaudium et Spes*, 22, in *Vatican Council II: Constitutions, Decrees, Declarations*, emphasis added).

constituting the divine being" and as a result, in the adoptive children of God, the fellowship of dignity and of life with God, is established in a way analogous to that of the natural son of God.[65]

The Spirit's indwelling leads Scheeben to declare that man's graced sonship is so mysterious and so profound that it actually "interlaces" *between* "adoptive" and "natural" sonship. And so he writes:

[The Holy Spirit] seals the relationship in which we stand to the Father not only alongside the only-begotten Son, but in Him as one Christ. Here He is given to us . . . as the pledge of the fatherly love with which the Father loves us in His only-begotten as His members, and as the pledge of the Son's love for the Father, which love the Son offers to the Father in behalf of us too, since we are

65. Scheeben, *Handbuch der Katholischen Dogmatik*, III/IV, 398: "Sie betrachtet die Einwohnung des Heiligen Geistes geradezu als das wichtigste konstitutive Moment der Kindschaft Gottes in dem Sinne, daß darin eine Teilnahme an der Substanz der göttlichen Natur, eine substanzielle Gemeinschaft und Einheit resp. Zusammenhang mit Gott enthalten ist, worin der Geist Gottes seiner Substanz nach in gewissem Sinne eine forma informans animam und eine forma constitutens esse divinum erscheint und wodurch in den Adoptivkindern Gottes die Gemeinschaft der Würde und des Lebens mit Gott in analoger Weise begründet wird wie im natürlichen Sohne Gottes." Similarly, Scheeben writes: "It is, as Thomas and Bonaventure say, not merely a love freely giving, but also a love freely accepting, as a result of which the creature is so blessed by God and favored by God, that it is received into to the deepest friendship, adopted to childhood, and chosen unto bridehood. And this love especially goes by the name of *gratia Spiritus Sancti* (grace of the Holy Spirit) because in it God spreads out his love over the creature, with which he embraces his only begotten Son and out of which the Holy Spirit proceeds, and through it his own life, whose breath the Holy Spirit is, is poured out on the creature" (Scheeben, *Handbuch der Katholischen Dogmatik*, III/IV, 276): "sie ist, wie Thom. und Bonav. sagen, nicht bloß ein amor liberaliter *donans,* sondern auch liberaliter acceptans, wodurch die Kreatur so von Gott begünstigt und zum Günstlinge Gottes gemacht wird, daß sie zur innigsten Freundschaft aufgenommen, zu Kindschaft adoptiert und zur Brautschaft auserwählt wird. Und diese Liebe führt auch ganz besonders den Namen gratia Spiritus Sancti, Gnade des Heiligen Geistes, weil in ihr Gott diejenige Liebe über die Kreatur ausbreitet, mit welcher er seinen eingeborenen Sohn umfaßt und aus welcher der Heilige Geist hervorgeht, und durch sie sein eigenes Leben, dessen Odem der Heilige Geist ist, in die Kreatur ausgießt." Scheeben writes: "For we are made like the natural Son of God not only because we are conformable to Him, but most of all because we personally possess within ourselves the very same Spirit that He possesses" (Scheeben, *Mysteries of Christianity*, 169): "Denn gerade dadurch werden wir dem natürlichen Sohne Gottes am meisten ähnlich, daß wir nicht bloß ihm gleichförmig sind, sondern auch denselben Geist persönlich in uns besitzen, den er besitzt; ebenso erscheint unsere Verbindung mit dem himmlischen Vater darin am glänzendsten, daß er seinen eigenen Geist in uns niedergelegt hat" (Scheeben, *Die Mysterien des Christentums*, 145, emphasis original).

His members. Hence the relationship whereby the Holy Spirit dwells in us as the *Spiritus Christi* is a hypostatic relationship through and through. . . . Moreover, it is the foundation and the crown of the divine sonship contained in grace itself: the foundation because our right to the pledge of God's fatherly love must draw down upon us the effects of that love; and the crown, *because it so closely interlaces adoptive sonship with natural sonship.*[66]

In the next section, we will take up the issue of Scheeben's Christocentricism and intrinsicism; here he captures the essential thrust of de Lubac's contribution on nature and grace.[67] Accordingly, the following section will bring our task to completion, since by establishing Scheeben's ability to incorporate the intrinsicist contribution of de Lubac—and given his clear congruity with the pure-nature tradition—it will be apparent that Scheeben's theology can reconcile the insights of both extrinsicism and intrinsicism. For this reason, he can provide the

---

66. Scheeben, *The Mysteries of Christianity*, 385, emphasis added. Here I will give a fuller citation in German, as here Scheeben ties a number of issues together; I will place brackets around the precise citation given above: "Auf ähnliche Weise treten wir als Glieder des Sohn Gottes eine festere und erhabenere, in *eine mehr persönliche Beziehung zum Heiligen Geiste*, als dies durch die Gnade an sich geschieht. Schon früher hatten wir gesehen, daß der Heilige Geist mit der Gnade der Kindschaft in seiner Hypostase als das Siegel dieser unserer Würde gegeben wird, indem wir eben in ihm in eine Relation zum Vater treten, die derjenigen analog ist, welche der Sohn zum Vater hat. Hier aber wird er unser Eigentum, indem wir als der Leib ihn als den Geist unseres Hauptes besitzen. [Hier besiegelt er das Verhältnis, in welchem wir nicht nur *neben* dem eingeborenen Sohne, sondern *in* ihm als ein Christus zum Vater stehen. Hier wird er uns geschenkt oder ist vielmehr 'ipso facto' unser eigen als das Pfand der väterlichen Liebe, womit der Vater uns in seinem eingeborenen Sohne als dessen Glieder liebt, und als das Pfand der Liebe des Sohnes zum Vater, die derselbe auch für uns als seine Glieder dem Vater entgegenbringt. Die Beziehung, wodurch der Heilige Geist als der 'Spiritus Christi' in uns wohnt, ist daher eine durchaus hypostatische; keine hypostatische Beziehung zum Heiligen Geiste brächte. Sie ist überdies der Grund und die Krone der in der Gnade selbst liegenden Kindschaft Gottes: der Grund, weil unser Recht an dem Pfande der väterlichen Liebe Gottes auch die Wirkungen derselben in uns herabziehen muß, die Krone, weil sie die Adoptivkindschaft mit der natürlichen so innig verflicht]" (Scheeben, *Die Mysterien des Christentums*, 319, emphasis original).

67. Here are the relevant biblical texts which have been cited earlier: "All things were created through him and for him . . . in him all things hold together" (Col 1:16–17); and no less: "The mystery of his will, according to his purpose which he set forth in Christ as a plan for the fullness of time, to unite [ἀνακεφαλαιώσασθαι] all things in him" (Eph 1:9–10). The following pages represent a small sampling of Scheeben's use of these very texts: Scheeben, *The Mysteries of Christianity*, 364–65, 401, 403.

most satisfactory resolution to the contemporary debate, and perhaps he holds the key to moving the debate beyond its current impasse.

Scheeben and Intrinsicism

The fundamental importance of intrinsicism and Christocentrism for nature and grace lies in securing the inherent connection between human nature and the supernatural order of grace. As we have seen, de Lubac accomplishes this task by way of his teaching on man's natural desire. As we will see, Scheeben on the other hand accomplishes this same goal, but by means of the Incarnation. In both instances, however, the effect is one and the same. Accordingly, Scheeben states: "The whole human race becomes the body of the Son of God when one of its members is embodied in the Son of God. . . . The whole human race is related to the person of the Son in a manner analogous to the way in which the humanity assumed by Him is related to Him."[68] For Scheeben, in other words, the Incarnation brings about a permanent relation between the Eternal Son and all of humanity, and this relation pertains to the entire human race. He writes:

> The entire race likewise becomes the body and flesh of the Word, not in a purely moral sense, but as truly and really as the union of the race with the humanity of Christ, and the union of this humanity with the divine person, are true and real. . . . Thus they [the human race] belong to Him more than to themselves, and in a larger sense form one person with Him, somewhat as Christ's own humanity, which entirely stripped of its autonomy, forms one person with the Son.[69]

68. Scheeben, *The Mysteries of Christianity*, 367–68; "Das ganze menschliche Geschlecht wird der Leib des Sohnes Gottes, wenn ein Glied desselben dem Sohne Gottes einverleibt wird. . . . *Das ganze menschliche Geschlecht verhält sich somit in analoger Weise zu der Person des Sohnes wie die von ihm in sich aufgenommene Menschheit*" (Scheeben, *Die Mysterien des Christentums*, 305, emphasis original). Though cited earlier, it is worth recalling the text of *Gaudium et Spes* no. 22: "For by His Incarnation the Son of God has united Himself in some fashion with every man." Pope John Paul II cites this very teaching with approval in his first encyclical several times. See John Paul II, *Redeemer of Man*, no. 8, 13, 18. Bl. John Paul II refers to this teaching of Vatican II in the encyclical *Evangelium Vitae* as a "wonderful truth" which "reveals to humanity . . . the boundless love of God . . . [as well as] the incomparable value of every human life" (John Paul II, *Evangelium Vitae*, no. 2).

69. Scheeben, *The Mysteries of Christianity*, 368–69; "Das ganze Geschlecht wird ebenfalls der Leib, das Fleisch des Wortes, nicht in einem bloß moralischen Sinne,

Scheeben goes even further, positing a *communicatio idiomatum* of sorts between the human race and the Eternal Son—in virtue of the

---

sondern so wahrhaft und reell, wie die Einheit des Geschlechtes mit der Menschheit Christi und die Einheit dieser Menschheit mit der göttlichen Person eine wahre und reelle ist. . . . so können auch die dem Geschlechte angehörenden Personen in einer höheren, in geheimnisvoller Weise das ganze Geschlecht durchherrschenden Person aufgenommen, mit ihrer eigenen Persönlichkeit dieser höheren angeeignet, von ihr umspannt und durch drungen werden, so daß sie ihr mehr angehören als sich selbst, und im weiteren Sinne auf ähnliche Weise mit ihr eine Person bilden wie die ihrer Selbständigkeit gänzlich beraubte ureigene Menschheit Christi" (Scheeben, *Die Mysterien des Christentums*, 306). In context, the language of Christ's humanity "being stripped of its autonomy" does not mean that Christ did not have a human will. Rather, what Scheeben is saying is that there is no *human person* in Christ, since Christ is one Divine Person with two natures (intellect and will flowing from each *nature*). Noteworthy also is the fact that Scheeben describes this relationship in a manner similar to the way in which de Lubac described the medieval Eucharistic controversies discussed earlier: namely, that "mystical" and "real" should not be set in opposition to one another (De Lubac, *Corpus Mysticum*, 223). Scheeben states: "The [human] race is usually styled the mystical body of Christ and Christ's own humanity is known as the *real* body of Christ, just as the union of the race with Christ is termed a *mystical* union, and that of His own body with His divine person is called a real union. . . . As the distinction stands, the adjectives 'mystical' and 'real' must be taken as opposites that mutually exclude each other. If such were actually the case, the union of Christ's humanity with His divine person would not be mystical, that is, mysterious and supernatural, and Christ's body would not be the body of God's Son in a mystical and mysterious manner. But how is this conceivable, since there is no more sublime, more wonderful, more mysterious union and unity than that between the Son of God and His humanity? And is it not true that the mystical character of the union of the race with Christ is based precisely upon the mystery of the hypostatic union? *Conversely, too, the union of the race with Christ is real and objective*, and is based on the real, internal unity of the race; further, it participates not only in the mysterious character, but also in the reality of the hypostatic union" (Scheeben, *Mysteries of Christianity*, 369, emphases added); "Das Geschlecht wird in der Regel der *mystische Leib* Christi, die Christus eigene Menschheit der *reale Leib Christi*, wie die Einheit des Geschlechtes mit Christus ebenfalls eine mystische, die seines eigenen Leibes mit seiner göttlichen Person reale Einheit. . . . Wie die Unterscheidung liegt, muß man die Prädikate 'mystisch' und 'real' als Gegensätze fassen, die sich gegenseitig ausschließen. Dann würde die Einheit der Menschheit Christi mit seiner göttlichen Person keine mystische, d. h. geheimnisvolle, übernatürliche sein, und der Leib Christi wäre nicht Leib des Sohnes Gottes auf eine mystische, geheimnisvolle Weise. Aber wie wäre das denkbar, da es keine erhabenere, wunderbarere, geheimnisvollere Union und Einheit gibt als zwischen dem Sohne Gottes und seiner Menschheit? Und beruht nicht auch eben der mystische Charakter der Einheit des Geschlechtes mit Christus eben auf dem Mysterium der hypostatischen Union? Umgekehrt ist auch die Einheit des Geschlechtes mit Christus eine reale, objective, in der realen Einheit des Geschlechtes an sich fußende, und partizipiert, wie an dem geheimnisvollen Charakter, so auch an der Realität der hypostatischen Union . . ." (Scheeben, *Die Mysterien des Christentums*, 306–7, emphasis original).

Incarnation—which is to say, even prior to baptism:

> Owing to our incorporation into His divine person and our union with His own humanity as the head of the mystical body, a *communicatio idiomatum* (interchange of properties) takes place between us and Christ similar to that which obtains between His own humanity and the divine person. And this interchange of properties is the best proof of the wonderful, mysterious union existing between the [whole] *human race* and the *Son of God*, who has entered in its midst.[70]

In Scheeben's mind, no less than a nuptial union has taken place in the Incarnation between the Logos and the entire human race. This marriage begins in the Incarnation and is later consummated through the sacraments of baptism and the Eucharist. Importantly, for Scheeben, this later consummation builds upon the *reality* of the former union established in the Incarnation. He writes:

> Because of the perfect hypostatic union of a member of the human race with the Logos, *the whole of human nature is wedded to Him in a very expressive sense of the word, and has become His bride.* The Logos, by assuming flesh from the flesh of the race and by making it His own, has become one flesh with all other persons of the race. The womb of the Virgin has become the bridal chamber wherein human nature has celebrated its ineffable nuptials with Him, and on account of its first fruit has been accepted by Him as His bride, and has become united to Him.[71]

70. Scheeben, *The Mysteries of Christianity*, 371, emphasis added; "Zwischen uns und Christus findet kraft unserer Eingliederung in seine göttliche Person und kraft unseres Anschlusses an seine eigene Menschheit, als das Haupt des mystischen Leibes, eine ähnliche 'communicatio idiomatum' (Austausch der Eigentümlichkeiten) statt wie zwischen seiner eigenen Menschheit und der göttlichen Person; und dieser Austausch der Eigentümlichkeiten ist der beste Beweis der wunderbaren, geheimnisvollen Einheit, die zwischen dem Menschengeschlechte und dem in seinen Schoß eingetretenen Sohne Gottes besteht" (Scheeben, *Die Mysterien des Christentums*, 308–9).

71. Scheeben, *The Mysteries of Christianity*, 373, emphasis added; "Daß gerade durch die volle hypostatische Einheit eines Gliedes der menschlichen Natur mit dem Logos die ganze Natur mit ihm im stärksten Sinne vermählt und seine Braut geworden sei. Indem nämlich der Logos Fleisch vom Fleische des Geschlechtes angenommen und sich zu eigen gemacht, sei er mit den übrigen Personen des Geschlechtes eins geworden in einem Fleische. Der Schoß der Jungfrau sei das Brautgemach gewesen, worin die menschliche Natur ihre unaussprechliche Vermählung mit ihm gefeiert habe, und durch ihren Erstling als seine Braut von ihm angenommen, ihm vereinigt worden sei" (Scheeben, *Die Mysterien des Christentums*, 310). Similarly, regarding ancient Israel's relation to the Son, Scheeben writes: "Even in the Old Testament the people of Israel

In the following, let us notice the ease with which he moves back and forth between describing the human race as the *"true* body of Christ," and describing the sacramentally "regenerated" people of God (i.e., the baptized) as the *"mystical* body of Christ." The reason he can do so is because of his teaching that the Incarnation itself has inaugurated a metaphysical relation between the Eternal Son and all of humanity. And so Scheeben writes:

> The divine dignity, which the humanity of Christ receives through its personal union with the Eternal Word, is reflected upon all the members of our race. As that humanity was made

---

was called God's son on account of its close connection with Christ, not as a mere type of Him, but because it was His own people by kin and formed one person with Him" (Scheeben, *The Mysteries of Christianity*, 370); "Im Alten Bunde schon wurde das israelitische Volk wegen seines engeren Verbandes mit Christus, nicht als bloßer Typus desselben, sondern weil es als sein Stammgeschlecht mit ihm verwandt war und eine Person mit ihm bildete, der Sohn Gottes genannt" (Scheeben, *Die Mysterien des Christentums*, 307). The allusion is to Exod 4:22 and Hos 11:1, the latter of which is cited in the New Testament in Matt 2:15. Using the words "virtual marriage" to describe this relation, he makes the same point here: "So far as the bodily union between God's Son and the human nature wedded to Him resulted immediately from the Incarnation, it is to be thought of primarily along the lines of the union which existed between Adam and Eve inasmuch as Eve was derived from Adam's side, but not according to the analogy of the union effected by their marriage as formally contracted or consummated. The latter kind of union is not established between Christ and us except by baptism and the Eucharist. But just as the derivation of the woman from the man's side served to prefigure and prepare the way for their marital union . . . *so likewise the assumption of human nature from the midst of the race is the foundation of the formal nuptials of God's Son with the human race* by baptism and the Eucharist. It is, so to speak, a *virtual marriage* . . ." (Scheeben, *The Mysteries of Christianity*, 374, emphasis added); "Daß die leibliche Einheit des Sohnes Gottes mit der ihm vermählten menschlichen Natur, insoweit sie unmittelbar in der Inkarnation selbst gegeben ist, zunächst bloß zu denken ist nach Analogie derjenigen, welche zwischen Adam und Eva insofern bestand, als Eva aus der Seite Adams genommen war, nicht aber nach Analogie derjenigen, welche zwischen Adam und Eva insofern bestand, als Eva aus der Seite Adams genommen war nicht aber nach Analogie derjenigen, welche erst durch die förmlich engegangene resp. vollzogene Ehe hergestellt wird. Letztere Einheit wird zwischen Christus und uns erst hergestellt durch die Taufe und die Eucharistie. Wie aber zur Grundlegung und Präformation der ehelichen Einheit das Weib aus der Seite des Mannes genommen . . . so ist auch die Annahme der menschlichen Natur aus dem Schoße des Geschlechtes beim Sohne Gottes die Grundlage seiner förmlichen Vermählung mit demselben durch die Taufe und die Eucharistie, sie ist gleichsam eine virtuelle Vermählung" (Scheeben, *Die Mysterien des Christentums*, 311).

the true body of Christ, so all of *regenerated* [i.e., baptized, cf. Titus 3:5] mankind was made the Mystical Body of Christ.[72]

For Scheeben, while faith and baptism confer the "rights and privileges" of man in a graced state,[73] this sacramental relationship builds upon the primordial union established already in the Incarnation. Accordingly, he states:

> Faith and baptism do not establish the simple union of the body [i.e., the human race as the body of Christ] with Christ; rather *they presuppose its existence.* If faith makes this union a living union, some material lifeless union must already be present as that which is to be vitalized. *The Spirit of the head cannot flow into us unless we already pertain to His body in some respect;* and on our part we cannot lay hold of Christ our head and clasp Him firmly unless He is already our head in a true sense, and *unless we already joined to Him in some way.* Further, since faith and indeed complete oneness of life with Christ can be present in us prior to baptism, some sort of bodily union with Christ must precede even baptism. *Baptism merely perfects, seals, organizes, completes, and consummates this union; but its foundation had been laid previously. The basis for our common sharing in Christ's goods and graces is His general relationship with the race as such.*[74]

---

72. Scheeben, *The Glories of Divine Grace*, 53, emphasis added; "Die göttliche Würde, welche die Menschheit Christi durch die persönliche Vereinigung mit dem ewigen Worte erhalten, strahlt auf alle Glieder des menschlichen Geschlechtes zurück. Wie jene der wahre Leib des Wortes geworden, so ist auch das ganze wiedergeborene Menschengeschlecht der mystische Leib des menschgewordenen Sohnes Gottes" (Scheeben, *Die Herrlichkeiten der Göttlichen Gnade*, 47).

73. Scheeben, *The Mysteries of Christianity*, 375.

74. Ibid., emphasis added; "Und der Taufe wird die Verbindung der Menschen mit Christus erst eine organische, eine an den Menschen äußerlich und innerlich hervortretende; in der Taufe drückt Christus ihnen das Gepräge ihrer Angehörigkeit an ihn auf und setzt sie dadurch in den Vollbesitz und Genuß der ihnen als Gliedern seines Leibes zustehenden Rechte und Privilegien. Aber beiderseits wird die einfache Einheit des Leibes mit Christus nicht nur nicht zuerst hergestellt, sondern geradezu vorausgesetzt. Wenn im Glauben die Einheit eine lebendige wird, dann mußte die materielle, die tote Einheit schon vorhanden sein als die zu belebende. Der Geist des Hauptes kann nicht in uns einströmen, wenn wir nicht schon in etwa zu seinem Leibe gehören, und wir unsererseits können jenes Haupt ist, und wir in etwa schon mit ihm verbunden sind. Da nun ferner der Glaube, ja auch die volle Lebenseinheit mit Christus vor der Taufe in uns vorhanden sein kann, so muß auch der Taufe schon eine gewisse Einheit des Leibes mit Christus vorausgehen. In der Taufe wird dieselbe nur ausgebildet, ausgeprägt, organisiert, vollzogen und abgeschlossen; aber grundgelegt war sie schon vorher. Die Grundlage der Güter und Gnadengemeinschaft mit Christus

On Scheeben's account, this teaching is no modern or medieval novelty, but finds its roots in the patristic inheritance of faith:

> The Fathers view the Incarnation itself as a marriage with the human race, inasmuch as it virtually contains everything that can lead to the full union of the Son of God with men. But the relationship of unity it sets up comes to full fruition only in the Church. Man is to attach himself to his divine bridegroom by faith; and the bridegroom seals His union with man in baptism, as with a wedding ring. But both faith and baptism are mere preliminaries for the coming together of man and the God-man in one flesh by a real Communion of flesh and blood in the Eucharist.[75]

On this point, Scheeben has an extended footnote, citing a number of Church Fathers, both East and West, who make similar claims regarding the Incarnation. For example, St. Hilary of Poitiers writes: "The Son of

---

ist sein allgemeines Verhältnis zum Geschlechte als solchem" (Scheeben, *Die Mysterien des Christentums*, 311). Elsewhere, he writes: "The Son of God, exerting the infinite attractive force of His divine person, took to Himself the race thus unified and made it his own throughout its entire compass. This He did by making His own and assuming to His person a member of the race that is ontologically connected with all the other members. *Thereby He becomes the new head of the whole race. . . .* Therefore, by taking complete possession of a member of the race, *He can draw the entire race to Himself, incorporate it in Himself* . . . because of the intimate, solidary union of this one member with all the rest, He [God, the Father] made all the other members [of the human race] His own through this one [Jesus Christ] and in this one [Jesus Christ]" (Scheeben, *The Mysteries of Christianity*, 366–67); "Das mit den übrigen in realem Zusammenhange steht, sich aneignet und in seine Person aufnimmt; und dadurch wird er das neue Haupt des ganzen Geschlechtes. . . . Sie eignet sich bloß eine menschliche Natur an, um sie zu beherrschen, um sie ihrer Persönlichkeit einzuverleiben, und so kann sie auch, indem sie ein Glied des Geschlechtes ganz in sich aufgehen läßt, das ganze Geschlecht an sich ziehen, sich einverleiben und beherrschen. . . . Weil er wegen der innigen, solidarischen Verbindung, in der dieses eine Glied mit allen übrigen Glieder sich angeeignet hat" (Scheeben, *Die Mysterien des Christentums*, 304–5).

75. Scheeben, *The Mysteries of Christianity*, 543; "Die Inkarnation an sich wird schon von den heiligen Vätern als eine Vermählung mit dem Menschengeschlechte dargestellt, insofern darin virtuell alles enthalten ist, ws zur vollen Vereinigung des Sohnes Gottes mit den Menschen führt. Allein das in ihr grundgelegte Einheitsverhältnis kommt erst in der Kirche zu Ausführung. Der Mensch soll im Glauben sich an seinen göttlichen Bräutigam anschließen, und dieser will in der Taufe seinen Bund mit ihm, wie durch einen Trauring, besiegeln. Beides geschieht aber nur dazu, um in der Eucharistie durch reale Kommunion des Fleisches und Blutes den Menschen und den Gottmenschen zu Einem Fleisch zu verschmelzen und dadurch in der vollkommensten Weise den Menschen mit der Gnadenkraft seines Hauptes zu befruchten" (Scheeben, *Die Mysterien des Christentums*, 447).

God assumed the nature of flesh common to all; and having thus become the true vine, *He contains within Himself the entire race of its offspring.*"[76] And likewise, St. Gregory of Nyssa: "From the whole human nature, to which was joined divinity, arose, as the first fruit of the common mass, the man who is in Christ, *by whom all mankind was united to divinity.*"[77]

As we have seen, this patristic and biblical inheritance appears also in the teaching of the Second Vatican Council: "For by His Incarnation the Son of God has united Himself in some fashion to every man."[78] For this reason, the link between de Lubac and Scheeben seems to lie—not just in their common outlook and sensitivity to, say, "mystery," "familial" logic, and the like—but even more importantly on account of their common indebtedness to the biblical and patristic heritage of faith. No doubt, herein is the source of Scheeben's intrinsicism, and herein also is the source of Scheeben's convergence with de Lubac.

This conclusion becomes all the more apparent when we take into account the fact that Scheeben's Christocentricism implies—not just that Christ is the head of every human being—but that He is the head of *all creation*. Let us recall here St. Paul's teaching again to this effect: "For in him all things were created, in heaven and on earth, visible and invisible . . . all things were created *through* him and *for* him" (Col 1:16).[79] Scheeben follows suit here without hesitation: "The God-man is associated with *all* creatures into whose society He has entered, and must on His part catch up *all* creatures into the mystery of the divine Trinity and Triunity."[80] The Incarnation, therefore, unites God intrinsically with all of creation, and so Scheeben writes:

---

76. St. Hilary of Poitiers, *Commentary on the Psalms*, cited in Scheeben, *Mysteries of Christianity*, 367 n. 3, emphasis added.

77. St. Gregory of Nyssa, *Commentary on 1 Cor 15:28*, cited in Scheeben, *The Mysteries of Christianity*, 368 n. 4, emphasis added.

78. *Gaudium et Spes*, n. 22, in *Vatican Council II: Constitutions, Decrees, Declarations*. See also Schönborn, *Chance or Purpose*, 129–43. Schönborn has a fairly extended treatment of Pierre Teilhard de Chardin in this chapter, drawing particularly on this theme from Col 1:16–17 (ibid., 132ff.).

79. "ὅτι ἐν αὐτῷ ἐκτίσθη τὰ πάντα ἐ τοῖς οὐρανοῖς καὶ ἐπὶ τῆς γῆς, τὰ ὁρατὰ καὶ τὰ ἀόρατα . . . τὰ πάντα δι' αὐτοῦ καὶ εἰς αὐτὸν ἔκτισται" (Col 1:16).

80. Scheeben, *The Mysteries of Christianity*, 364, emphasis added: "Der Gott-mensch ist verflochten mit allen Kreaturen, in deren Gemeinschaft er eingetreten, und soll seinerseits alle Kreaturen in das Mysterium der göttlichen Dreifaltigkeit und Dreieinigkeit verflechten" (Scheeben, *Die Mysterien des Christentums*, 301).

He is in truth God and man. As man He is at one with the whole human race, indeed, *with the created world*, for He is its head. As God . . . He raises the world up to the closest proximity, the most intimate union, with the eternal Father; on the other hand, *the union which He has with the Father, He extends outside of God, and conveys to the entire world.* He links God and God's creature together in so close a union and mutual relationship . . .[81]

81. Scheeben, *The Mysteries of Christianity*, 406: "Der Gottmensch ist die persön-liche, hypostatische Einheit der Gottheit mit der Menschheit; er ist in Wahrheit Gott und Mensch. Als Mensch ist er eins, ein Ganzes mit dem ganzen Menschengeschlechte, ja mit der geschaffenen Welt, die er als Haupt in sich trägt; als Gott steht er in der realsten, innigsten Verbindung mit seinem Vater, von dem er ausgeht, und mit dem Heiligen Geiste, den er aushaucht. In der Welt stehend, eins mit der Welt, ragt er in das Innerste der Gottheit hinein, ist selbst Gott und eins mit dem Vater und dem Heiligen Geiste. Folglich hebt er in seiner Person die Welt in die nächste Nähe, in die innigste Verbindung mit dem ewigen Vater empor und trägt anderseits die Einheit, die er mit dem Vater hat, weiter nach außen und leitet sie über auf die ganze Welt. Er verflicht miteinander Gott und seine Kreatur durch eine so innige Einheit und Wechselbeziehung, daß dadurch nicht allein jede Trennung der Kreatur von Gott durch ihren Abfall, sondern auch der unendliche Abstand der Kreatur von Gott, in dem sie schon von Natur, d. h. also abgesehen von ihrem Falle, steht, überwunden und aufgehoben wird" (Scheeben, *Die Mysterien des Christentums*, 336). Scheeben even suggests that Christ' self-offering on the Cross is the offering—not just of humanity back to the Father—but of all creation as well. The entire cosmos is in a sense "in" the Son and is therefore offered back to the Father on the Cross. In this light, *in Christ*, the redemption of *all* creation takes place: "Christ as the head of the human race is truly a priest, the representative of all His members in the worship of God. Hence He offers His sacrifice as head of all His members, *primarily in the name of the human race*, [but] *secondarily in the name of the entire universe*" (Scheeben, *The Mysteries of Christianity*, 438, emphasis added); "Christus ist, wie wie früher gesehen, als Haupt des Menschengeschlechtes wahrhaft Priester, Vertreter aller seiner Glieder im Kulte Gottes, und soll daher auch als Haupt aller seiner Glieder im Namen des Menschengeschlechtes zunächst, und weiterhin im Namen des ganzen Universums sein Opfer darbringen" (Scheeben, *Die Mysterien des Christentums*, 361–62). Scheeben similarly writes that as "the head of all creatures," Christ "officiates in His sacrifice as a priest in the absolute sense of the word, reproducing in the creature, by the mutual surrender of boundless love, that mutual surrender which necessarily takes place between the Father and the Son. . . . We are naturally led to ascribe to that sacrifice a universal significance for the whole of creation. . . . What is more natural than to suppose that this supreme sacrificial act, which is offered in the heart of creation and enables it to achieve its ultimate purpose, is performed in the name of all creatures, and that creation in its totality shares in it?" (Scheeben, *The Mysteries of Christianity*, 444–45); "das Haupt aller Kreaturen" (Scheeben, *Die Mysterien des Christentums*, 368); "Und indem er durch seine Auferstehung, in welcher er die Wahrzeichen seiner Selbstvernichtung bewahrt, als das von Anfang geschlachtete Lamm in Ewigkeit vor den Augen Gottes steht und so das in der Fülle der Zeit gesetzte Opfer zum ewigen macht, fungiert er in seinem Opfer als der Priester im absoluten Sinn des Wortes, der die wesenhafte Wechselhingabe

Clearly, Scheeben wishes to embrace the intrinsicist insight that reality is at its core unabashedly Christocentric—just as the Letter to the Colossians has it: "all things were created *for* [Christ]" (Col 1:16). For this reason, Scheeben's theology is singularly poised to reconcile intrinsicism and extrinsicism; and as acrimonious as the nature-grace debate was at mid-twentieth century, his contribution here is perhaps more timely now than ever.

Accordingly, our aim in the following chapter is simply to point out why this is indeed the case. Hence, it is our hope and modest conviction that this project will become more than merely an academic exercise, but rather one which might contribute in some small way toward Scheeben's becoming a more central figure in this discussion. And so let us now turn to our conclusion.

---

zwischen Vater und Sohn in der Kreatur durch die Wechselhingabe unermeßlicher Liebe zur Darstellung bringt.... So muß es ganz natürlich erscheinen, ihm weiterhin die universalste Bedeutung für die ganze Schöpfung beizulegen.... oder was ist natürlicher als diesen höchsten Zweck derselben erfüllt, im Namen der Gesamtschöpfung gesetzt und die letztere in ihrer Totalität an ihm beteiligt zu denken?" (ibid., 368, 366).

7

Conclusion

We have argued that the theology of Matthias J. Scheeben is best able to capture the Christian mystery of nature and grace in all its fullness, both in its Christocentric dimension, as well as in regards to the necessary distinction between nature and grace. Our claim is that Scheeben can reconcile the most important contributions of both intrinsicism and extrinsicism, which is to say that he can reconcile the most important contributions of de Lubac and the pure-nature tradition.

As we mentioned at the close of the previous chapter, Scheeben's singular contribution on this issue is particularly relevant at the present time, as the Church moves beyond the postconciliar era. This is especially the case for the following reasons: (1) the polemical character of the nature-grace debate has subsided, which no doubt greatly strengthens the prospects that the present discussion will bear fruit; (2) as we have noted throughout, there has been a noticeable increase in interest and activity regarding this debate, a point which is witnessed by the very publication of the works of Lawrence Feingold and Steven A. Long.[1]

---

1. Long, *Natura Pura*; Feingold, *Natural Desire to See God*. John Milbank's, *The Suspended Middle* is an example of a negative review of Feingold. More recently, D. Stephen Long has reviewed Steven A. Long's book above in a negative light as well. D. Long, review of *Natura Pura* by Steven A. Long, 695–98. On the other hand, just as recent is the following article which makes explicit the author's indebtedness to both Long and Feingold: Malloy, "De Lubac on Natural Desire," 567–624. Malloy concludes his article this way: "I owe enormous thanks to Lawrence Feingold and Steven Long for their assistance on matters pertinent to this article" (ibid., 624). Also noteworthy is Portier, "Thomist Resurgence" a review of *Twentieth-Century Catholic Theologians* by Fergus Kerr, 494–504. Guy Mansini has recently attempted to correlate Feingold's work with that of Bernard Lonergan (1904–1984). Mansini, "Lonergan on the Natural Desire

195

While these works have received both positive and negative reviews, let us note that even the negative reviews are indicative of an intellectual climate that recognizes the paramount importance of this issue; and finally, (3) Scheeben is yet to be considered as a significant interlocutor in this debate, as one who is poised to make his own unique contribution, and so our work here hopes to rectify this lacuna.

For all of these reasons, the present context provides an opportune time for introducing Scheeben to the present discussion on nature and grace. For both the freshness of his analysis, as well as his uncanny ability to reach both sides of the spectrum, make him a formidable candidate. Quite possibly—at least such is our contention—Scheeben could recast the entire debate in a whole new light, allowing for a reconciliation of the most important aspects of each side.

Indeed, Scheeben can rightly be said to have presaged what Reinhard Hütter has recently described as a "Ressourcement Thomism,"[2] a term which describes not only a renewed appreciation of the pure-nature tradition, but one which seeks to cede to de Lubac his full due, as one who in some respects has made a permanent contribution to the Church, even and especially on the matter of nature and grace.[3] Scheeben, we suggest, is just such a model, one no doubt certainly well ahead of his time.

While Scheeben is certainly an avowed Thomist, he is no less steeped in the Christocentrism of the Bible and the Church Fathers; and likely for this reason, no one captures the nature-grace dynamic better than he, as a mystery comprised of both distinction and unity. The contemporary discussion will be well served by his contribution; for as we have argued here, the key to resolving the contemporary debate seems to lie in no other than the theology of Matthias Joseph Scheeben.

And so here we come to the end of our journey, one which has spanned several centuries, but always with the same goal in mind: namely, to capture the fullness of the mystery of nature and grace—both in its Christocentric dimension, as well as maintaining the requisite

---

in the Light of Feingold," 185–98. See also: Mettepenningen, *Nouvelle Théologie–New Theology*; Thompson and Long, *Reason and the Rule of Faith*; and Mulcahy, *Aquinas's Notion*.

2. See Hütter, "Catholic Theology in America," 539–47.

3. The work of the Dominicans of Toulouse also captures this sentiment well. Bonino, *Surnaturel*.

distinction between nature and grace. No one brings these aspects together as well as Scheeben; and so with both humility and conviction, we look forward to the fruit of his contribution, as the Church unceasingly continues its mission of service and evangelization, articulating to the culture at large the nobility of man's nature and the sublime dignity of his calling in Christ.

Bibliography

Alberigo, Giuseppe, and Komonchak, Joseph A., eds. *History of Vatican II, Vol. 1: Announcing and Preparing Vatican Council II: Toward a New Era in Catholicism.* EnglishVersion. Maryknoll, NY: Orbis, 1995.

Aristotle. *Aristotelis De Anima.* Edited by W. D. Ross. Oxford: Oxford University Press, 1963.

————. *Aristotelis De Caelo.* Edited by D. J. Allan. Oxford: Oxford University Press, 1965.

————. *Aristotelis De Generatione Animalium.* Edited by H. J. Drossaart Lulofs. Oxford: Oxford University Press, 1965.

————. *Aristotelis Ethica.* Edited by I. Bywater. Oxford: Oxford University Press, 1920.

————. *Aristotelis Physica.* Edited by W. D. Ross. Oxford: Oxford University Press, 1966.

————. *The Complete Works of Aristotle.* Edited by Jonathan Barnes. 2 vols. Oxford: Oxford University Press, 1984.

————. *Nicomachean Ethics.* Translated by Terence Irwin. 2nd ed. Indianapolis: Hackett, 1999.

Athanasius, Saint. *On the Incarnation.* Translated and edited by a Religious of C. S. M. V. Crestwood, NY: St. Vladimir's Seminary Press, 1998.

Aubert, Roger. *The Church in a Secularised Society.* New York: Paulist, 1978.

Augustine, Saint. *Confessions.* Translated by R. S. Pine-Coffin. Penguin: New York, 1961.

Aquinas, Thomas, Saint. *Commentary on Aristotle's Nicomachean Ethics.* Translated by C. I. Litzinger. Notre Dame: Dumb Ox, 1993.

————. *On Evil.* Translated by Jean Oesterle. Notre Dame: University of Notre Dame Press, 1995.

————. *Questiones Disputatae de Veritate.* Translated by Robert W. Mulligan. Chicago: Henry Regnery, 1952.

————. *Summa contra Gentiles.* Translated by Anton Charles Pegis. Notre Dame: University of Notre Dame Press, 1991.

————. *Summa Theologica.* New York: Benziger Bros., 1948.

————. *Thomas Aquinas: Selected Writings.* Edited and translated by Ralph McInerny. New York: Penguin, 1998.

Balthasar, Hans Urs von. *Seeing the Form.* Translated by Erasmo Leiva-Merikakis. San Francisco: Ignatius, 1982.

————. *The Theology of Henri de Lubac.* Translated by Joseph Fessio and Michael M. Waldstein. San Francisco: Ignatius, 1991.

————. *The Theology of Karl Barth: Exposition and Interpretation.* Translated by Edward T. Oakes. San Francisco: Ignatius, 1992.

Báñez, Domingo. *Commentarios inéditos a la Prima secundae de Santo Tomás*. Vol. 1, *Scholastic commentaria in primam partem*. Edited by Vicente Beltrán de Heredia. Madrid: Matriti, 1942.

Biblia Hebraica Stuttgartensia. Stuttgart: Deutsche Bibelgesellschaft, 1997.

Blanchette, Oliva. *Maurice Blondel: A Philosophical Life*. Grand Rapids: Eerdmans, 2010.

Blondel, Maurice. *L'Action*. Vol. 1, *Le Problème des Causes Secondes et Le pur Agir*. Paris: Presses Universitaires de France, 1949.

———. *L'Action*. Vol. 2, *L'Action Humaine et Les Conditions de son Aboutissement*. Paris: Presses Universitaires de France, 1963.

———. *L'Action: Essay on a Critique of Life and a Science of Action*. Translated by Oliva Blanchette. Notre Dame: University of Notre Dame Press, 1984.

———. *The Letter on Apologetics and History and Dogma*. Translated by Illtyd Trethowan. Grand Rapids: Eerdmans, 1995.

Bonino, Serge-Thomas. *Surnaturel: A Controversy at the Heart of Twentieth-Century Thomistic Thought*. Translated by Robert Williams; translation revised by Matthew Levering. Naples, FL: Sapientia, 2009.

Cajetan, Tommaso de Vio. Commentary on *Summa theologiae*. In *Sancti Thomae Aquinatis Opera Omnia*. Leonine edition. Vols. 4–12. Rome, 1888–1906.

Catechism of the Catholic Church. 2nd ed. Vatican: Libreria Editrice Vaticana, 1997.

Cessario, Romanus. *Christian Faith and the Theological Life*. Washington, DC: Catholic University of America Press, 1996.

———. *A Short History of Thomism*. Washington, DC: Catholic University of America Press, 2005.

Chadwick, Owen. *The Secularization of the European Mind in the Nineteenth Century*. Cambridge: Cambridge University Press, 1975.

Coffele, Gianfranco. "De Lubac and the Theological Foundation of the Missions." *Communio* 23 (1996) 757–75.

Cunningham, Conor. "*Natura Pura*, the Invention of the Anti-Christ: A Week with No Sabbath." *Communio* 37 (2010) 243–54.

Dansette, Adrian. *Histoire Religieuse de la France Contemporaine*. 2 vols. Paris: Flammarion, 1948–51.

———. *Religious History of Modern France*. Translated by John Dingle. 2 vols. Edinburgh: Nelson, 1961.

De Lubac, Henri. "Apologétique et théologie." *Nouvelle Revue Théologique* 57 (1930) 361–78.

———. *At the Service of the Church*. Translated by Anne Elizabeth Englund. San Francisco: Ignatius, 1993.

———. *Augustinianism and Modern Theology*. Translated by Lancelot Sheppard. New York: Crossroad, 2000.

———. *Augustinisme et théologie moderne*. Paris: Les Éditions du Cerf, 2008.

———. *A Brief Catechesis on Nature and Grace*. Translated by Richard Arnandez. San Francisco: Ignatius, 1984.

———. *Catholicism: Christ and the Common Destiny of Man*. Translated by Lancelot C. Sheppard and Elizabeth Englund. San Francisco: Ignatius, 1988.

———. *Catholicisme: Les aspects sociaux du dogme*. Paris: Cerf, 2003.

———. "The Church in Crisis." *Theology Digest* 17 (1969) 312–25.

———. *Corpus Mysticum: L'Eucharistie et l'Église au Moyen Âge*. Paris: Cerf, 2010.

———. *Corpus Mysticum: The Eucharist and the Church in the Middle Ages*. Translated by Gemma Simmonds. Notre Dame: University of Notre Dame Press, 2006.

———. *De la connaissance de Dieu.* Paris: Témoignage Chrétien, 1941.

———. *The Discovery of God.* Translated by Alexander Dru. Grand Rapids: Eerdmans, 1996.

———. *The Drama of Atheist Humanism.* Translated by Edith M. Riley, Anne Englund, and Mark Sebanc. San Francisco: Ignatius, 1995.

———. *Le drame l'humanisme athée.* Paris: Cerf, 1998.

———. "Duplex hominis beatitudo." *Communio* 35 (2008) 599–612.

———. "*Duplex Hominis Beatitudo* (Saint Thomas, Ia 2ae, q. 62, a. I)." *Recherches de science religieuse* 35 (1948) 290–99.

———. *Medieval Exegesis: The Four Senses of Scripture.* Vol. 2. Translated by E. M. Macierowski. Grand Rapids: Eerdmans, 2000.

———. *Medieval Exegesis: The Four Senses of Scripture.* Vol. 3. Translated by. E. M. Macierowski. Grand Rapids: Eerdmans, 2009.

———. *Méditation sur l'Église.* Paris: Les Éditions du Cerf, 2003.

———. *Mémoire sur l'occasion de mes écrits.* Namur: Culture et Vérité, 1989.

———. *Le Mystère du Surnaturel.* Paris: Cerf, 2000.

———. "Le Mystère du Surnaturel." *Recherches de science religieuse* 36 (1949) 80–121.

———. *The Mystery of the Supernatural.* Translated by Rosemary Sheed. New York: Crossroad, 1998.

———. *Petite Catéchèse sur Natur et Grâce.* Paris: Fayard, 1980.

———. "Le problème du developpement du dogme." *Recherches de science Religieuse* 35 (1948) 130–60.

———. *Proudhon et le Christianisme.* Paris: Seuil, 1945.

———. *Splendor of the Church.* Translated by Michael Mason. San Francisco: Ignatius, 1986.

———. *Sur les chemins de Dieu.* Paris: Cerf, 2006.

———. *Surnaturel: Études historiques.* Paris: Desclée de Brouwer, 1991.

———. *Theological Fragments.* San Francisco: Ignatius, 1989.

———. *Théologie dans l'histoire.* Paris: Desclée de Brouwer, 1990.

———. *Theology in History.* Translated by Anne Englund. San Francisco: Ignatius, 1996.

———. *The Un-Marxian Socialist: A Study of Proudhon.* Translated by R. E. Scantlebury. New York: Sheed & Ward, 1948.

Denzinger, Henrich. *Enchiridion symbolorum definitionum et declarationum de rebus fidei et morum.* Quod emendavit, auxit, in linguam germanicam transtulit et adiuvante Helmuto Hoping edidit, Petrus Hünermann, Editio XXXVII. Freiburg: Herder, 1991.

Denzinger, Henry, ed. *The Sources of Catholic Dogma.* Translated by Roy J. Deferrari. Fitzwilliam, NH: Loreto, 2002.

Derfler, Leslie. *The Dreyfus Affair.* Westport, CT: Greenwood, 2002.

———. *The Dreyfus Affair: Tragedy of Errors?* Boston: D. C. Heath, 1963.

———. *Socialism since Marx: A Century of the European Left.* New York: St. Martin's, 1973.

———. *The Third French Republic: 1870–1940.* New York. D. Van Nostrand, 1966.

Dupuis, Jacques, ed. *The Christian Faith in the Doctrinal Documents of the Catholic Church.* 7th rev. ed. Staten Island, NY: Alba, 2001.

Feingold, Lawrence. *The Natural Desire to See God according to St. Thomas Aquinas and His Interpreters.* 2nd ed. Naples, FL: Sapientia, 2010.

Garrigou-Lagrange, Réginald. "La nouvelle théologie où va-t-elle?" *Angelicum* 23 (1946) 126–45.

Gilson, Etienne. *Letters of Etienne Gilson to Henri de Lubac.* Translated by Mary Emily Hamilton San Francisco: Ignatius, 1988.

The Greek New Testament. Edited by Barbara Aland, Kurt Aland, Johannes Kravidopoulos, Carlo M. Martini, and Bruce Metzger. 4th rev. ed. Stuttgart: Deutsche Bibelgesellschaft, 2001.

Hauerwas, Stanely. "How Risky Is *The Risk of Education*? Random Reflections from the American Context." *Communio* 30 (2003) 79–94.

Healey, John W. *Jansenius' Critique of Pure Nature.* Rome: Pontificia Universitas Gregoriana, 1964.

Hütter, Reinhardt. "Aquinas on the Natural Desire for the Vision of God: A Relecture of *Summa Contra Gentiles* III, c. 25 *Après* Henri de Lubac." *Thomist* 73 (2009) 523–91.

———. "Catholic Theology in America: *Quo Vadis?*" *Nova et Vetera* 9 (2011) 539–47.

———."Desiderium Naturale Visionis Dei: Some Observations about Lawrence Feingold's and John Milbank's Recent Interventions in the Debate over the Natural Desire to See God." *Nova et Vetera* 5 (2007) 81–131.

John Paul II. *Evangelium Vitae.* Boston: Pauline, 1995.

———. *Fides et Ratio.* Boston: Pauline, 1998.

———. *The Redeemer of Man.* Boston: Pauline, 1979.

———. *Veritatis Splendor.* Boston: Pauline, 1993.

Kasper, Walter. "The Theological Anthropology of *Gaudium et Spes*." *Communio* 23 (1996) 129–40.

Kerr, Fergus. *Twentieth-Century Catholic Theologians: From Neo-Scholasticism to Nuptial Mysticism.* Oxford: Blackwell, 2007.

Komonchak, Joseph A. "Theology and Culture at Mid-Century: The Example of Henri de Lubac." *Theological Studies* 51 (1990) 579–602.

Körner, Bernhard. "Henri de Lubac and Fundamental Theology." *Communio* 23 (1996) 711–24.

Lapomarda, Vincent A. *Jesuits and the Third Reich.* Lewiston, NY: Edwin Mellen, 2005.

Larkin, Maurice. *Church and State Affairs after the Dreyfus Affair: The Separation Issue in France.* London: Macmillan, 1974.

———. *France since the Popular Front: Government and People 1936–1996.* 2nd ed. Oxford: Clarendon, 1997.

Lewis, C. S. *Miracles.* San Francisco: Harper Collins, 2001.

Long, D. Stephen. Review of *Natura Pura: On the Recovery of Nature in the Doctrine of Grace* by Steven A. Long. *Modern Theology* 27 (2011) 695–98.

Long, Steven A. *Natura Pura: On the Recovery of Nature in the Doctrine of Grace.* New York: Fordham University Press, 2010.

———. "Obediential Potency, Human Knowledge, and the Natural Desire for God." *International Philosophical Quarterly* 37 (1997) 45–63.

———."On the Possibility of a Purely Natural End for Man." *Thomist* 64 (2000) 211–37.

Lossky, Vladimir. *The Mystical Theology of the Eastern Church.* Crestwood, NY: St. Vladimir's Seminary Press, 1976.

Luther, Martin. *Selections from His Writings.* Edited by John Dillenberger. New York: Doubleday, 1962.

MacIntyre, Alasdair. *After Virtue: A Study in Moral Theory.* 2nd ed. Notre Dame: University of Notre Dame Press, 1984.

————. *Three Rival Versions of Moral Enquiry: Encylopaedia, Genealogy, and Tradition.* Notre Dame: University of Notre Dame Press, 1990.

Malloy, Christopher J. "De Lubac on Natural Desire: Difficulties and Antitheses." *Nova et Vetera* 9 (2011) 567–624.

Mansini, Guy. "The Abiding Theological Significance of Henri de Lubac's *Surnaturel.*" *Thomist* 73/4 (2009) 593–619.

————. "Lonergan on the Natural Desire in the Light of Feingold." *Nova et Vetera* 5 (2007) 185–98.

Maritain, Jacques. *Degrees of Knowledge.* Notre Dame: University of Notre Dame Press, 1999.

McBrien, Richard P. *The Church: The Evolution of Catholicism.* New York: HarperCollins, 2008.

McManners, John. *Church and State in France: 1870-1914.* New York: Harper, 1973.

Mertens, Herman-Emiel. "Nature and Grace in Twentieth Century Catholic Theology." *Louvain Studies* 16 (1991) 242–62.

Mettepenningen, Jürgen. *Nouvelle Théologie–New Theology: Inheritor of Modernism, Precursor of Vatican II.* New York: T. & T. Clark, 2010.

Milbank, John. *The Suspended Middle: Henri de Lubac and the Debate Concerning the Supernatural.* Grand Rapids: Eerdmans, 2005.

Mulcahy, Bernhard. *Aquinas's Notion of Pure Nature and the Christian Integralism of Henri de Lubac.* New York: Peter Lang, 2011.

Nichols, Aidan. *Romance and System: The Theological Synthesis of Matthias Joseph Scheeben.* Denver: Augustine Institute, 2010.

————. "Thomism and the Nouvelle Théologie." *Thomist* 64 (2000) 1–19.

Nicolas, J. H. *The Mystery of God's Grace.* Dubuque, IA: The Priory, 1960.

Nietzsche, Friedrich. *Beyond Good and Evil.* Translated by Helen Zimmern. Amherst, NY: Prometheus, 1989.

Oakes, Edward T. "Catholic Eschatology and the Development of Doctrine." *Nova et Vetera* 6 (2008) 419–46.

————. "The Paradox of Nature and Grace: On John Milbank's *The Suspended Middle: Henri de Lubac and the Debate Concerning the Supernatural.*" *Nova et Vetera* 4 (2006) 667–96.

————. "The *Surnaturel* Controversy: A Survey and a Response." *Nova et Vetera* 9 (2011) 625–56.

Ockham, William [of]. *Quaestiones in librum quartum Sententiarum (Reportatio).* Vol. 7 of *Opera philosophica et theologica.* St. Bonaventure, NY: Franciscan Institute, 1984.

Owens, Joseph. *An Elementary Christian Metaphysics.* Houston: Center for Thomistic Studies, 1963.

Paxton, Robert O. *Vichy France: Old Guard and New Order 1940-1944.* New York: Alfred A. Knopf, 1972.

Peddicord, Richard. *The Sacred Monster of Thomism: An Introduction to the Life and Legacy of Réginald Garrigou-Lagrange.* South Bend, IN: St. Augustine's, 2005.

Pelikan, Jaroslav. *The Christian Tradition: A History of the Development of Doctrine.* Vol. 1, *The Emergence of the Catholic Tradition (100-600).* Chicago: University of Chicago Press, 1971.

————. *The Christian Tradition: A History of the Development of Doctrine.* Vol. 4, *Reformation of Church and Dogma (1300-1700).* Chicago: University of Chicago Press, 1984.

Pinckaers, Servais. *Sources of Christian Ethics*. Translated by Mary Thomas Noble. Washington, DC: Catholic University of America Press, 1995.

Pius XII. *Humani Generis: Encyclical Letter of Pope Pius XII: Concerning Some False Opinions Which Threaten to Undermine the Foundations of Catholic Doctrine*. Washington, DC: National Catholic Welfare Conference, 1950.

Portier, William L. "Thomist Resurgence." Review of *Twentieth-Century Catholic Theologians: From Neoscholasticism to Nuptial Mysticism*, by Fergus Kerr. *Communio* 35 (Fall 2008) 494–504.

Rahner, Karl. *Theological Investigations IV*. Translated by Kevin Smyth. London: Darton, Longman & Todd, 1966.

Ratzinger, Joseph. *Christianity and the Crisis of Cultures*. Translated by Brian McNeil. San Francisco: Ignatius, 2006.

———. *The Ratzinger Report: An Exclusive Interview on the State of the Church*. Translated by Salvator Attanasio and Graham Harrison. San Francisco: Ignatius, 1985.

Richardson, Cyril C. *Early Christian Fathers*. Austin, TX: Touchstone, 1995.

Rioux, Jean W., ed. *Nature, the Soul, and God: An Introduction to Natural Philosophy*. Eugene, OR: Cascade, 2004.

Rondet, Henri. *The Grace of Christ: A Brief History of the Theology of Grace*. Translated by Tad W. Guzie. New York: Newman, 1966.

Russo, A. *Henri de Lubac: Teologia e dogma nella storia; L'influsso di Blondel*. Rome: Studium, 1990.

Schall, James V. *The Regensburg Lecture*. Chicago: St. Augustine's, 2007.

Scheeben, Matthias Joseph. *Die Herrlichkeiten der Göttlichen Gnade*. Freiburg: Herder, 1941.

———. *Die Mysterien des Christentums: Wesen, Bedeutung und Zusammenhang derselben nach der in ihrem übernatürlichen Charakter gegebenen Perspektive dargestellt*. Freiburg: Herder, 1951.

———. *The Glories of Divine Grace: A Fervent Exhortation to All to Preserve and to Grow in Sanctifying Grace*. Translated by Patrick Shaughnessy. Rockford, IL: Tan, 2000.

———. *Handbuch der katholischen Dogmatik*. Freiburg: Herder, 1945–61.

———. *The Mysteries of Christianity*. Translated by Cyril Vollert. St. Louis: Herder, 1946.

———. *Natur und Gnade: Versuch einer systematischen, wissenschaftlichen Darstellung der natürlichen und übernatürlichen Lebensordnung im Menschen*. Freiburg: Herder, 1949.

———. *Nature and Grace*. Translated by Cyril Vollert. St. Louis: Herder, 1954.

Schindler, David L. "Christology and the *Imago Dei*: Interpreting *Gaudium et Spes*." *Communio* 23 (1996) 156–83.

Schönborn, Christoph. *Chance or Purpose? Creation, Evolution, and a Rational Faith*. Translated by Henry Taylor. San Francisco: Ignatius, 2007.

Suárez, Franciscus. *Opera Omnia*. Edited by D. M. André. Paris: Vivès, 1856–1878.

Sylvester of Ferrara, Francis [Franciscus de Sylvestris Ferrariensis]. "Commentary on *Summa contra Gentiles*." In *Sancti Thomae Aquinatis Opera Omnia*, vols. 13–15. Leonine edition. Rome, 1918–1926.

Tanner, Norman P. *Decrees of the Ecumenical Councils*. Washington, DC: Georgetown University Press, 1990.

Thompson, Christopher J., and Steven A. Long. *Reason and the Rule of Faith: Conversations in the Tradition with John Paul II.* New York: University Press of America, 2011.

Vanhoozer, Kevin J. *Is There a Meaning in this Text? The Bible, the Reader, and the Morality of Literary Knowledge.* Grand Rapids: Zondervan, 1998.

Vatican Council II: Constitutions, Decrees, Declarations. Edited by Austin Flannery. Northport, NY: Costello, 1996.

Voderholzer, Rudolf. "Dogma and History: Henri de Lubac and the Retrieval of Historicity as a Key to Theological Renewal." *Communio* 28 (2001) 648–68.

———. *Meet Henri de Lubac.* Translated by Michael J. Miller. San Francisco: Ignatius, 2008.

White, Thomas Joseph. "The 'Pure Nature' of Christology: Human Nature and *Gaudium et Spes* 22." *Nova et Vetera* 8 (2010) 283–322.

Wilken, Robert Louis. *The Spirit of Early Christian Thought.* New Haven, CT: Yale University Press, 2003.

Wojtyla, Karol. *Love and Responsibility.* Translated by H. T. Willetts. San Francisco: Ignatius, 1981.

Wood, Susan. "The Nature-Grace Problematic within Henri de Lubac's Christological Paradox." *Communio* 19 (1992) 389–403.